STRANGE THINGS HAPPEN

STRANGE THINGS HAPPEN
A LIFE WITH THE POLICE, POLO, AND PYGMIES

STEWART COPELAND

harperstudio

An Imprint of HarperCollins*Publishers*

FIRST EDITION

Designed by Jaime Putorti

Library of Congress Cataloging-in-Publication Data

Copeland, Stewart.
  Strange things happen : a life with the Police, polo, and pygmies / Stewart Copeland.—1st ed.
    p. cm.
  ISBN 978-0-06-179149-9 (hardcover)
    1. Copeland, Stewart. 2. Rock musicians—England—Biography. 3. Police (Musical group) I. Title.
  ML419.C67A3 2009
  782.42166092—dc22
  [B]

                                                                            2009030667

09 10 11 12 13   OV/RRD   10 9 8 7 6 5 4 3 2 1

CONTENTS

PART I
STRANGE THINGS HAPPEN

Tarazi, Lennie, me, Aragoosie (1965)

Tarazi with UN bunker (1998)

CHAPTER 1

A LETTER TO A CHILDHOOD FRIEND

2009

Dear Iskandar,

A lot has happened since we broke that branch off of old Abu Tannous's olive tree, behind the Tarazi Palace. Do you remember our little town in the Lebanese hills overlooking Beirut? That was back in 1965. The Russians had just made it into outer space and I was playing in my first band. I wonder what you and your mom are up to now.

We parted rather suddenly when my dad evacuated us after his CIA cover was blown. Do you remember that English kid, Harry Philby? Well, his dad's cover was blown, too—as a double agent for Russia!

So we got pulled out of the American Community School in Beirut, and I was packed off to boarding school in England. Out in the misty wilds of Somerset, at Millfield School, I kept on blasting on the drums whenever I could. It was difficult because of the noise they made. Wherever I could find a cellar or an attic, or a distant outbuilding I *would drag in my four big heavy cases, unpack my kit, and blaze away like fury. It never lasted. Someone was always annoyed by my art, and I would be cast out again.*

But I got pretty good at it. By the time I left college, I could get into a semifamous group, and pretty soon I could break out with a little band of my own. We were called The Police and ended up playing huge stadiums. Our songs were glued to the charts. It was a blast! We struggled for two years, surged for four years, and then just sat there at the top of the world for another two years before walking away.

So now I've got a real job, a real family, and a real life! I write and record the music you hear in Hollywood movies. I have seven *kids! No idea how that happened. Life is pretty settled now, but I keep having these strange adventures. Odd opportunities are attracted to celebrity, even when it's much faded.*

As I write this Lebanon is rebuilding. Again! Last time I checked, the old palace was still standing. But that was one war ago. If you get a chance, could you check it out for me? You're probably a banker in Dubai by now.

Best wishes,

Stewart

CHAPTER 2

WARDROBE

SUMMER, LATE 1980s

One fine morning, I step out of the shower, peer into my wardrobe, and realize that my life is over. I'm looking at an exotic collection of leather pants, hostile shirts, and pointy shoes. Problem is, I'm a forty-something father of four, and I'm feeling kind of mellow. I'm not angry about anything, and as a tax-paying, property-owning, investment-holding lotus-eater, I am in disagreement with what my clothes are saying to the world. The thrill has gone from frightening the natives. I care not that the world be unruffled by my passage through it.

So what do I wear? What have I got in my closet that doesn't say "FUCK YOU! I'M GOING TO BURN DOWN YOUR WORLD!" For so long, I have had to be worthy of the stares and furtive glances that follow rock stars. It would be unprofessional of me to walk out of my hotel room looking like I'd be safe with children. But now what?

All my life I have lived in self-imposed exile from the normal world. My arty friends and I feel like we are the only humans in a world of robots. A business suit is like the carapace of an insect. Conformity is surrender. Even long hair is a cop-out. Mine has had all color peroxided out of it—heaven forbid that I should be mistaken for a nice hippie.

But I have discovered that some humans are merely disguised as robots. Under cover of conformity strange personalities can emerge. I have started to experiment with other uniforms and disguises. My main circle of friends is the polo set of Gloucestershire. It's only natural that my first attempt at a new mufti would start here. They wear the same clothes that I used to wear in boarding school. Problem is, my career was fueled by a desire to burn down my old school. I get even stranger looks than usual when I show up at the club bar in a blazer, with handkerchief in the pocket. Out on the street, the usual double take is followed by a look of confusion.

The fact is that my dream of lapsing into the countryside in my post–rock star years is not panning out. The flashbulb-popping, tabloid-screaming, chart-topping, crowd-roaring express train of fame may have blazed off over the horizon, but strange adventures still befall me. From dancing the Ndele Banga with the Kamba of Tsavo to elbowing royalty on the polo fields of Cirencester, to sweaty jam sessions in Havana clip joints and black-tie curtain calls at my opera premieres, stuff still keeps on happening to me. Only now that I'm off the train, I can play with these things as they go by.

Here follows a collection of strange tales about the things that can happen as I walk in the constant company of a distantly remembered mythical being. Twenty years ago there was this kid with my face up there on the screen, the whole world got a pretty good look at him, and he still hovers just over my shoulder. He's mostly invisible after all these years, unseen by passersby, but in some settings, everyone can see him. In fact they see him and not me. And the strangest things happen.

▲ Happy in leather.

CHAPTER 3

LEBANON

1957–67

Life and times of a diplo-brat in Beirut:
Cowboys and Injuns in the Crusader castles.

Pete Karnif is looking for us. My bass player buddy Greg and I are skulking in the shadows, but it's time for us to get up there and do it. I'm shaking with fear because I'm twelve years old and I'm about to start getting what I wished for.

There isn't any stage, just some Selmer amps and my drums in a corner of the ballroom at the American Embassy Beach Club in Beirut, Lebanon.

All of the American, British, French, and other European expatriate kids are crammed into the room. In enclaves like this they have re-created an approximation of the teenage life that they should be living back home. They're dancing the Twist and the Mashed Potato and the Frug, whatever that is. My brother, Miles, should know. Even though the cool Mediterranean air breezes across the beach into the open room, the atmosphere is hot hot. These Western kids are desperate to be Western. They don't want to miss any of the teen boom that is happening back in the First World. Ian is lurking

somewhere nearby. He got me into this and is getting a huge kick from it.

At my tender age I don't have any idea what it means, but I can feel the buzz. Michele Savage is here. And Connie Ridgeway and Colleen Bisharat. All of the yearned-for fifteen-year-old women—so far above my lowly prepubescent but ardent station—are gyrating to Fats Domino right in front of the gear. I push past them to my drums. Pete is plugging in, and his amp is squawking. The hubbub of voices in the room immediately hushes, and all eyes are on us.

Actually, since I'm sitting down at the drums all I can see is the first row of kids, who look like grown-ups to me. Pete counts us in. . . .

"One, two—"

I never hear him finish the count. I have already embarked on the headlong joyride that is my life of drumming. Whatever we rehearsed is gone from my head, but the motor has started. I'm on a pulse and the band is ragged but connected. The kids are dancing to

"It's My Life" and I'm driving it. It's My Groove. Somewhere in the years ahead I'll learn how to be exulted and collaborative at the same time. For now though, there is only one thing on the planet, and that is Janet McRoberts dancing in front of me. Her eyes are wide with astonishment. The big girls are moving with seductive intent, and Janet is moving with me. She's being moved by me.

It was just yesterday that I got my first inkling of what music was going to do to my life. At the shawerma stand on the beach I overheard two of the big girls talking about The Nomads.

"I heard they've got a new drummer—you'll never guess who. . . ."

"Yeah I heard, it's Ian's kid brother!"

"Oh I can't wait to see him—is he as groovy as Ian?"

Well, I'm not even close to being as groovy as Ian. Never will be. I'm a skinny twelve-year-old, and these girls are fifteen. They are talking about a mythical being. They're already pouring their young imaginations into the chalice of music idolatry. I badly want to drink undeservedly from that cup. My chest is rising with the idea that the subject of their fancy is nerdy little me.

I've got my hand on the snare and my foot on the kick. The noise makes me big. It grows me up, like a shortcut to manhood. Primatologists studying gorillas and orangutans have established the connection between male dominance behavior and noise. Well, here I am, the skinny runt of the litter, but as long as I drive the beat, I'm a hairy-assed silverback motherfucker banging tree trunks. I'm swinging through the trees. My voice is a manly roar.

FAST FORWARD TO 2001

Ian is looking up at the bullet holes that have scratched the otherwise pristine facade of our old home in the hills overlooking Beirut. The city is spread out behind us as we gaze up at the wisteria-clad arches. It's a beautiful old Levantine building with soaring ceilings, grand stairways, and baronial galleries. Since my

brother and I were last here a half century ago, Lebanon has endured invasion, civil war, occupation, massacre, siege, and pretty much every form of human madness. The neighborhoods where we played have been corroded by warfare, sprayed by automatic rifle fire, plugged by RPGs, or leveled by bombs.

But our old villa Tarazi has just these five bullet holes that we can count. Ian figures that a militia gunman must have stood where he is now standing and just sprayed one blast upward. To get someone's attention, no doubt.

I'm standing there with a tear in my eye as Ian disappears. In a moment he is hailing us from the front balcony, a giant terrace that wraps around the top of the house. He has climbed up the wisteria vines just outside his old room and sneaked back into the house just like he did when he was a teenager returning from the lam. I'm right up there beside him in a flash. We're looking out over Beirut, standing right in the spot where my first drums were set forty years ago.

The drums had a faded champagne sparkle finish. Dad had rented them from a store in town, maybe reluctant to buy any

STEWART COPELAND

more musical instruments. Our home was a graveyard of abandoned music toys. My three older siblings, Miles, Lennie, and Ian, had passed right by our father's inducements and exhortations to follow him into music; so when I showed interest he was a little wary at first. My mother bought me a snare drum because I wouldn't leave her alone. It was a white pearl-finished Lefima drum made in Germany, of all places. I've never since seen another drum with that brand.

When my rat-tat-tat became a prolonged irritant to the family, my father began to discern the elemental urge that is the signature behavior of a budding musician. I just could not stop. The power of the noise was endlessly thrilling and empowering. When I wasn't drumming I was air drumming, or worse, I was that kid who drives everyone insane with persistent foot tapping and thigh slapping. It was the nervous twitch from hell.

One day Ian roars up the driveway on his motorcycle with some of his ragged crew. It's his buddies in the band, who have lost their drummer. On the basis of Ian being the coolest kid in town, his kid brother must be at least worth checking out as a replacement.

Here they are up on the balcony, The Nomads, snarling at me to do something hip on my drums. I start flailing at the drums in the worst possible way, and since they too are just callow youths, they're impressed by the ferocity and volume. They are the first in a long line of musicians who have no idea what they are in for when they let me into the band. My father made sure that I had every kind of proper musical training and technique, but no one was ever able to teach me when to shut up.

 1965

Harry Philby is terrified. The staircase in the old crusader castle has fallen away, but the outer wall, also ruined, provides a jagged few steps up to the next level of the tower. It would be easier to scramble up there if it weren't for the cardboard crusader shield strapped to one arm and the long plastic sword in the other hand. But the plucky young Englisher makes it, and now it's my turn. It's a little easier for me, having watched Harry's route, so soon we are on the top of the tower, two miniature crusader knights ready for battle.

Down below, in the little bay that the castle protects, our parents are lolling on the boat that my father hired to bring us here. Harry's dad, Kim Philby, is kind of a boozy old slob, but his American stepmother, stretched out in her bikini sunbathing on the deck, distracts us from our holy war for a minute. We are looking almost vertically straight down at them. Neither of us boys has any inkling of it yet, but both of our fathers are spies, mine for the "Old Glue Factory" (CIA) and his for the Soviet KGB. Right now they are head-to-head by the tiller down below, chuckling about something. One day soon old man Philby is going to escape in the dead of night on a Russian ship.

There are many advantages to Crusaders & Saracens over Cowboys & Indians. For one thing, the helmet, shield, and sword are cooler than a cowboy hat; and the castles provide powerful set dressing. The crusaders were about raw dumb power. They are remembered in these parts for their suicidal courage and their ignorant cruelty. Their mission here is regarded as a quixotic failure. The magnificent stone castles—much heavier and more business-like than their European counterparts—couldn't protect them from the wily Saracens. Unlike the natives of North America, the Arab natives were able to evict the colonists. Children like us playing in these relics learn something about the impotence of empire.

All over the Middle East there are layers of discarded military hardware from every age, from axe heads to tank turrets. Pretty much everyone of note has washed over this land, which leaves the current natives as the most variously flavored population in the Western Hemisphere. They are the true

▲ Tyre Castle with Spy Daddy and Gene Trone

descendants of Abraham, Moses, Nebuchadnezzar, Ramses I–XI, Cyrus, Alexander, Constantine, Jesus, Muhammad, Khalil Gibran, and Yasser Arafat.

As a WASP I'm a little humbled by this ancestry. All we've got is King Arthur, Julius Caesar, and Norman.

CHAPTER 4

MUSIC

DECEMBER 1968
WELLS CATHEDRAL

*In darkest Somerset, Millfield School celebrates
Christmas in the huge stone church.
I learn to serve the gift.*

A thousand voices echo up the stone arches that frame the ancient stained glass windows. Floodlit from the outside, these
twelfth-century images of obscure piety combine with the soaring
hymns to sear the art receptors in my adolescent brain. There is
nothing more beautiful than music. All of the magnificent architecture that towers overhead is just a vessel for the sound that sweeps
through me.

In fact the sound forgives the overall creepiness of the church
experience. All afternoon while I set up my drums amid the school
orchestra and wait for the Christmas service to begin, that guilt of
alienation creeps around me, pervading the cold damp air. Few
places are chillier than an English church without its congregation. The cold stone statues are impassive, but they know that I am
apostate.

Now it's evening, and the cathedral is warmed by the bodies of
the students, teachers, and parents. The giant candles are lit,

▲ Second drum set

golden flames reflecting off the brass and glass. Flowers are every-where. To still my autistic tip-tapping on the drums, Mr. Fox has banished me to the furthest corner of our arm of the cross. We are set up in the south wing, the choir is in the north wing, and the folks are in the stem. All of the religious stuff is happening around the corner in the head of the cross. The mumbling prayers and the shuffling of the congregation from kneeling to sitting to standing are prelude to the rustling of the hymnbooks. The singing starts off ragged but builds and swells as the magic takes hold. Breathing and singing together, the thousand souls become one mighty sound.

And did the Countenance Divine
Shine forth upon our clouded hills?
And was Jerusalem builded here
Among these dark Satanic Mills?

I doubt it, based on what I know of Levantine cities. This bit of Blake is the *least* daft of the hymns and carols that are sung. Most of the lyrics are mumbo jumbo. It's the music combined with ritual that thrills the air.

In the final cadenzas of each song the school choir kicks in for the descant, providing a silvery lining to the bellowing flock. The angels are dancing in a shimmering cascade above our heads as a shattering glory of voices lifts the roof.

Mr. F. raises his eyebrow to give me the nod; finally, it's my moment to join the ceremony. The previous hymn has echoed off into silence and the enraptured congregants are creaking in their pews, waiting in the candlelight. They are eager to be touched by the next wave of the shaman's wand.

I'm so ready.

Tum
Tadada
Tum, Tum
Bumpumpum . . .
Tum
Dadada
Tum, Tum
Bumpumpum . . .

The tom-tom reverberates with a sonorous boom. Up until now drums have been about assertion and empowerment but this is new. Into my young quavering hand has been placed the rudder of this sacred ship. I can only be a servant of the powerful emotional force that has been created in this ancient stone shrine. All of us are joined at this moment by the momentum of our shared ritual, and I am the beating heart. I am nothing, no one. Just the beating heart of a larger body, enveloped by the soul of the faithful. A synapse closes in the mind of the enraptured protoshaman.

Next morning, when my head clears, it seems obvious that music isn't just a tool or weapon, it's what my life is for. It's powerful juju, and I want to own it as much as it owns me.

The gatehouse lodge to the old Millfield estate is where Mr. Fox rules the music kingdom. In an annex to this quaint little house are the piano rooms, where the music geeks pore over their finger exercises and ear training. This is where the seed planted by my sister, Lennie, back at Tarazi starts to grow. Lennie taught me the connection between the music on the page and the keys on the piano. My good fortune is that my position in the school orchestra means I can schedule piano time, even though my instrument is drums—which unfortunately won't fit into the tiny piano rooms. The school, faithful to my father's wish, has fixed me up a drum tutor in the nearby town, but I can already play my paradiddles better than he can, so this "practice" time is my own.

I can even skive off stables duties by skulking here in music world. I can faintly hear Mozart stammering through the thinly soundproofed walls, but in my slot, I'm hammering two-finger ostinatos of unknown origin.

Bring me my bow of burning gold;
Bring me my arrows of desire:
Bring me my spear! O clouds unfold!
Bring me my chariot of fire!

I'M LEARNING MORE THAN I ever intended to about drums.

My London tutor, the venerable Max Abrams, has never shown me his paradiddles. He exhausts my brain with endless reading and coordination exercises. He's off drinking tea somewhere no doubt while I plod through Glenn Miller charts, learning to recognize rhythmic patterns expressed as dots on a staff. My father is grumpy about the Glenn Miller. Although he played in the Glenn Miller Army band during the war, he considers it to be a blot on his musical résumé. My dad would have preferred Stan Kenton or Woody Herman. I couldn't care less, they all lacked raging guitar.

Breathing in the stale air of the London Underground, I'm staring blankly at my shoes. The coordination exercises are the most exhausting part of the tuition. Learning to uncouple the hands so as to free them for independent activity is the goal, but uncoupling my brain is the result. As I stagger home I'm aware that my "gift" is making heavy demands.

Still, after a lethargic dinner I'm soon down in the basement blazing away on my own drumming agenda. There is no discipline or inducement involved; it's an unquenchable urge.

1973
COLLEGE

It turns out that life can be lived in almost constant sunshine. The surfers of Southern California can hardly imagine any other kind of life. Everybody here in Ocean Beach is so laid-back that I feel like I'm stuck in permanent fast-motion. I'm not used to this relentless ease. Don't these people realize there is Cold and War and Want in the world? I have been "American" all my life, but this is effectively the first time that I've actually been here. My daddy took us off to Egypt when I was two months old. From out there in the world people are watching America, but America is not watching them. So it turns out that I'm kind of a foreigner here, too. I'm getting used to being the guy in differently shaped jeans.

Every other day I head downtown to the San Diego School of Performing Arts for piano time and composition classes. The music department takes up the bottom half of the stately old building.

The music students are the usual nonsporty stick-insect types, but compared to the theater and ballet geeks, we are like raging bulls in the basement.

In the piano rooms I'm conjuring music that has gone way beyond what I can actually play with my hands. In fact my intelligent designer omitted to give me the gift of pianitude. I did get the genes for stringed instruments and mallets (guitars and drums), which I find naturally easy to play, but my fingers just don't do keyboards. No matter how many hours, years, or decades I spend composing on the keyboard, my hands just can't find their cunning.

I can find the notes that my head dictates and check them against one another to build harmony, but I can't play them in rhythm. I can play the rhythm of the notes I want but can't find the pitches fast enough. I can play my music with good rhythm and wrong notes or with correct pitches and no rhythm.

At least back home in London, my dad's Beocord open reel recorder allowed me to record two parallel tracks of guitar. On the left track I could record the rhythm chords, and then on the right track I could record an accompanying tune. Then came the trance of listening to my music while my hands lay idle. There is no greater glow of narcissistic validation than receiving my own art. I slay myself—always have and hope I always will.

Here in California I'm a college kid tangled up and yearning for the mysterious golden girls, but that glow of validation is dim. I can strum on my guitar, but there is bigger stuff raging around in my head. I'm not even a professional musician yet, but I'm already dreaming up concept albums. In the piano rooms I can try to work things out on paper, but I can't love my music by looking at it on the page. I just have to sing it in my head and let it go by.

In class I'm kind of the runt of the litter, again. Almost all of the other composition students are pianists from the other side of the universe. In fact, music study has always been of music that has never attracted me. Music classes cured me of Mozart, and my father cured me of jazz—meaning that I'm immune to the charms of both. The music that I do listen to doesn't exist here in music school.

Dr. Mary K. Phillips is at the piano playing our homework. All of us geeks are twitching as she points out the mistakes of voicing and spelling. The assignment was to write sixteen bars of four-part harmonic composition observing the rules of figured bass. As a practical matter I have always found that the rules could only be applied as a retrofit. The music comes out of my brain and lands in the material world—and then I can figure out what rules apply. So my sixteen bars derive from some larger opus of the piano room that have been retrofitted with the rules of Dr. Phillips's class.

The focus of the group is the mechanics of harmony. The other student pieces sound like they are supposed to sound, like pale Mozart, and no one seems to mind that they are meaningless sequences of chords. The point is to grasp the laws of harmonic movement.

When she gets to my piece she plays it down like a breeze, and I'm basking in the beauty of hearing it for the first time as a listener, without having to limp through playing it myself. But I know that she will crush me with the inevitable technical errors. When she reaches the end the room is unusually silent. She turns to me and says:

"Stewart, you have parallel fifths in measures three, seven, and eleven, but more important, this is actual music. You have a voice."

Well, that may seem like faint praise, but it puffed me right up. Some part of the feverish grandiose exultation that I get from my own music is actually discernible to a dispassionate ear! Some part of the voodoo actually works.

She was right about those sixteen bars that I wrote for her homework assignment. They stuck in my head and eventually even reached my fingers. I could play that string of expertly voiced chords together with a scrap of lyric, and a few years later record it with The Police. The song was called "Does Everyone Stare the Way I Do?" I imagine the royalties from just that one song—flagged by Dr. Mary K. Phillips—must have paid off all my years of music education.

 1985

NIEBAUM RANCH, NAPA VALLEY

Francis leans back heavily and speaks calmly to the producer. The dark screening room is lit by a film frame frozen on the screen.

"Yeah . . . couple places, we need strings."

Damn. This had been going really well. As we screened the scenes that I had scored, Francis Coppola had been rumbling with approval. The director and the other postproduction chiefs had been chuckling and nodding sagely over the callow charm of my first attempt at film music. The lack of finesse suited Francis's sense of atmosphere for this film. Since I had no idea how movies had been scored since the dawn of film I had had to invent the wheel for myself. The important thing was that Francis was able to infuse me with the mood that he needed in each scene. With my bare hands, on guitar, marimba, bass, banjo, and kazoo, I could make that mood.

From the start Francis has been talking about using rhythm as a dramatic device in this film, *Rumble Fish*. With the classic film *High Noon* as a template, he wants to build a sense of impending, implacable doom. The story is of a countdown. Matt Dillon, Mickey Rourke, Laurence Fishburne, Dennis Hopper, Diane Lane, and Tom Waits all have an appointment with fate in reel twelve of the movie. Francis wants the audience to sweat every second of the journey to that place.

Well, I don't know much about drama, but rhythm is a thing of mine. With the help of two teenage Coppolas, Roman and Gian-Carlo, ferreting through the sound effect libraries, I was able to start a collection of rhythms created by machinery, animals, and people. Pile drivers, barking dogs, typewriters, and car crashes all have rhythm if you look closely.

At the Long Branch Studio in Tulsa, Oklahoma, I have recordings of these sounds on magnetic tape. If I cut the tape with a razor at the beginning and end of, say, a burst of dog barking, then I can join the two ends of the strip of tape and create a loop. Threading this loop onto the tape machine is easy enough, but we have to set up tape spools on mic stands around the room to keep the tape untangled as we play the loop and record the repeating pattern of dog barking onto a second tape recorder. One day, a decade or so in the future, someone will invent computers.

The latest breakthrough in audio recording today is technology that can synchronize and dependently lock two tape machines. This enables us to build up a web of sound effect rhythms. By tweaking the speed of the playback machine I can synchronize each new layer of repeating noise to groove in some way with the collection on the recorder.

▲ Happiness is a Stratocaster plugged into a Marshall stack.

For every reel of the movie—of which there are twelve—I have a tapestry of rhythmatized and synchronized sounds. On each of eight tracks there is a groove. On track four, for instance, there is a pile driver pounding incessantly. On track six there is a billiard ball break looped to create a strange rhythm. This can be used as a subliminal effect in the pool hall scene. Or to presage the scene, or to refer back to the scene later in the movie. Richard Beggs, who is the overall soundmeister of the movie, is in on the plot. Every scene of the film has a rhythm chugging somewhere in the soundscape. The clock is ticking.

Upon these rhythms I build the music with guitar, drums, banjo, bass, marimba, and piano. There is a scene in which Matt pays an evening visit to his girlfriend, Diane, at her parents' house. He is met on the front porch by the young Sophia Coppola, who plays the precocious kid sister.

The scene needs to carry the underlying tension of impending, implacable doom but also to lighten up for a minute to play some romance. In the background, the train whistle blows at almost imperceptibly regular intervals. Closer, there is a broken fan that we can feel vibrating. Over these vaguely sinister rhythms a tinkling progression of chords on a toy piano is all it takes to combine with Matt's yearning performance to create a wave of poignancy.

I have no idea how you are supposed to score a movie, so I just made this whole scheme up as a theory of a practical solution to an artistic problem. It turns out that my method is so far from how you're supposed to do it that no one has ever done it like this— which makes me the Che Guevara of film scoring.

So far, so good. I don't even realize yet how rare it is to have a director who will give anyone this much rope. This is the Francis method—find people with the right instincts and turn them loose with the tools.

Now he wants some conventional orchestral score to leaven the rather astringent high-concept layers that I have produced. Violins, oboes, that sort of thing. Some premonition of a career in Hollywood alerts me to a door opening. Strings?

I had already chased off competition from other musicians, arrangers, and composers that Francis had gathered in Tulsa during the shoot. This suddenly looks like a new opportunity for an interloper. Some fool of a studio hack can come on board and sweeten all of my cool stuff! The director wants instruments that I can't play myself!

In a split second I'm an orchestral arranger.

"Strings? . . . Sure, yeah, lemme rustle up some strings and nice orchestra stuff in a couple of places," says I.

2000

YEARS LATER AT PARAMOUNT STUDIO M

Behind me in the huge control room is the director, his producer, and a couple of studio bosses. In front of me is the seventy-channel mixing console nursed by a five- or six-man recording crew.

Through the glass in front of us we can see the orchestra. There are video monitors everywhere that show us the movie, the recording status, and each other. The score is on my desk in front of me. Jeff Seitz, my man from Juilliard and collaborator of two decades, runs the recording crew while I run the band, and the director behind me runs the executives.

The conductor is on the podium, facing the slickest orchestral talent that money can buy. In his headset he can hear dialogue, metronome click, and me:

"Let's go to 1m6, measure 25. We'll drop you in at bar 27. Tacit, please, brass until 32. And you can take them down one dynamic, say . . . mezzo forte until 36. Everybody play ink at 36. Show me when you're ready."

Through the twenty or thirty microphones we can hear the rustling of scores as the sixty players turn to the spot. Pete on the podium conveys the instruction for the horns, trumpets, trom-

bones, and tuba to not play for the specified six measures and to play slightly less loudly when they do enter. Rustle, Rustle.

He raises his baton. The room stills.

"Roll tape."

The chatter behind me stops, and the scene is playing on everyone's screens. At exactly seven minutes, eighteen seconds, and twelve frames into the reel a bright yellow streamer appears on the screen and a loud clicking indicates the tempo of the incoming music. After four clicks the band strikes up—although we can't yet hear it. We're listening to music that we recorded on the last pass, as the orchestra plays along in parallel. At measure 27 the recordist hits his red button, and seamlessly we are now hearing the new recording of the current performance.

All this is in response to the client behind me, who wants his favorite line of dialogue to be more clearly audible through the din of sound effects and thrilling music. This is an easy one; all

I have to do is carve off some of the orchestra to clear audio space for the dialogue. The mood of the scene is playing well so I don't have to rewrite the music and put new charts on the stands.

But it does happen sometimes, that a hitherto undisclosed producer will show up at the orchestra date with a brand-new perspective on the scene. This is the last high-octane, thousands-of-dollars-per-minute event of the film production, so distant functionaries whom I've never before met will arrive for one last piss on the tree.

"Wait a minute!" such a producer might say. "This scene is supposed to be happy-sad! I'm only hearing sad!"

By the time we get to the hyperexpensive scoring stage the relative happy and sad have been fully calibrated to the satisfaction of the director and more immediate producers. But now this guy wants more happy in this scene. That's when you have to put the orchestra on a fifteen-minute break, sprint over to the keyboard, and start figuring.

With modern software it's not too hard to immediately print up new parts to put on the stands. The tricky part is manipulating the emotional message of the chords, melodies, rhythms, and timbres. The film composer has to work very decisively and quickly to hit the precise emotional spot. Composing for full orchestra on the fly separates the men from the boys. I've had to learn how to do it with the clock ticking. It's been the formal part of my music education—and I've been paid for all of it!

CHAPTER 5

CURVED AIR

1975

My first pro rock band.

Dear Sirs,
I recently had the exquisite joy of experiencing a Curved Air concert and was most impressed by the exceptional talent of their new drummer. . . .

Dear Sounds,
Curved Air are BRILLYANT!
What's the drummer's name?

To whom it may concern,
Wow! Me and some mates went to see Curved Air at the. . . . Incredible . . . especially the drummer. . . .

I'm writing all of these letters to music magazines myself, using different handwriting, styles, spellings, and stationery. After playing a show we usually pull over on the edge of town to gas up for the drive back home to London, so while Darryl pumps gas into

▼ Phil, Mick, Sonja, Darryl, me. I loved those boots.

our Ford Zodiac, I find a letterbox and slip another piece of skulduggery into the system.

I have no faith that the crown of fame and fortune will be justly placed upon my deserving brow. For some reason I'm desperate, even though I'm only twenty-three. I'm in too much of a hurry to wait for the apples to drop, so I must shake the tree. In a strange kind of way I'm more proud of plunder grabbed than honor bestowed.

We're having a great time in Curved Air. I'm in a big pro band now—as a member of the band. I've had many other jobs in show business—roadie, tour manager, journalist, promoter, radio disc jockey—but now I'm back on this side of the line. I'm the product, not the producer.

When big brother Miles got to London and started building bands, I latched on to any of his projects that had a free seat in the van. I carried amps for Wishbone Ash. I drove for Renaissance, did lights for Cat Iron, and tour managed Joan Armatrading.

In college my drumming had actually lapsed in favor of composing and publishing. I started a little magazine in Berkeley called *College Event*. Actually it was more of a tip sheet than a magazine. I published letters by college concert promoters, who were students like me. I pooled their experiences with the industry professionals and artists—and then sold advertising to the same industry people. It was kind of a journalistic protection racket—a concept that Miles had dreamed up and perfected in England.

But those drums just came back and got me. I was about to finish up college in California when Miles called from London with an opportunity to get in a band with Darryl Way, the virtuoso violinist of the long disbanded Curved Air. Even though my drum fervor had faded a bit, I jumped on the next flight to London and immediately sparked a connection with Darryl. He was looking for players with passion at a time when everyone else was looking for plush. He had kept enough of a reputation going that we could form a group called Stark Naked & the Car Thieves (a name borrowed from Ian's Vietnam tour) and start playing shows.

Just as we were about to get serious, maybe three or four shows into our push, Darryl and each of the other members of Curved Air got tax bills that had been bequeathed them by previous insect people. Since all of the Curvians were in the same predicament, they were able to patch up their differences and reunite for a tour to pay the bill. It did put our new band on hold for about a month, but at least I was able to cross back over the line and weasel my way into the Curved Air tour as tour manager. I'm the only guy I know (OK, except Henry Padovani) who could ever work both sides of the camera.

THE FIRST SHOW OF the tour is a college gig in Reading. After dropping the band off in their dressing room I go up to the stage to check the crew. They are in the usual first show panic. For its day, this is a high-tech band, with banked synthesizers and special effects gadgets. The stage is a tangle of gear and wires. I let each of the roadies unload his tale of woe and then let them get on with it. Classic roadies—they bitch . . . and then just do it. I'm just a kid, but I've done the job of every man on this crew.

At least the promoter is happy. Massed college kids are straining at the doors, and the show is going to be packed.

Back onstage the crew is finally ready for a few minutes of sound check before the doors must open. I bring the band up for a panicked run-through of one song. There are still uncontrolled buzzes from the amps and unintended screeches from the PA, so everyone is tense. Sonja Kristina, the singer, is absolutely calm, smoking a cigarette as she surveys the crew's raging spaghetti fight.

We can't hold the doors any longer, so I hustle the band off the stage. I have to pry Francis Monkman's fingers from the keyboards. Some musicians are *never* finished with their sound check.

It's much easier to manage a band than to be in a band. There isn't any of the nervous sweat. I can leave them in the dressing room to stew until showtime while I go see what fires I can put out onstage. The crew are a little calmer now, and the griping is down to a grump. They're much happier now that the support act crew are setting up and can be lorded over. The room is filling up fast. Whatever noise comes out of the amplifiers, this show is going to start with some momentum.

When I take this news down to the band, their mood brightens and they start to puff up with the mojo. While the other band thumps away over our heads, laconic drummer Florian rat-tat-tats his hand exercises, Phil rattles his bass, and Darryl arpeggiates furiously on his violin while Francis frets mysteriously. Sonja is in another room doing chick singer stuff with her wardrobe and makeup posse.

It's showtime. The other band has cleared off, our stage is set, and the crew is ready. I go down and give Darryl the nod, and he's raring to go. He leads the guys up to the wings, rapping on Sonja's door as he goes by. I head up to shake some payment out of the promoter before the band plays a note. Gigs these days can be shifty.

I was supposed to meet Darryl in the wings before the band went onstage, but before I make it back to the hall he has already started up. He opens the show with some heavy rhythmic scrubbing on his electric violin as an attention grabber, and then the band kicks in for an instrumental romp through some slightly classical, vaguely Verdi riffs.

They do have something here, this band. They immediately have the crowd moving. There are a lot of groups out there these days that are sophisto-classical, but these guys actually rock. And that's not all.

After blizzards of virtuosity from Francis and Darryl the band cuts down to a low throb. They hold the groove for a minute, and the kids are yelling. I can see why. My own hackles are on end. Sonja Kristina has arrived on the stage. Suddenly there is no band, no stage, no college kids. Just Sonja glinting in the green light. She moves like smoke across the stage, hardly seeming to move at all, but undulating in slow motion. Who cares what the band is doing? As a muso I've never bothered with singers, considering them to be musical passengers. How wrong I've been! She's not even singing yet, and she owns everything.

SIX MONTHS LATER SONJA is squeezed into the backseat of the Zodiac between myself and Mick Jacques, and we are chuckling off down the motorway back to London after a show. We're a happy band and we have just killed another crowd. After the Curved Air tour wrapped up, Francis and Florian went back to their lives, leaving Sonja and Darryl to consider the value of their band brand. It seemed like a no-brainer for Darryl to bring in the Car Thieves and continue as Curved Air with Sonja, Phil, Mick on guitar, and me on drums.

Who could ever expect that Sonja will one day become my first wife and mother of three of my four sons?

Melody Maker **reprint: After a rather sudden and mysterious avalanche of readers' letters, this one was printed in the "Any Questions?" section. My First Ink, and I scammed it myself.**

▲ Fourth drum set

CHAPTER 6

TAGGING LONDON

1977

Fuck! . . . is that a cop car?"

Paul Mulligan and I are lurking in a cleft in the cityscape, peering up the rainy night street and trying to discern the threat to our endeavor. Stashing our spray cans in our coats we, for the umpteenth time, interrupt our mission and pretend to be normal until we can see that there are no protuberances on the approaching vehicle. We're still nervous because this is our first crime wave.

We started out with a stencil, but ended up getting more paint on ourselves than the walls. And the logo, THE POLICE, just wasn't dominating the canvas with enough pride. So we ditched the soggy, dripping cardboard stencil and have been spraying the band name in uneven capitals on suitable walls around London. The word tagging hasn't yet been invented, but that's what we're doing.

The inoffensive car passes on down the street, and we are about to resume our insurrection when a couple of pedestrians come around the corner. Damn. After a reflexive lurch back into the shadows, Paul lights up a smirk.

"Do you think they could give a damn? Fuck 'em," he says as he strides out into full lamplight and draws his can. The pedestrians pass by with not a sideward glance. They completely ignore Dalí and Picasso flagrantly spraying on their city walls.

It dawns on us that the shade of night is more of a hindrance than a shield. If we do this in broad daylight, we can see cops from further off. We can certainly see them better than they can see us. Everyone else on the street, whether on foot or in cars seems to be blind to us. We're invisible! So we get bolder and soon are out at high noon plastering posters and spraying our turf like any male mammals. Paul, eager to invest in show business, lent us £400 to record our first single. We both have high hopes for a return on his gamble.

CHAPTER 7

KLARK KENT

1978

My first hit record was as an artist who hid behind a mask. The mask reveals the true identity.

I'm never going to make it home. I'm driving through the night and not getting anywhere. Lost somewhere in London, or maybe I'm not even in London anymore. No matter. My ears are glued to the speakers in my car. The music coming out has me transfixed because of course it's my own. Really, *really* mine.

After years of home-recording my guitar riffs, today was the first time that I've had the chance to professionally record my guitars, bass, and piano over real drums—my drums!

In my car, lost in the night, I'm listening to a thrashing band that hangs together with unholy cohesion.

It's been a busy day. At the crack of dawn (10:00 A.M. for my kind) I loaded my trusty Gibson SG guitar, Fender Telecaster bass, a tiny little Fender Champ amp, a cheesy drum box, and my real drums into my purple VW and drove down to Surrey Sound Studio. Nigel Gray is the owner and chief engineer. We're working with state-of-the-art sixteen-track one-inch recording tape.

The first track that we lay down for each of the three songs is the cheesy drum box pattern, as a glorified metronome. This machine was designed to accompany lounge singers who are too cheap to hire a drummer. It has preprogrammed rhythms, of which most are rumbas, sambas, and the like. But it does have "Pop 1" and "Pop 2," which gives me two serviceable rhythms that I can use.

Then I plug in the SG and work my way down the songs, chugging the rhythm guitar parts in time with the drum box. It's already sounding amazing compared with my home recordings. Just having someone else to hit the record button for me is a big luxury. But I don't get too carried away with the guitar yet. Next, Nigel puts up a microphone for me to quickly yodel out a guide vocal track, which helps navigation during the whole process. I have three songs on tape.

Now it's time for the real recording, starting with the drums, which are the foundation upon which any modern music is built. Very carefully Nigel arranges the microphone tree around my drums and I lay down the beat, with the guide tracks in my earphones. It's the easiest drum session I've ever done, since the guitarist has exactly my sense of rhythm. But drums are still the most demanding aspect of band recording—even if I am the band.

It's about four o'clock, but I'm just getting started. It's time to get serious with the guitars. My little Champ amp would never be big enough to play with a band, but for overdubs, with near and distant mics, we can get a big, raging guitar sound. After the slog of all that drumming now I'm in Guitar Hero heaven, and that drummer on the tracks is just the perfect guy. . . .

All of the parts that I've been noodling over at home now come to life in full stereo studio sound. There is no greater joy than this. When I'm working at home, engineering my own sessions, I spend most of the time fussing over wires and connections so when I finally strap on my guitar, my head is still engineering. With Nigel at the controls I can spend all day getting deeper and deeper into the pocket. Music is like that. Inspiration and vibe gather momentum. Guitars, bass, piano, even a bit of wild kazoo as fake brass, and I've got three tunes thrashing. The band sounds pretty thick when you consider that there are just two guys in the building—and one of them is the engineer.

Tomorrow I'll do vocals, but now I've got the backing tracks going around and around on the cassette player in my car. I don't ever want to get home.

I CAN'T SEE VERY well out of this mask, but I'm enjoying very much the befuddled amusement on the face of the journalist before me. Most of my experience with interviews has been watching the artists that I have worked for stammering their way through boring responses to standard questions. Now it's my turn, and I'm doing it a little differently.

I'm wearing a thick rubber mask, a long black coat, and thick gloves. On my way over to the record company press office I have

concocted another bogus persona, life story, and scam. This time I'm an escapee from a government scientific program involving radiation synapse crevulation—I hope you are wearing your lead diapers! Under this mask I'm still glowing. . . .

Everybody wants to talk to the masked man of mystery, but the last thing I want is for anyone to identify me. How do you like that? My first brush with honestly earned fame, and I'm sneaking!

For one thing, my reputation in London right now is suspect, and I don't want to taint this new brand that is working so well for me. I'm the chief mercenary behind that fake punk band The Police, and while the musicians here generally respect our chops, the rock press has already written us off as not cool. The Police is actually kind of dead in the water right now—which is going to change because Stingo, out of nowhere, has started writing some pretty incredible songs. Andy's joining the band has really woken him up. There's this one new song that we should record called "Roxanne."

So, since I am nothing and no one, how about if I use a mask to suggest that I'm someone and something? When confronted by the mask folks might ask, "What's he got to hide if he's not somebody?" It's what my sly father taught me: If you want to create a rumor, start by denying it, as in: "I swear that I *never* slept with Diana. . . ."

Which would be academic of course if the BBC Radio 1 hadn't picked up one of my Klark Kent songs, "Don't Care," and started playing the hell out of it all over the country, thereby anointing me with a bona fide (though modest) hit single—my first ever. I'm twenty-six and had almost given up hope that real mojo would ever be mine. Curved Air was a good first step out of college, but it was like being the last man to climb aboard the sinking ship. The Police right now is just another scabrous London band, albeit one with a secret nuclear weapon hatching.

THE BBC TV PRODUCER has that same look of befuddled amusement on his face, but he's much redder. We're all in masks. Even

Miles, who has identified himself as Melvin Miltoss, my manager. He's sounding a bit nasal through his pig snout, but he's trying to reason with the TV people—who swear they have never seen anything like this.

Top of the Pops is *the* national television opportunity in the UK. Appearing on this show is an automatic five-point bump in the charts. I figured that bands look cooler than solo performers on TV, so I brought a band to mime along with me, comprised of Sting, Andy, Florian, and Kim Turner. None of us has ever been on TV before, this is the big one, and we're all in masks.

Behind his disguise, Miles is unhinged. Released by anonymity and unburdened by his sterling reputation he's having the time of his life, alternately blubbering, exhorting, and suavely negotiating. The thing is that they have a problem with close-ups of a singer in a rubber mask. The whole show is mimed to playback, but miming behind a mask is pushing it. Miles wheedles them into a compromise, which is for me to wear some kind of camouflage makeup. They escape from our dressing room just as Miles is winding into a sobbing flood of histrionic, clutching gratitude.

Up on the tiny TV studio stage we're all clutching guitars that aren't plugged in, and Florian is checking out the plastic cymbals that they put on his kit. Looking at them, they are not remotely realistic, but the crew assure us that under the lights and through the cameras they look "better" than real ones. The point of them, however, is that they make no sound other than a damp *thut*.

With drums it's hard to pretend that you are playing without making a fearful racket—which makes it hard for the other players to stay in sync with the playback. The television viewer can see if a cymbal is struck, so the drummer pretending to play must actually strike something—and if he actually strikes, *thut* is better than CLANG!

Considering the enormity of the show, the stage is tiny. The cameras like us all to be pressed up close to one another so the screen always has multiple players. We each have a little spot marked on the stage beneath our feet. Behind their masks my buddies—even Sting, who is usually so cool—are jigging about in their little spots. Each one must boogie in his own square foot.

Up front I'm staring into the big camera lens facing, for the first time, the world on national TV. In front of me is a tiny dance floor with twenty or thirty fake groovy teenagers waiting glumly for their cue. They are pushed over to one side while the cameras work out their positions. It's all business for the moment. I'm just standing there under the intense light. Over there I can see a monitor that is flitting from close-up to wide-angle shots of me in the dumb makeup that they made me wear. In the makeup room it looked like pretty deep camouflage, but on camera you can see right through it.

"OK . . . let's try one . . . everybody on *one* please. . . . PLAYBACK!"

The crowd directors wave up the fake teenagers who are suddenly whooping with joyous teenage hysteria and dancing like fury as the crazy lights swirl and the cameras are sweeping overhead. After three loud pops my track starts, and I'm dancing around pretending to sing my song. I'm jitterbugging, I'm gyrating and gallivanting. I'm hollering, high-rolling, and Holy Moly! I am ON TV!

Well actually, not yet. That was just a run-through, a camera rehearsal. The fake teenagers immediately droop off back to the side, and I stand inert once more under the lights while they figure more shit out. This time, I'm soaking wet. It's not just my first time on TV, it's also the first time I've ever thought of myself as a singer let alone pretended to be one in front of people. I have decades of youthful experience with air guitar, but singing? It feels like cross-dressing.

Miles sidles over. For years we have both been exhorting artists to be more animated, but he's coaching me now to calm down. My brother with his pig mask is a reassuring presence. Behind me Andy and Kimbo are goofing off, freed from inhibition by their masks, striking outrageous guitar poses. Sting is biding his time. Just standing there he looks cool, even with the monkey mask.

"OK, Quiet Please! Everybody on one . . . thank you . . . and . . . Cue Audience!"

"WROUAGH!" shout the fake teenagers as the crazy lights swirl and the cameras sweep.

This time I'm trying the stillness-is-movement concept. I'm rigid while singing, with occasional twitches for punctuation. This is still only the second time ever in my life that I have been a singer. First time was ten minutes ago. But this is going to become a pattern. Living and learning right in front of everybody, on TV.

In their homes around the nation people are hearing the real deal—a music soundscape entirely created by just one hard-workin' fool. But they're watching a fake performance on fake instruments in front of a fake audience. Even the mask—which doesn't hide anything—is fake. But the ever humble feeling in my heart is real, as I pretend to shout out the lyric into the fake microphone:

"I am the coolest thing that ever hit town. . . ."

A Sounds *magazine reprint of one journalist's impression of the young cipher.*

WHO WAS THAT MASKED MAN?

Goddamit, I knew I should have worn my Bazooka Joe mask—confronting me across the table in the A&M interrogation room is Klark Kent, who in spite of his biography isn't a church organist from Wales or a bank clerk from Tyneside, nor even a computer programmer from Brooklyn. What he definitely is: blond, six foot three, American, around twenty-five to thirty years of age (he has too much time perspective to be younger) wearing white projectionist's gloves, a black greatcoat, and this goddamn Jimmy Carter mask, none of which he removed in the incognito ninety-minute conversation, playing the secret identity trip to the hilt. What you will know about him is that he has a hot single out called "Don't Care" with "Thrills" and "Office Girls" gracing the B-Side of his green vinyl wonder. First issued on Kryptone Records (get it?), an offshoot of the small independent Faulty Products, it has been snapped up and rush-released for mass purchase by A&M because, according to Mr. Kent, "I threatened to snap Tom Noble's neck if he didn't." After all, you don't fool around with Superman, do you?

The possibility of the single becoming a hit is actually pretty good, it has received suitable airplay, and was even Paul Burnett's pick of the week a while back. "Don't Care" is an incredibly catchy satire about this guy who knows (not believes, you understand) that he is the greatest thing in the universe, and its main message is not that he doesn't care, but that everybody is the star of their own life and should act accordingly. Kent also plays all the instruments himself, with such a remarkable ability that it leads us to the main question: who the hell is he really?

Now there are several possibilities—he could be an extremely famous American superstar trying to find out if he can cut it without the instant status and having a good laugh at the same time, but this Klark sternly denies. The story he would have you believe goes something like this:

Born of English and American parents, who were archaeologists, he spent many years in Lebanon, where he became involved with a local religious group by the name of the Druze. He says he was accepted by them because of his "high intuitive matrix." The Druze, he claimed, are particularly interested in the development of emotion and believe that God is a manifestation of art. He will not be more explicit about this religion other than to say his main interest was not the religion itself but their techniques for stimulating creativity in the individual.

Because of the civil war in Lebanon he was forced to move back to the States, where he worked for a private firm (probably computer electronics or communications) who paid him highly for his skills. He left suddenly in 1976 to come to England, where he felt the change in climate in the music scene, felt cold toward it, and immediately bought a Gibson SG, a Fender bass, a drum kit, and a couple of tape recorders, and within a month he had taught himself to play them, apparently using skills he developed from the Druze.

Ask why he persists with the masquerade, he tells you, "This is important for personal, creative, and business reasons, not to mention legal ones." By which I infer that if the American firm knew where he was they would probably sue the ass off him, probably to give back any information he may possess that they don't want on the loose. Still, becoming a rock star is an unlikely way to hide, isn't it, so maybe he is just a rich prankster.

Klark Kent remains an enigma. During the course of conversation the topics included various aspects of art, religion, radio, the social security system, what Britain needs to do to survive, the sinister motive behind the Soviet arms buildup, expansion of human potential, and a thousand other nonmusical topics, and interesting as they are I can't really go into them here. He's a very erudite gentleman, he may or may not be a superman, but I'm sure we're definitely going to be hearing an awful lot more of him.

—RAB

CHAPTER 8

A QUICK HISTORY OF THE POLICE

1976–78

As narrated in my film Everyone Stares.

It's 1976,
and this thing called punk rock
has just raised its ugly head in London.
Sting, Henry Padovani, and I
have formed a group called: The Police.
We cut our hair, put on shades,
and have adopted the hostile posture of the day.
It's a chaotic scene
so most of our gigs
are from cancellations by other bands.
We're the only guys who know how to hire a truck
and get to the show.
Our fee is £30 sterling:
5 for the truck,
10 for the PA,
and a fiver each for the three of us.
With 400 quid from my buddy Paul,

we recorded our first single
and sell it ourselves, by the box,
to record stores around the country.
I am president of Illegal Records
and chief salesperson.
Sting has his doubts.
He gets a buzz from the energy of the scene,
but pretty much hates the music,
including ours.
So Andy shows up,
with his harmonic sophistication,
and Sting starts writing these big songs.
A sound of our own is beginning to hatch.
Problem is,
the cognoscenti are onto us.

▲ **Hungry professionals**

They know that we're just carpetbaggers.
I have a dark past with the long-hair group, Curved Air,
and Andy Summers has consorted for years
    with the enemy generation.
We are unloved.
But something strange is happening.
A mysterious, masked American has turned up in London
with a couple songs
    that got him a modest hit on the English charts.
He goes under the name of Klark Kent,
but no one knows who he is.
He plays all of the instruments,
writes, sings, and produces the songs.
So, since no one can think of anyone else
    who could do all that,
they are starting to point the finger at me.
Well, it's the first time I've ever been blamed for a hit
    of any kind,
and I'm all for it.
This is the big time.
At last.
But it never would have happened like this
for that known charlatan,
The Police drummer,
so the lesson is clear.
The Police needs to regain its virginity,
to shed the leprous scab of its wretched history,
to shake loose the chains and sally forth
to the promised land of America,
where people are kind of anticipating
something new out of England.
We've been together for two years.
Arriving in New York City
with our gear as hand luggage,

we're ready to start all over from scratch.
My brothers, Ian and Miles, have hatched a scheme
where they are connecting up a string of clubs across America
where un-hippie, rebellious youth
      can be part of a brand-new scene.
It's 1978, and the hippie thing is way old.
Everybody's looking at this New Wave,
which actually is mainly characterized by a new hairdo.
Short hair is the dividing line.
So Ian finds a club in every city
where we can play to the fifty or hundred kids
who have heard of this new thing.
And Miles makes sure the radio guys are there.
Out on the road,
it's the three of us in a van
with my childhood chum Kim Turner at the wheel.
But things are picking up pretty quickly.
There's a buzz about the band.
Shows are filling up,
The clubs are getting bigger.
Best thing about that is, roadies!
Man, I am sick of carrying
those fucking drums around!
It also means that our sound is better,
and we can play fresher.
We're getting pretty good.
Something about the way Andy hits those chords
and the way Sting pumps that bass
just lights me right up.
And in the winter of 1978,
just as America is beginning to notice us,
and with pretty much the first spare change
      I have in my pocket,
I got this Super 8 movie camera. . . .

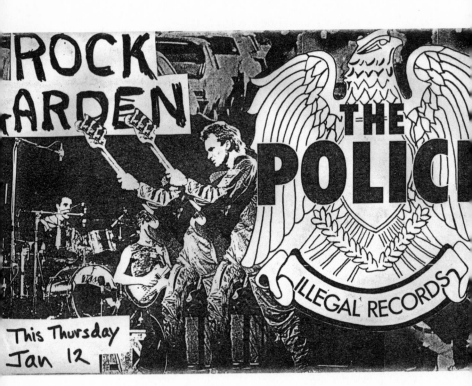

CHAPTER 9

POLICE RULE

1979–84

The Police took up only eight of my fifty-seven years, and those years went by fast. They were big years, and they left a mark; but the really important things happened outside of band life.

Re-entry into the civilian world after band life took a long time. From the day I left college I had never lived in the real world that most people inhabit. Musicians live apart from society, maybe because of our vaguely shamanistic role in life. Office hours are our weekends, and we work while society plays. Saturdays and Sundays are a problem for us because on these days we have to share everything with the civilians, who, since they are crowding the parks and boulevards, are not at their stations making our world function. On Monday everything is ours. Thank God it's Monday!

On Sundays we can't bitch at our managers and there is no laundry service at the hotel. The populace is loose on the streets! The starving musician merely turns up his collar against the world and shuns the light, but the wealthy shaman can build a fortress.

I certainly needed one. When the first money hit, after buying an inexhaustible supply of jet black jeans, I claimed a nice little house on a quiet London street. The sidewalk in front of it immediately became a sacred grove for young fans who, when school got out, would congregate on the neighbor's stoop singing Police songs. They would oooh and aaahh at the tiniest signs of life coming from my house. Inside I was a charging bull who was feeling intimidated by a bunch of girls. I wished I were still in our Ottoman fortress above Beirut. I'd snarl at the congregants ferociously as I came and went.

It may have been inconvenient, but this was what I had come for. Notoriety is an odd by-product of music but essential. The music transports the musician himself first of all but bewitching others is really what it's about. Music is an amplifier of one's self. If it doesn't capture attention, then the magic is sterile. So being stared at is part of the deal, and at first it was just fine to create a stir just by existing.

There would be a rustle of recognition and the "S" sound.

"Isss it him? . . . PoliCe . . . SSting. . . . SSStewart . . ." I'd be wondering if I was just hearing things, then there would be someone praying at me for a photo or an autograph, or a blessing.

One reason to be cheerful was that I got pissing rights over pretty much everybody. At least in the music universe. The combination of chart success and validated musical prowess (other musicians respected us) meant that I had a rank that was right alongside the graven images that I myself worshipped.

That's how I felt the night I took my dad down to the West End in London to see the Buddy Rich Big Band at Ronnie Scott's Jazz Club. My daddy raised me on Buddy Rich, and it was a thrill, not just to get to see his show and experience the most spectacular manifestation of my craft on the planet, but also for my father and me to be treated like royalty in Buddy world. Backstage after the show I was saved from gushing over the master by his band surrounding me for autographs. His players were all the hottest young cats straight out of Juilliard, and they grooved to The Police. It was a pretty perfect Christmas moment in my heart as Dad and Buddy reminisced about bygone bandstands, notorious bandleaders, and legendary big band players from back in the day. They were contemporaries and had inhabited the same world before my father was swept away by the Second World War into a life of international skulduggery. Every now and then after the war was over, he would pull his trumpet out of its battered case and blow some soul over Lebanon from the terrace of our house in the hills. It was a big glow to see him now, backstage at the swank jazz club, getting respect in the world of his unrealized dreams from my most exulted music deity.

But living with idolatry is strange, even for those who seek and expect it. You notice that people act oddly in your presence. There is heightened tension. Veins throb in people's foreheads. People laugh nervously, particularly at any gag from the Known One. The tiniest acts of kindness, wisdom, or wit are rewarded with undue enthusiasm. The palest sigh or frown can be an excruciating laceration on the soul of the faithful.

People apologize for all manner of imperfections, as if it is their duty to maintain the pristine quality of my environment. People offer their seat, their place in line, their daughter, wife, or mother. Folks seem to assume that I deserve a better shake than they get. Somehow I'm special, although there is not anything remotely sacred about me. In Los Angeles, where many really luminous stars live, civilians are actually discomfited when they see stars unpampered, even if they snicker about it and exaggerate the anecdote later. It's hard sometimes to know how nice or not people really are. Everybody is on best behavior.

Although most people really don't know or don't care about the cult-head, there are some who strenuously pretend not to. They are usually the people who are most drawn by the strange social magnetism and overcompensate as they resist it. You can see the struggle to tamp down the butterflies. It looks like a kind of hysterical nonchalance. At the other end of the scale are the folks who are so bewitched that they think they are in the presence of an apparition. Two of them will stand in front of me and talk about me as if I'm a painting on a museum wall.

"Gosh he's tall!"

If I move or speak directly to them they will still conduct their dialogue about me as they interact with the avatar.

"Tell him he's tall. . . ."

As I was starting to experience this I was pretty sure it wasn't normal, but for the moment it was the role I had chosen. It didn't occur to me until years later that I'm just some guy.

It was getting claustrophobic. Privacy deprivation is something like sleep deprivation. The love that surrounds you becomes vexatious.

I often wished that I could merely turn my collar up and shun the light.

A wall went up. Suddenly I could afford a country estate, so off I went to green Valhalla in darkest Buckinghamshire. The ivory tower grew like a beanstalk. Old friends gave up trying to get through. When they did, I had to put them at ease by downplaying everything. And so there was I, overcompensating.

Fame has its comforts but is intermittent in its use as a tool or key. Sometimes it deserts you. You can't plan ahead on the basis that it will work for you. Sometimes the maître d' at the most critical restaurant will light up and throw rose petals as he escorts you to the best table, sometimes not. When confronted by nonrecognition it is perilous to pull rank—because it's not real rank anyway. How the mighty crash and burn to be overheard saying:

"But don't you realize that I'm—?"

On the whole, things turn out better when the mojo is working than when not. When the eminence is recognized, doors open to the rarefied zones and the blessings of this world are more freely offered. It's like being extremely lucky in an inordinate number of instances. When the mojo is lit you just get dealt better cards and any roll of the dice is a winner.

It does lose its fizz, however. If you are an alligator, then the dankest swamp is just plain white bread. If you are an eagle, you're probably over having the world right there on the end of your talons. It's just another day in the boring old sky. And so it was that I tried to remember my most yearning youthful fantasies about the ultimate Olympian state of grace that should be rock star life. When I looked around, all I could see was the same old everyday world. Of course, my life was blessed, but why did I have to keep on reminding myself?

One day, on my way to the airport, my limousine takes a detour through a leafy neighborhood with children playing on the lawns and guys playing baseball. I look out the window at the splendor of a glamorous life. I've seen this world in a thousand cereal commercials and am enthralled by its simple, easy, wholesome charm. I'm sick of Valhalla. I wish I could live on this street. I wish everyone could live on this street.

It took getting off the jet to start being able to catch stuff as it went by. The strangest things happened when I jumped ship and crawled onto dry land.

PART II
LEARNING TO BE NORMAL

CHAPTER 10

CONGO

JULY 1984

*Far up the Congo River, in the heart of Africa, is a
tributary called the Sangha, on the banks of which
we're shooting a movie.*

Jean-Pierre Dutilleux, the mad Belgian explorer, is shouting at
me through the clattering drums and chanting natives. The jungle
is alive with music.

"Go with the shaman!"

He's pointing to a dark hut across the clearing. I scramble
through the dancing frenzy of the massed Pygmies and duck into
the tribal Holy of Holies. The shaman is there, suiting up for the
big party.

Outside the hut, two or three hundred Pygmies are cutting it up
on the dance floor, singing their swaying melodies and banging
their elephant skin drums. There are more Pygmies gathered than
have ever been seen before—even by Pygmies. The scene is lit by
bonfires and by big klieg lights that we have borrowed from the
French logging crew whose camp has been our base down here in
the deep jungle of northern Congo.

It's dark in the hut, but light from the fire is streaming through
the leafy walls. The shaman is rustling his relics as I stumble in.

I'm crouching under the low roof and mumbling some supportive incantations of my own. Just to put him at ease, you understand. We're in the same business, after all.

"Jesus loves you, this I know," I venture.

He peers at me without much expression and then returns to his preparations. I'm about as relevant to his business as a man from Mars. He dons a grass cape that covers his head and drapes down to cover his feet. Brushing past me, he steps out into the clearing.

As one, the voices rise to a higher-pitched fever as the shaman twirls among them. The strands of his headdress splay around him as he spins. Behind him your correspondent is grooving along for the ride, trying to fit in and dancing up a little improvised frenzy of my own. The throng is so dense that most of my gyrations are confined to waving my arms above their heads.

JP and the crew are there with the cameras, but I can see over the bobbing heads of the natives that he has lost our love interest. The scene we are trying to shoot calls for her to be discovered, at last, by the Rhythmatist in the deep jungle. She is found among the lost Mboroo tribe and has been entranced by their strange music. Our heroine is played by JP's fiancée, Tisch.

But the shot is not going as planned. These are real Fourth World natives, and they really are entranced by their strange music. Tisch, daubed with paint and festooned with feathers, has been adopted by the women of the tribe. They have surrounded her and are wailing at her, imbibing of her outlandish blond pallor. She too is wailing.

"JayPeeeee! They won't let me through!" she beseeches, struggling to get to the men's circle, where she can be discovered by the intrepid Rhythmatist. Pygmy social rules are very strict about this, as it happens. Women only dance with the women.

JP is in more of a frenzy than anyone. He's a director who wants his shot. He clears a path through the womenfolk and drags Tish over to the men's side—where I'm still thrashing away.

Actually by now I've got kind of a groove going with my new brothers in music. The rhythm is tricky but the pulse is clear, and I have pretty much got the hang of it. The melody is otherworldly and rhythmically harder to fathom. Somehow their voices fuse in choral waves and spirals, swirling up to peaks and swooping down to deep earth tones. I'm just chanting Beach Boy songs and swooping along with them.

"Ooooweeeoooweeeoooooo!"

The story we are trying to tell in this odd movie we are making is kind of improvised. And JP is improvising now, inflamed no doubt by the general hubbub.

"OK, now ravish her!" he shouts to me.

"Whuh?"

I was midswoop, but now I have paused, trying to hear him through the din.

"Keep dancing! And then ravish her!"

"JayPeeee!" wails Tisch.

"Radish?"

JP is on a mission, and he won't quit until he has me transgressing upon his babe in front of the astonished Pygmies. The music abates momentarily while the natives process this new information about the White Giants; but then they get the drift and are back into full swing as I perform my thespian duty on the director's girlfriend.

I'm sure if we had any idea what we were doing before we got to Africa this movie would probably make more sense, but I'm also sure that we wouldn't be having anything like this amount of fun shooting it. We're just making this up as we go along. There are just five of us in two Land Rovers. JP and I are in front, trailblazing and searching out locations for our ever more flimsy "plot"; behind us are Richard, Paul, and Lorne on sound, camera, and everything else. In the first vehicle our story conferences are becoming ever more feverish as we struggle to imagineer all of the cool stuff that's happening around us into some kind of plausible "story." The only plot point that we can agree on is that the love interest is lost and can't be found.

Neither of us knows a thing about plot development or denouement or epiphany, but JP sure does know how to sniff out adventure. This intrepid Belgian is the real Indiana Jones—even though I'm not sure if it's a case of art imitating life or vice versa. He's got the leather jacket and the indefatigable hat (just like the movie) and even sometimes uses a long whip for flicking mosquitoes and tarantulas; but when you are carving your way through the deep jungle, JP is the real thing. He can sidle up to anyone, Samburu chief or customs agent, and work something out. With his Babel of languages and patois he can cajole and barter us into (or out of) anywhere. It's his easy tongue and tight fist on the wallet that is stretching our two-week budget into two months across the Dark Continent.

And we are arguing the whole way. I'm after musical/cultural truth, and he wants to shoot a Hollywood blockbuster. That's because he has spent his life documenting the cultural truths of the vanishing Fourth World beyond the last frontiers of the planet. The Holy Grail for most of his life has been contact with the last and most remote tribes. He's been hit by every form of tropical disease, snake, tsetse fly, and scorpion in the swamps and jungles of his day job. Now he's ready for the comforts of show business, and I'm his ticket.

Off the east coast of Africa we have found a scenic little slaver island called Lamu. From this spot Arab traders would venture into the heartland to spread Islam and capture humans. Of course that's all forgotten now and the modern islanders are a cheerfully roguish mix of Africa and Islam. The wealth from the bad old days is still evident in the fine Arab architecture with its lavish filigree, but the sandy streets have never seen cars.

While the crew hunker down in Mombasa to clean their gear, JP and I catch a boat out there and discover that it's the perfect location for a chase scene. We figure that the black-clad Rhythmatist arrives with his sampling equipment and is just about to discover . . . (we'll think up something) but the natives become agitated by the strange ritual music emanating from his black-clad traveling lab.

Which gives you a pretty good idea of how thinly we spread the logic as we built this cinematic masterpiece. Never mind how we got here, this locale is perfect for a chase, so let's have a chase. When the crew arrives we hire some donkeys and start rolling. It's Ramadan, when faithful Muslims fast by day and feast by night, so the local extras are photogenically grumpy as they wave scimitars and swarm after me on a horde of donkeys. Of course the wily black-clad Rhythmatist is too slick for them and his donkey is the sleekest. He gives them the slip before we lose the light and then go feasting with the erstwhile bad guys. Deep into the night we laugh as we languish on the lamplit streets of Lamu.

▲ Logo in Lamu

In the bar of the Nairobi Sheraton, JP sniffs out a huge game reserve and ranch owned by the billionaire Khashoggi family. In no time at all he has sidled up to young Khalid Khashoggi and scored an invitation to shoot there. It's perfect for our story—whatever that might be—so we load up the Rovers and head out there. One of the toys at the ranch is an excellent black ex-polo horse that Kahlid offers as a prop. It's certainly an improvement on the donkeys. We devise a scheme to shoot an establishing shot of the black-clad Rhythmatist traveling across Africa on his quest for . . . we're still arguing about that. Anyway he's traveling, and as he travels he comes alongside a herd of giraffe and rides along poetically with them.

Before sunrise the trackers are out over the savannah, and they have located the perfect herd. The giant herbivores are deep in

acacia cover for the night, but the beaters gently coax them toward an open plain where the black-clad horse groover is waiting. As the gray dawn grows I'm astride this dark mare with my ears stretched out to the sounds of the wild. Over yonder in the mist, JP is yelling something from his perch on top of one of the Land Rovers. He wants the giraffe to emerge from the thicket and majestically caravan in front of the camera with the far-seeking Rhythmatist sojourning scenically alongside.

My horse hears the giraffes before I do, and she's not wild about it. By the time I can see them towering through the early light, the mare is spooked out of her skin and is trotting and prancing with fear. Horses don't safari for pleasure. They aren't interested in anything that might come crashing through the bush. But I've got her more or less steady when the giraffes appear. My attempts to persuade the horse to snuggle up to the herd, however, are not anything you would see in a cowboy movie. The black mare is struggling to trot backward away from the wild giraffes or, if I can get her to move forward, is making a tight circle. She has no interest in the giraffes at all. And I'm not looking that sage myself.

I'm technically the boss in this relationship, so I get her moving toward the tall ones. But she's so full of fear that if she's going to do anything for me, it's going to be at a gallop. So now we are charging toward the gentle giants. As soon as they catch sight of us, they are off across the open plain—with me and my steed in pursuit. Wow, this is fun! Now that the horse is at a flat-out gallop, she's much calmer and soon catches up with our quarry. The giraffes are huge and beautiful. As the horse gallops alongside, they appear to be in slow motion. I have to be careful not to get too close, though. One kick from Jimmy Giraffe would take me out of the saddle and turn my skull into peanut butter and jelly.

Man, I'm in heaven. We are charging right along the equator where the dawn happens very quickly. The sun is bursting over the edge of the Maasai Mara as the posse of giraffes, horse, and Rhythmatist takes flight across the open savannah. Now this is the real cowboy movie. The brilliant golden side lighting of the rising sun against the dull blue awakening sky finds me galloping free over the distant African plain with the theme to *Bonanza* ringing in my ears. This is truly one of the Great Designer's more intelligent moments. Sometimes the concentrated beauty of a moment can make even the craftiest professional shaman stop and thank.

My rapture is interrupted suddenly by the advent of an acacia thicket, into which the giraffes continue their canter without breaking stride. End of adventure. The prickles on those acacia tree are like nails. The giraffes don't seem to mind and can plow right through, but for me on my horse those needles are at face level. "Whoa, Nelly!" I cry, tugging the reins and leaning back against the stirrups. My agile little mare puts four hoofs in front of her and stops like a polo pro. She would have bounced me right out the front door if I hadn't been ready.

Problem is that the giraffes broke cover and headed off totally in the wrong direction, away from the cameras. So while I was free-birding with my tall giraffe brethren, JP was over the horizon, howling profanities. Later, when I return sheepishly to HQ we arrange to try again tomorrow morning.

It actually takes us two more glorious mornings before we are able to line up the giraffes, horse, and camera. We end up with twenty-three seconds of wild ride on film. It doesn't look much like a traveling shot, so we'll have to think up another dubious plot point to explain the Rhythmatist's relationship with the galloping giraffes. Maybe something to do with rhythm and the herding instinct . . . gimme a minute.

Another of the Khashoggi toys is a pride of lion who live in a large compound surrounded

▲ Polo logo

by fourteen-foot-high chain-link fencing. The whole animal thing is a little distracting for us since the Rhythmatist is a musicologist not a biologist, but we are broad-minded when it comes to dumb plot turns that put our hero next to photogenic stuff. Lions? Um . . . OK, he's got to commune with the lions who are the last mammals to have seen the girl who has disappeared (or has been kidnapped, or who has gone on a spiritual quest, or . . . something).

Young Khalid also has, in one of the air-conditioned sheds at the ranch, a full set of band equipment—guitars, amps, PA system, and drums. Those Saudi kids love to jam! The drums are a little obvious, but what the heck. We load them up, drag them out to the lions, and set up a shot.

Now lions are best avoided but aren't usually a problem out in the bush. For some reason they regard humans as superior predators, or at least one or two rungs up the food chain. If you are in a vehicle they pay no attention at all, but if you are on foot they will generally move away with majestic caution, unless you surprise or corner them. Cubs are less cautious, more playful, and way scarier than the adults. Lions actually become more dangerous when they have greater contact with humans because they lose their fear. Perhaps they start noticing ours.

Within the lion's enclosure is another area sectioned off with a ten-foot-high wall of chain-link. In this area a chicken wire cage has been constructed in which my drums are set for me to serenade the lions. I'm sure JP actually thinks that we're going to get the lions grooving to the beat. We have both studiously avoided any talk of what relevance any of this might have to our film.

I notice that there is no top to my little chicken wire cage. This amuses both our crew and the Khashoggi ranchers.

"Show no fear!" they chortle.

I insist that I want full chicken wire coverage, and they start rigging while still snickering about the scaredy-cat black-clad guy. The wranglers are dubious that the big cats will come anywhere near the noisy drums, so the feed truck arrives full of fresh kill with which to festoon the cage. It is hoped that the meat show will inspire the beasts to enjoy the music. Or at least to get close enough for us to get our shot.

As soon as the lions get a whiff of the meat truck they are over the ten-foot fence in a twinkling. They have to be shouted at and coaxed to back off while I climb into my cage and the wranglers festoon it with fresh gazelle. The lions retreat snarling as the guys wave sticks and throw rocks at them. As the ranchers finish their set dressing and clear the shot, the lions come right up for dinner. But when I hit my drums they stop dead in their tracks. They do *not* like my music. JP can shout "Action!" till he's blue in the face but Simba ain't coming anywhere near my racket. Their ears are back, and they're cowering. So I have to stop hitting the drums and just pretend to play. The deep culture of this transports me. Just like a Britney Spears video. After waving my arms for a while in the direction of my drums, being very careful not to hit them, the wild beasts pluck up courage and begin to approach the cage. Soon they are swiping at the treats and JP has the cameras rolling happily.

One lion has discovered that he can reach under the cage. In fact, as his forearm advances under the chicken wire toward my bass drum the whole side of the cage is coming adrift! Just as the consequence of this is dawning on me there is a huge crash next to my head where one of the tawny brutes is climbing onto the roof! The totally inadequate-to-bear-the-weight-of-a-lion roof of my chicken wire cage is just beginning to sag when, faster than thought I'm the loudest drummer on the planet blazing away with terrified fury on the Khashoggi drums. I think it's the only drum solo that I've ever played in my life—can't stand drum solos—but I'm hammering now! The lions back off with an expression on their faces that reminds me of a certain singer that I know. . . .

I'll have to tell the Maasai about this trick. All they have to do is carry a chrome snare drum with them when out in the bush protecting (or rustling) the cattle. For myself, I'm relieved at the lions' poor taste in music.

■

WE SQUABBLE ENDLESSLY OVER the finer points of the plot as we cross Africa but we are of one mind as we grab every opportunity to interact with the music that is everywhere. Africans apply rhythm to life as if it were flavoring. Any physical activity has a groove, particularly if it's a coordinated team activity like handling a boat, loading a truck, or enjoying life.

My theory is that I should be able to find the antecedents of American music here on this continent. By American music I mean modern popular music that is in four-four rhythm with a backbeat and uses the flattened seventh, or "blue note." I'm looking for the ingredients of our music that don't come from Mozart. It's a useful thing for me to know about since I make a living as a purveyor of this uniquely American mix of Africa and Mozart and which we Americans export all over the world. It's my (far from unique) *Out of Africa* theory of why American music rules.

We generally steer clear of the cities in our quest, mostly because JP is too cheap (with my money) to pay city prices. Air-conditioning is for pussies. For JP drinkable water is for pussies. Out in the villages there is music everywhere. The first thing about Africa is that it's not one place. It's a giant continent with huge diversity and many different places. The urgently tight polyrhythms of the coastal Giriama, the throaty war music of the Maasai, the heavy drums of Burundi, and the transcendental chanting of the Pygmies are just some of the wildly contrasting styles that cross our path as we follow the equator from east to west. But *none* of them sound like Chuck Berry.

One city that we can't avoid is Kinshasa, Zaire. This town is the wildest rodeo in Africa. There is a splendid dictator holding the country together while his cohorts help themselves to everything in sight. The guys with guns are running everything, that is, if anything is being run at all. Getting into Zaire is easy. Just pay the Man and keep walking. Getting out is more of a problem.

We're on our way to Gabon, where JP knows a guy who is tight with President Bongo. Before us is the Congo River, fast flowing and croc-infested. On the other side is the sleepy little Belgian-flavored Brazzaville. On this side is bedlam at the quayside. A large riverboat—more like a city on a raft—is disembarking, and the men with guns are in charge of threatening, herding, obstructing, and abusing the river people. This entrepôt is where the wealth of the hinterland comes down the river to the capital and the goons get to tax it. The multitudes are heaving this way and that under the lash of the bosses.

We manage to thread the throng and get aboard the crowded ferry. As the ship pulls out into the current we can see a chain gang of criminals being off-loaded from the river raft. They are herded onto trucks, and we shudder at their fate for a moment before turning our gaze to the approaching shore. Brazzaville. We can see tree-lined boulevards and cheerful-looking citizens as the vessel nears the quiet little harbor.

With glad hearts we're soon down the ramp and JP is head-to-head with the customs guy. But it's not going well. For some reason he's not responding to our blandishments. Soon there are several uniforms leaning over our passports with furrowed disapproval on their brows. This is bad because now any bribery has to be public, which totally takes the savoir faire out of it. You just don't know how the group will respond. So we learn, with heavy hearts, that we must cross back to Kinshasa and get proper Zairian exit visas.

And the ship is now casting off. We need to be aboard, so JP zips up his silver tongue, and we're on our way back to crazy Kinshasa. Around us the river air is thickening and with equatorial speed, night is falling in darkest Congo. This is the last boat before the crocodiles take over. We'll spend the night in Zaire.

At the customs shed the last of the river people are being processed, scolded, and fleeced as we get to our turn with the Man. He's just plain pissed off. His has not been a good day. Our documents are just the final and worst insult after a day of river scum.

We have just come from Brazza? But we couldn't enter Brazza? What was our problem in Brazza? As he considers the weight of our implausible story, other passports and documents are being thrust at him from every angle. The African customs official is a multitasker. Standing in line must be a European invention because you don't see it much here. Any dealing with officialdom is shared with other supplicants who are weaker than you. Stronger ones are ahead of you. When the official hits a problem document, he merely bats it away and plucks another from the multitude that bobs before him.

He has batted ours away several times now, and the throng around us can smell our weakness. They clamor over and around us. JP is raging through his repertoire of Gallic persuasions, temptations, and damnations. But Kinshasa Man is not having it. Suddenly his eyes slacken and he hunches forward.

"Go sit over there!" he commands.

Foolishly, we're not having it either, dammit. We're still talking.

"Over THERE!" he shouts. Then he's standing up and shouting as he bangs the desk with his power stick. Now we are dancing cheek to cheek with the men with guns as they drag us over to the side of the room. Our buddy is still shouting orders, so the heavies take us outside and handcuff us to a bench. Just like that, we are fucked. Chained to a bench pending further review, at the pleasure of our new friend. The soldiers wander off, but we're still chained to the bench. The crowds have begun to thin, and the dimly lit quayside is slowing down.

The human traffic is just a trickle when we spy a skinny white man and manage to catch his attention. He nods but keeps moving. Not much he can do on his own. JP is shouting "Belgique!" to the back of his head as the stranger fades off into the night.

Soon it's just JP and me, chained to a bench and deep into our usual "story conference." He's got me convinced that ours is an "elliptical" film, whatever that means. The evening around us has become dark and quiet. But not completely quiet. During a pause in our debate, while I consider the magnitude of his concept, I hear music.

It's a lilting, throbbing, bouncing, laughing, dancing, and romancing kind of music. It's nothing like the stuff we have been hearing out in the bush; this is city music. It has those ingredients that I have been looking for. Of course it does, because it's the return voyage of Chuck Berry. I'm hearing guitar, bass, and drums—American instruments, rhythms, and harmony—having traveled back to Africa.

It's coming from a radio inside the building. It dawns on us that we've actually been forgotten. About an hour ago there was a changing of the guard, with a lowering of flags and a clanging of gates. Our friend never came for us. Heck, he's probably got people who pissed him off chained up all over town. The night shift probably doesn't even know we're here.

In our most dulcet tones we start shouting out to the guys in the building.

"Hel·LO, oh," we call, with friendly charm.

Soon the night guys are peering at us from behind their flash-lights. It seems boorish to go into details of our misunderstanding with the day shift. With these guys we feel that we can make a fresh start. What's that music? I inquire in my lame French.

"Ahh , Franco Franco!" they reply, and one of them goes back inside to turn it up.

▲ Swinging through the trees with my Pygmy friends.

Just when we have the Bantu chiefs more or less mollified, we get a welcome visitor. The Belgian embassy was contacted by the passing stranger, and this is the ambassador himself coming over to investigate the report of two of his compatriots chained by goons down at the dock. The guards are impressed by his stature as he drops names of the most senior and most heinous thugs in government. Best of all, he brought beer.

Soon we are all grooving to the Lingala music. The party has moved inside the building and we are unleashed, with cheerful apologies all around.

Things are a lot more comfy, and we're out of bondage, but the soldiers can't exactly let us go. If Ahab locked us up, he had better see us there in the morning or the night guys might get trouble. Regretfully, we must stay.

Well, we're here among friends now, and the hotels we stay at generally aren't much better than this anyway, so sure, this is good. And I could listen to this music all night.

Next morning the ambassador returns. Phone calls have been made, and now Ahab is all smiles as he stamps our passports and waves us on. Once more our hearts are glad as we pull into Brazzaville, although JP is sniffing with disapproval as I drag him straight to the Sofitel Hotel and, for the first time in weeks, slap out my plastic. After our night with the mosquitoes in the shed I need a shower, hard liquor, and soft sheets.

JP, the mad Belgian explorer, is already down at the bar. He has sidled up to some guy who's got a plane flying upcountry to bring supplies to the logging companies near Ouésso. That's right in the middle of Pygmy country. . . .

CHAPTER 11

HORSES

JUNE 1987

*Ten years after scraping the streets of London
as a starving musician, things are looking up.*

Hey, Rock Star!" a large voice is booming across the polo field. I look up from my pony inspection to see a pin-striped, extravagantly mustachioed Sikh striding across the grass toward me. "I have a team for you," he announces. This must be Kuldip "Collin" Singh Dhillon, about whom I have heard jealous rumors. In person, he is the most affably energized person that I've met in the polo world: big smile, easy laugh, and a jaunty style. Butter wouldn't melt in his fangs.

I'VE BEEN HOLED UP on my country estate for several years now. This place seemed like the obligatory destination of my success in music. Apart from basic financial security, this was the best I could come up with as a dream to realize. It contains the recording studio of my dreams and every musical instrument that I ever dreamed of owning. It even has a couple of horses.

I had almost forgotten about horses. At Millfield I learned to

ride the hard way—hours of cantering around a paddock without stirrups. We also played polo. I was never much good at the game, but did seem to have a good seat on a horse. The riding program was so enveloping, with the cantering, tack maintenance, horse maintenance, and mucking out the stables, that riders tended to exist in a world that was removed from the rest of the school. For a while, horses even crowded out my obsession with music.

Music just came into my life and dragged me into its world. Since there was no room in the wretched struggle of my music career for horses, I forgot about them. Years later, when I got the country estate I was excited to rekindle the horse thing. Now there would be no one barking at me, and I would be able to play with my own horses without having to shovel their shit.

The only problem was that after I cantered around my fields a few times and clopped along the country lanes around my village, I pretty quickly ran out of things to do on my horses.

ON AN INVITATION OF an old friend to attend a polo game at the Guards Polo Club in Windsor, I am reminded of the most fun thing of all to do on horses. With the riders uttering strangely familiar cries as the horses gallop past me on the emerald expanse of the Windsor polo ground, the bulb blinks on in my head, and I am striding up to the clubhouse with a whole new hobby hatching.

The first person I see inside is a swooning young woman, who points me to the back office where I must talk to the boss, a Major Ronald Ferguson. This is still in the height of The Police ascendancy, and I'm wearing leather pants and a violent shirt. My hair looks like I'm being electrocuted.

The major is mystified by my presence in his office. "Are you a member of the HPA?" he asks, squinting suspiciously beneath his outthrust eyebrows. "USPA?" he ventures, upon hearing my American accent. As a nonmember of any known polo association, he tells me regretfully that I am an unknown quantity and therefore am presumed to be unsafe on the polo field. The horses are moving fast out there, and there is very real danger if a player is not qualified. Also this, by the way, is an ancient military club; it is the apex of the polo ziggurat, with a membership waiting list of generations.

So with a little research I find the Kirtlington Park Polo Club in Oxfordshire, about forty minutes away from my house. I arrive as quietly as possible, but Rupert, the club manager, erupts with enthusiasm. In a twinkling he has rustled me up a horse and helmet and has thrust me out onto the field for a chukka. Well, it's like a pillow fight in the harem. At this entry level of play, hardly anyone can hit the ball and some of the players are kind of loose in the saddle. So there is much swinging of mallets and cursing at horses but not much galloping. If the ball goes through the goalmouth, a horse probably kicked it. By some strange miracle, however, all I can think about when it's over is how to get more of it.

It doesn't take long to scare up some horses (horse dealing is the second-oldest profession), and soon I'm out there every Tuesday, Thursday, Saturday, and Sunday, with thoughts of nothing else for the remainder of the week. In England, summer afternoons last forever. The late sun catches the greens and golds of the fields in a particular way that lights up the Saxon heart.

Sometimes my teenage son Sven rides out to the games with me, bringing along some of his suave boarding school friends. Sometimes my smaller boys, Patrick, Jordan, and Scott, pile into the car and swarm the horse box while I play. None of the lads seem interested in the horses, but they all love the truck that they travel in. So do I, for that matter; it's my favorite vehicle. I can load six horses in the back, Margaret Churchill, who runs my horses, and her crew drive up front, and in the middle is my little traveling clubhouse. For a great view of the game I can climb up on the roof with deck chairs. The boys are all over that truck, although they don't spend much time in the deck chairs watching Daddy's game.

It's a faintly familiar alien world. My new polo chums are just like my old schoolmates, but I've been around the world ten times and they haven't. They are like the cast of a Merchant Ivory movie, and I'm from another planet. They are very impressed that I'm a Millfield boy, which surprises me. My old school was no Eton. It was most notable for the raffishness of the parents (King of Thailand, Elizabeth Taylor, various bin Ladens, and other nouveaux riches) but also for its sports programs. In the polo world, Millfield is second in prestige only to Sandhurst. In fact I soon learn that one of the biggest heroes of English polo is none other than my old school buddy Sniffer Kent. At Kirtlington I can dine out on just having met the man.

At first, I assume that among this rural crowd, I'm regarded as just a mysterious American with a clean slate and odd hair. But one day in the clubhouse, someone blurts out, "So what's it like to be a pop star?" Oh well, they were on to me from day one and were just being polite. Pretty soon the conversation goes back to horses.

These are the first people that I've met since high school who aren't in show business. Even in college I shrank from the light of "straight" society, and I've been underground ever since. These country polo folk are kind of insular themselves with their über-straightness, V-neck sweaters, corduroy pants, and Old World charm. Although they are feared and despised by the British middle class, they seem completely harmless to an American like me. The accent gets me every time. They live with frowsy grace in beautiful country estates and are extremely vague about their jobs. If you already own several acres of Twinkishire, it doesn't take much to throw a couple of horses into one of the fields. If you have grown up in the country with plenty of time for such pursuits, you can make your own polo ponies and be equipped on Sunday afternoon with enough of a string to earn your gin and tonic. These folks are not so much wealthy as leisurely.

Kuldip Singh Dhillon is a contrast to this. There is no subtle mystery about his wherewithal at all. He is that most dreaded creature of all in the country set: the self-made man. He may have started off selling jeans in the market stalls of Manchester, but now he's an unstoppable force. Somewhere out there in the world he's a slash-and-burn real estate developer. In polo world he's just having fun as he chews up the gentle folk. But his personal magnetism is such that they grudgingly enjoy his company. Hard not to.

Also out there on the polo field are the triple-alpha-type big shots. It doesn't just take money to play polo. If you work for a living, you need to be able to walk out of the office on weekday afternoons for matches around the country. For this you need to own the office. These are the guys who show up on the field in Ferraris with hot second wives and slick livery. They are used to winning and love the idea of polo, but most are learning to ride as they try to master the game.

And this isn't the kind of riding that you do on rented trail horses. These horses are revved up and hog-snorting for fast galloping, sudden stops, mad turns, and explosive acceleration. You need your horse to go exactly here, or there, so you can hit the ball or push someone else away from it. And then there is the strategy of the game. You actually haven't got time to think about the horse. You read the play and race to hit your mark. The horse is on a hair trigger. You communicate with leg and bit but your mind has to be on the game, not on the horse.

In the winters, I go to Argentina and buy horses. My friend Adrian Laplacette has a ranch there, and every day is spent in endless polo. The speed of play is terrifying but smooth. The Argies start young, and by the age of twelve have complete command of horse and ball. Any other player at my level is either eleven, or not Argentine. Unlike the free-for-all melee of the Kirtlington players, the Argies all hit the ball accurately with strategic purpose, and can turn on a dime as they read the play.

The game is divided into eight-minute chukkas. Actually with stoppages for penalties, they take longer, and by the end of one chukka the horses are soaking in sweat and breathing hard. The players leap onto new mounts and roar off to the next period. The spent horses are quickly stripped of gear, hosed down, rubbed, and then walked until they are calm and dry. Better treatment than I get after a show.

The best horses are made in Argentina. They mix the right amount of thoroughbred for speed with a dab of American quarter horse for muscle. They have enough stock that they can be very selective and throw out (to the cattle ranches) anything that doesn't have a natural talent for the game. Pretty soon there are twelve equine athletes lined up in my string.

To play on a team with Collin will be a step up for my polo involvement. I had been content to play with my horses at practice chukkas at my sleepy little club, but have recently been bringing my string over here to the higher-octane Cirencester club for faster play. Over here, the talk is of tournaments, qualifying matches, and storied trophies.

At Kirtlington, my club, I play formal games on the weekends as arranged by the club, but it's just Sunday fun. There is no urgency to the competition, no ongoing rivalry with enemy teams. Kirtlington Sunday polo on the main ground is about fun with horses combined with Pimm's cup, the scent of fresh-cut grass, the wooden clubhouse, and that beautiful tinkling music of clipped British accents. Not many settings are as beautiful as a golden afternoon in rolling Oxfordshire with the sound of the horses hoofs thundering softly, accented by posh military expostulations, "Oh bloody buggering hell!"

Kirtlington does have one team, the official club team, captained by the formidable John Tyler. In the club bar players tell war stories about heroic away games on fabled fields. It all sounds very sexy, but no one ever asked me to play on this team. Decades of brownnosing are required to make the cut, and I have only been out here for a year or two.

So Collin's proposal is interesting. It will be him and me with two professionals to make up the four-man team. It will be my team, so I get to think up a cool name, choose some colors, and get the shirts made. And I pay for one of the pros.

Entry-level team competition is at the "eight-goal" level. This means simply that the combined handicaps of the four players cannot exceed eight goals. The polo handicap system is the opposite of golf. As a beginner, you start at –2 and then work your way up to a pinnacle of 10. There are maybe six living 10-handicap players in the world. Amateur players can be mighty proud of a 2 handicap. You can start getting paid to play at a 3 handicap and up. I am rated at –1, which means that I gaze down upon about half of the players at Kirtlington but barely qualify for practice chukkas at Cirencester.

▲ Not a great horse for polo.

Collin has a handicap of 1. Add that to my −1, and we must hire eight goals' worth of pro to make up the eight-goal team. How about if we call the team Outlandos?

With a careful eye he has recruited two quietly underhandicapped big hitters for our team, one at 3, the other at 4, which is only seven, but good enough. Philip Elliott is a professional from Australia, and Johnny Kidd is a natural from old money.

Collin hasn't just chosen me for my wallet, nor for my autograph. He and I are under the radar, undiscovered by the HPA, and are also underhandicapped. We have both been building up strings of fast horses by sneaking down to the Argentina ranches. Strangely, horses make a big difference in polo. No amount of investment in a tennis racquet will make you win at Wimbledon, but, as we are about to find out, fast horses can get you to Windsor.

When other kids were developing hand-eye coordination, I was more into my ears I guess. I've never been very good at connecting with a ball. In fact polo is the only ball sport that I have ever worked at. In this sport the ball is addressed from the back of a charging beast, which is a kind of leveler at least. Although my control of the ball is patchy, I'm pretty good at getting to the spot. Some rhythmic part of my brain is in tune with the way horses move, and my fancy boarding school taught me the technique. So on the right horse I can at least get to the ball first, or sometimes more important, deny it to the enemy pro. I may not be able to hit the ball so far, but he ain't gonna be hitting it at all!

Collin is somewhat better. When he connects, the mighty Hammer of the Punjab strikes terror into the hearts of the enemy as the ball flies overhead. The fighting Sikh is fearless and will charge invincibly along the line of play, scattering all before him.

So with me confounding the enemy and Collin intimidating them, Philip and Johnny calmly make the plays.

The big tournament of the season at our level is the Archie David Cup, which is played at Windsor. It's the most coveted trophy of the semipro polo world. At clubs all across the land teams are mustered and qualifying matches are played. The competition to make the final eight is endless.

First we pick off the riffraff, the local lads on their homemade horses. These guys are generally quite sanguine about getting thrashed by our hired assassins because they probably haven't got the horsepower to get very far in the tournament anyway. They're just having a jolly good try. With so many games to play it's hard on the ponies, so you need many.

Slightly more challenging are the Porsche drivers with their assassins. They are not sanguine at all. These qualifiers are not the beautiful Sunday games. They're played during the week on distant back fields. There are no ladies in beautiful dresses out here; just flinty-eyed grooms and trucks full of horses. Since every game is a knockout, we can't lose a single one.

Every match scrapes us past another team. Our cohesion improves. My job at No. 1 is to play forward. I must harass the enemy defenses and clear openings for our big guys. Collin at No. 2 and Philip at No. 3 combine to score goals, while Johnny at No. 4 plays our back door and stops any enemy attack. He's about six foot four and has been playing polo at the family ranch on Barbados since childhood. Philip is an industrious player and led by Collin's raw aggression, keeps us moving inexorably closer to qualifying for the big tournament.

Finally we get to the last qualifier, which is against the official Kirtlington Club team with the formidable John Tyler at the helm. This game is played on Sunday on the main ground, attended by all my chums at my home club. Most of them were on the crap teams that Outlandos has been thrashing so they are jeering as they cheer us on. And we win! Well, Pimm's cup has never tasted so sweet. It feels like stealing the head prefect's tuck. We're going to Windsor! Sixty-odd teams have been whittled down to eight.

We manage to win the quarterfinal without incident. I think the other team must have exhausted their horses in the qualifiers because we run circles around them. Not so the next team that we have to play in the semifinal. For this game we are up against the best horses in the country. The enemy trucks and grooms are like an army. Actually, it's the cavalry. The patron on the opposition sort of owns the ground we are playing on, or at least will one day be king of it. For the moment he's just the Prince of Wales.

Lucky for us, he's a little out of sorts, having just pranged his Aston Martin into my Range Rover at the side of the field. He's playing back for his team, which means that he's my opposite number. I'm supposed to shut him down so that Collin and Philip can score. Well, he's got me completely outhorsed, but I'm able to screw him up just enough for us to win the game. Profane language has a special panache when issued from royal lips.

Next day, my engineer Jeff Seitz is a mystery celebrity. He was at the wheel of my car when Sir clipped it. I was elsewhere at the time. It just so happens that the papers have recently been full of the latest royal tiff. At Ascot recently, Prince Charles was overheard speaking a tad more gruffly than intended to Princess Diana to order her off sitting on his blessed Aston. The photos of the tragic princess scorned have lit up the nation. So now here is the future king bending the same precious fender against a car owned by an unidentified American polo player. The headlines are howling. Jeff has a little extra swagger to him after his brush with royalty. He's a big Diana fan.

By the time we get to the big final match of the Archie David Cup, the club knows whose Range Rover that was, so I'm greeted by my old friend the Major Ronald Ferguson. And sure enough in his view, I have survived to dent royalty. Exactly the sort of problem you get when you let pop stars in. Since I wasn't anywhere near the incident, he can't do much more than harrumph me with those saberlike brows. And getting through to the final of this tournament that he's hosting does confer a certain shred of mojo. My quantity is more known.

We have barely made it. Of my twelve horses, only four are fully fit. The others are either exhausted or dented.

Every night I've been on the phone with Margaret Churchill. Part of her job is to protect the animals against my overuse, but she is as engaged in winning the tournament as I am. Inevitably horses get whacked by ball, mallet, spur, and other horses. In fact nothing nice happens to them on the field, which you would never suspect given their enthusiasm for the game. They are always eager to play. One technique that the polo player has to learn early on is the trick of running backward on one leg while mounting an eager horse. They run out to the game and exert themselves to the max, charging into other horses if need be. They can hear the crack of the ball, and they leap to follow the line. But they do get dented. Big and bony as they are, they're quite fragile. The bruises take time to arise, however, so my conversations with Margaret are like a tally of bumps, scratches, stiffnesses, and sorenesses. We consider which ponies will be ready for the next game and try to plot a course that gives me the hottest ones when I need them. Right now they are all overplayed. We had to win the semifinal yesterday, so I put my best stock on the field to defeat the royal team. Today we get to play on what's left.

It's a big day, but the weather is terrible. The ground is a soggy, slippery mess. As we charge desperately up and down the field, mud is flying from hooves and the ball is bouncing off huge divots. The other team has been on the same endless journey to get here and are looking just as rangy as us. Their assassins are monsters, and even the patrons are gnarly. Our Collin is in a homicidal rage. Under the brim of his helmet his mustache is on fire.

Neither team is able to hold the advantage. We score, then they do, then us, and so on for four chukkas. The bell goes, and it's a tie. Now we go into sudden death: first team to score wins. Well, for this fifth chukka I have to pull out a horse that has already played today. This is where horsepower is critical. Zola can do it. She's my lightest and fastest but most used horse. She's exhausted, but so is everyone else. We can see that the other team is not exactly rushing back out onto the field, so hopefully they are having problems, too. This chukka is just a panic. Everyone has lost their minds and no one can score. Collin is apoplectic. The bell rings again. Still no winner!

We are all so covered in mud that it's hard to distinguish the teams as we limp off the field to find horses. The next chukka is like the fourth day at Woodstock, in a driving rain. We are beginning to wear the other bastards down and are driving the game toward their goal, but they get a lucky break, and in an instant are in our goalmouth. Johnny is there! He cuts the ball away, but the whistle blows. No one is sure what happened, but a foul is called against us. A thirty-yard free shot at our undefended goal is awarded. Aahhh, shit!

The meanest and flintiest of the enemy team lines up the ball for his shot. I'm sitting on my drooping horse behind the back line, soaking in the dull rain. Philip is the only member of our team who isn't wallowing in certain defeat. The umpire has his back to the wet wind and calls "Play." The enemy is still tapping the ball into position for his coup de grâce. Suddenly Philip is over the back line spurring his screw to a gallop! The bad guy just has time to look up in surprise before our good guy cracks the ball away and is off up the field with Outlandos in ragged pursuit. You see, after the umpire says "play" you get one free shot—which ought to be right into the open goalmouth. So the enemy stud's next tap was that shot, and now it's our turn. He should have been listening.

Philip's moment of lightning genius is overcome by exhaustion of course, and our progress up the ground is not beautiful, but we get there. Because of our shambolic progress the attack is blunted by a last dogged defense by the rotters. It's an Agincourt of flying mud, squealing horses, and hoarse curses. We're shouting and straining and swinging but have lost the ball. Finally someone connects with a healthy whack. The ball flies . . . hits a horse . . .

bounces . . . Collin swings . . . misses . . . and then a horse kicks the damned ball over the back line into the goal, and we are victorious!

The good news is that we have won the Archie David Cup and pretty much a lifetime of bragging rights. The slightly mixed news is that Collin and I have been spotted. When you win big tournaments, your handicap goes up. So Collin goes up to 2 and I go to zero, which sounds pretty lame but is better than –1. This slows down our progress for the season now that we have to trade one of our big players in for someone lesser. We carry on winning though, and before the end of the summer I get put up again, to 1. Way better than being a zero, even if we don't end up winning any more games.

One day, in the semifinal of the County Cup at Cirencester, having a great game on a hot day, I ask my horse to turn right when he's just about to turn left. He crosses his front legs, trips, and is suddenly somersaulting. I am obliged to dismount—headfirst out the front door. The important thing to consider during this nanosecond is the full bony half-ton of horse that is sharing your trajectory through space. You don't wish to cushion at all the impending impact of beast and turf. You don't want to be where he hits the ground. When you come down with speed you hit the ground at an angle and can deflect damage by rolling. Before hitting the deck you are already scrambling to keep moving and dodge the horse.

But this is a relatively slow tumble so my own angle of impact with the field is hard. Even though I roll like a ninja and am back on my feet before the horse is, there is something wrong with my shoulder. My collarbone has a new flexibility in a place that it shouldn't. Damn! It's broken. The horse is fine, but there is no more polo for me this summer. Pity also about that Police album that we were just about to record.

The following summer we are so overhandicapped that we can't even get past the local lads into any of the big tournaments. But

Outlandos has gone international. With our chums Bruce Green and Robert Hanson we play all over the world. Kenya, Switzerland, Japan, Jamaica, and across America we show up, and the local oligarchs and masters of the universe entertain us on their yachts, chalets, hot rods, and horses. They get sponsors and have a big day playing "England"—as in Denver vs. England—and the home team gets to win every time. We are on their horses and are hungover from their entertainment, and they are playing in front of their friends, girlfriends, and wives.

Collin is an excellent social climber and more than compensates for my natural laziness in this regard. This is how one glorious July Fourth I find myself on the main ground at Cirencester locked in polo combat again with the Prince of Wales. This time it's just a Sunday game with no big trophy at stake. But for me it's a matter of national honor. I'm the most patriotic American on the planet as I aggress directly upon British royalty on this Independence Day. We are being protected by Secret Service men around the field as, with elbow, knee, and horse, I confound his play in any way that I can.

"No Taxation! . . ."

Bump!

". . . Without Representation!"

Bump!

"Boston Tea Party!"

Bump!

He takes it with pretty good cheer. With his fine horses he's able to escape my colonial embrace and have a pretty decent day anyway and, unlike his ancestor George, is able to at least tie the game.

CHAPTER 12

OPERA

HOLY BLOOD, CRESCENT MOON

SEPTEMBER 1989

*I never imagined, when I first discovered music
that I'd end up commissioned to write a grand opera.
Of course it had to be about the Crusades.*

Just the other day I was a punk rocker, but now I'm an opera composer. So when I walk the stormy Chiltern Hills with the wind in my hair and a torrent of music raging in my head, I have the companionship of Puccini and Wagner to puff me up. My friends are perplexed. Opera?! A guaranteed career killer, even more ruinous than jazz. Opera generates no income but burns up hours, days, years of creative energy. I earn a living flogging film scores in the gaps between orgies of opera composition. Artistically, opera is a natural progression for a film composer. In the same way that the central creative authority in a movie is the director, in opera the composer is boss of everything. I think this tradition comes from the fact that most opera composers are safely dead.

It all began as a cute anecdote. When Michael Smuin, the fight director of my first film (Francis Ford Coppola's *Rumble Fish*) became the director of the San Francisco Ballet, he commissioned me for a ballet, which was performed there in 1984. At a postshow press conference I was asked if I would ever write another ballet.

The flippant reply was, "Sure, when I finish my opera." It got a laugh in a room full of hardened critics, and landed me with this commission. Cleveland Opera director David Bamberger's son, Steven, picked up the quote on national TV and harassed his father into contacting me. David now likes to joke, "I send my son to Duke University, give him a million-dollar opera, and now he wants a car!"

It seemed easy at first. The first idea was to turn the ballet (*Lear*) into an opera, but it just didn't work. I had used up my enthusiasm for Lear and his wretched daughters. The Crusaders seemed like a better way to go. Their ignorant fanaticism and their wild superstitions seemed just perfect for overwrought singing.

The only person I knew who had ever seen an opera was my friend the playwright Susan Shirwen. She introduced me to that melodious word *libretto*. It has a ring to it: *Librrrettto*. She took me to *Salome* (awful), *Calisto* (fun), and *Mask of Orpheus* (incomprehensible). The problem was that I couldn't discern any music in all the yodeling. Is that soprano capable of uttering melody? Perhaps an audiophysicist could find a tune there under the vibrato, but I was unmoved. English, Italian, German, or Welsh—they were all shouting at one another. I could never have sold that hackneyed score to any of my directors. But with an eager heart I got started anyway, sustained by the brazenly arrogant idea that there wasn't anything wrong with opera that a good opera couldn't fix. Ha!

The exercise of setting dialogue to music, however, turns out to be deeply engrossing. With my computer I can conjure up a facsimile of the music. For the vocal parts, I have to sing everything myself—all of the parts. I quite fancy myself as a baritone, but nobody will ever want to hear my soprano renditions. It's a very ugly falsetto. I get through the first act—about an hour of music for full orchestra, choir, and soloists—without the benefit of external inspiration. I'm loving what I'm doing, but just don't get what the masters have done.

A light dawns when I happen across Richard Wagner's Ring Cycle. It is often said that Wagner's music is only for adepts; I can't imagine why. What sentient being wouldn't respond to Siegfried's funeral music? It's the real, hairy-chested stuff: cerebral, majestic, everything. Oh Siegmund, *where* is that sword? Now I begin to understand what this is all about and can write the second act.

FOUR YEARS AFTER MY first conversation with David Bamberger, I have a two-hour opera score on paper, on the stands in front of sixty players of the Cleveland Opera orchestra.

In a giant rehearsal room, up behind the State Theatre, we are working our way down the chart; after years of toil, I'm literally Facing The Music.

Everything is pretty much working as I had hoped, although the orchestra has contrived a few extra battle scenes and the odd car crash, most of which are my fault. I'm wondering about the wisdom of some of the tricky-dick rhythms. This material is a little more involved than the football notes I generally give to Hollywood studio orchestras. The easy sections sound fantastic and the bars that they play correctly (out of three thousand) are worth the four years of composition. The band has been sight-reading up until now and the heroic conductor, Imre Palló, assures me that they will be able to figure it all out by showtime. These first readings are really only to check the parts for spelling mistakes. After to-day's rehearsal the players can finally take their parts home and learn them. It's going to be fine, *inshallah*.

The vocal rehearsals are a different story. David has semistaged a complete, uninterrupted run-through for the benefit of librettist Susan Shirwen and me. The big rehearsal room is filled with choristers and principals, some of whom are cheerfully waving plastic Crusader swords as they sing the Crusader songs. Harry Philby would have loved this.

The chorus is strong enough to lift the roof. Mitchell Krieger, the chorus master, has them tight as a brass section—like Tower of Power. The sound is huge and the atmosphere of the company is exhilarating. They applaud the arias in rehearsal and there have been cheers after the big chorus numbers. They also like the end of act one, in which the sixty choristers and forty supernumeraries ("extras" to you) swashbuckle around the stage in a battle scene that lasts three minutes, ending with a big victory song. It's an organized riot, with the band hammering in the pit. The other battle scene in act two features my humble self leading the wily Saracens over the wall. I slash, I smite, I leap from the parapet, and, at a big musical moment, I throw my dagger clear across the stage (smoke and mirrors) to skewer King Tancred, who in his death throes pulls down a big tapestry. The ecstasy of a fine operatic death.

One dimension that's a big revelation is the visual effect of the acting and staging. What the singers do with their bodies while they sing and how they react to one another are facets that are new to me. It's inspiring to watch David meticulously manipulate the soloists, choristers, and supers around the stage to find nuances of the plot that are not in the libretto or music. The plot unfolds with a dramatic power beyond my wildest dreams. They *can* sing it. I have a sore throat from the lump that has been in it all afternoon. They almost have me weeping at my own music (no great feat).

Meanwhile, at the box office, ticket sales are slow! The State Theatre holds 3,100 and we are at about 1,000 heads per show over the next five nights. The perception seems to be that it must be sold-out; or the ticket prices must be high. I would very much like to know who has bought tickets—opera regulars or pop fans.

So Alletta Kriak has me running ragged on the promotion trail that Kathy Schenker in New York has worked up. I miss the *sitzprobe* (first time singers and orchestra meet) on Sunday because of promotion duties in New York. I talk to CBS, *Time* magazine, MTV, VH1, Associated Press, National Public Radio (who are

broadcasting the show), and several regional papers over the telephone. I tell the highbrow media that this is *not* a rock opera; I tell the rock media that this is the Megadeath of opera. I tell the story of how the work was commissioned by David Bamberger's son as-the-result-of-a-flippant-remark story at least twenty times. I explain that the piece was written on a computer, not by a computer. We get some pretty big coverage: *New York Times Magazine*—five pages with the headline ROLL OVER WAGNER, *Newsweek, Rolling Stone, Opera, Elle, Taxi, Spin,* CBS morning news, etc. etc.

Back in Cleveland in time for the first piano tech, David meets me in the lobby of the theater, and he starts preparing me for some lumps. This is the first time that the cast gets to work on-stage with the newly arrived sets, so we can expect some navigational issues. It drags into five hours of utter chaos. Set changes for which I have written thirty-six seconds of music take half an hour. The battle scene is still raging furiously at the point where the music calls for the Christian victory song. I almost lose my front teeth in my dive from the parapet. "Dead" Muslims have to scramble for safety when the curtain descends. The gigantic tapestry of Christ has him severely cross-eyed. Dahlia's Muslim costume looks distinctly Romanian (the four gorgeous dresses—for before and after ravishing and for each of the mezzos in this double cast—cost six thousand dollars *each*). Her twelfth-century maid appears onstage in a sombrero, which is accurate but looks weird. With David's reassurance in mind, I laugh hysterically at the snafus, but at 1:00 A.M., when it's over, David is looking very tense. Just to get comfortable with the worst-case scenario, I'll write my own review:

> *One gropes for words. Mr. Copeland's sad attempt at grand opera falls flat as a Belgian baritone. Rhythms that go nowhere, random sprinklings of notes within a pointlessly shifting key structure, and cement-minded bass lines define a music, which obviously owes more to accident than design. Was Copeland laughing at us as he pressed "random access" on his fabled computer? The general effect is a cross between Carl Orff and Donald Duck.*
>
> *If you were mystified by the mindless meanderings of minimalism, all will become clear with this opera. The world has gone completely mad. Cleveland Opera has sunk so low in its hunger for notoriety as to throw huge resources onto the lap of this entirely undeserving dilettante. Did I hear correctly that this man is the drummer (excuse me, "percussionist") of a pop group? Surely in all the fine music schools there are young composers*

with the proper training who could have used these fine sets, magnificent costumes, talented singers, brutalized orchestra, and monumentally broad-minded conductor to give us an opera worthy of the name.

The sheer misery emanating from the pit is surpassed by the gruesome farce onstage for sheer idiocy. The plot is warmed-over Shakespeare of the Romeo and Juliet *variety although in this one, as an ingenious twist, the soprano lives and has to suffer through the bitter end while retaining her dinner. The plot seems to revolve around opportunities for swashbuckling and kung fu fighting. In one (of many) battle scenes, the composer himself gets into the fun, culminating his appearance onstage by slaying a perfectly good bass baritone. The other voices are walking wounded by this time anyway. If only one of the supernumeraries could have slain the perpetrator. . . .*

 OCTOBER 10, 1989
HBCM world premiere! "International Music Event of the Year!"

The house is sold-out by midday. A close shave, but a sellout—that's 15,300 tickets for 15,000 seats—standing room only for all five shows. The dress rehearsal was brilliant. I'm not too nervous. We all know that the first act is a bit lumpy, but if the second act doesn't kill 'em, I'll have to write another opera.

The lights go down, the tune begins. First the imam comes out raving, then the mezzo sings a song. Polite applause. During the first scene there are many moments when the audience is not sure if they should applaud. But they do—dutifully. Then we switch to a Christian sound for an orchestral interlude of two minutes' duration, which ends in a nifty scene switch when a large tapestry of Christ becomes the interior of a Christian tent. This arouses the first vocal noise from the audience. A few cheers. Not sure if this is for the music or for the set. Soprano aria—good applause, no cheers. The chorus comes on and things start to happen.

TEMPLAR KNIGHT: *Saracens!*

CHORUS: *No! No!*

TEMPLAR KNIGHT: *Overwhelmed him. . . .*

CHORUS: *No!*

A large sound is coming from the pit and stage and I can feel a thrill around me as I sit in the balcony front row. But the scene drops energy at the end and the curtain goes down. Good applause, no cheers.

Scene three is slow and difficult for the orchestra. Fiddly Arabic rhythms and definitely too many notes. You live and learn, sometimes in public. There is good applause for the mezzo. She gets one of the only real arias, a real tearjerker. Response is good but doesn't bring the house down. I'm listening for cheering and stomping feet but have to remember that this is an opera. How much cheering does one hear at the English National Opera during a performance? Anyway, I'm stuck here in my seat in the audience. There's nothing I can do about it from here.

Scene four hits suddenly with swordplay, urgent dialogue, and the big battle scene. For three minutes the chorus and supernumeraries chase each other around the set yelling while conductor Imre and the band let rip. The battle choreography finishes early. The chorus is in position for the victory song sixteen bars before the music pays off, so they continue braying and sword-waving for eight bars, then wonder what to do for another eight bars, and then hit their big number at a full gallop:

For Jesus!
For Jesus!
The Mighty Lamb of God!

Where I grew up we always thought that the Crusaders had kind of missed the point of their own religion. The curtain comes down on the scene, and now the audience is yelling. Not stomping but yelling. Definitely cheers . . . yes, they are cheering!

During the composition of act one, scene five, I discovered Wagner and it shows. There are no holes for obligatory applause, the action and music are continuous. The audience makes no sound—it is engrossed and this is actually a more interesting atmosphere in the theater. But the scene and act finale don't quite pay off. Staging is difficult, and by the time we get the "dead" Muslims onto their resurrection stand, we run out of music. If only I had put a repeat sign around bars 1,671 thru 1,683. Alas! The crescendo is incomplete. The act ends with good applause, no cheers.

Before the lights come up I dash backstage for makeup and wardrobe for my operatic debut as a supernumerary. The atmosphere back in the green room is jubilant. Much back-slapping and photos with the choristers. Then it's time for the little battle scene, known to the crew as "Stewart's Leap." I climb up the battlements like when I was a kid. This time I'm a wily Saracen. The magnitude of the whole adventure hits me as I peer out from under an inch of pancake makeup down at the stage heaving with battle and the orchestra pit surging with my music. And about three thousand head of punters—wide-eyed and slack-jawed.

The curtain comes down on the scene with its heavy velvet, too thick to hear the response on the other side. Scrubbing off the incredibly thick stage makeup is more difficult than painting it on, so I don't get back into the house until the final windup of the opera. There is a deeply engrossed atmosphere and the finale builds with intense concentration from the audience. At the climax, the drama switches with a loud bang. The tables are turned! The opera ends with a piquant little duet lament from the mezzo and the soprano. There is a chord that I am rather proud of. The curtain comes down on the opera.

I am out of my seat running down the stairs for the curtain calls. As the audience recedes behind me, my practiced hungry ears are tuned. . . . Very good applause, a few cheers. Well, shit! Come *on*! At the wings I can see the chorus are onstage bowing. Very good applause. Even better when the soloists start going on. The four Templar Knights get a big cheer, and it builds for the mezzo, soprano, and tenor. There is a big shout and sustained applause for the conductor Imre that carries through David and the central production figures. David comes to get me, brings me out on the stage and, God bless my soul . . . the audience is on its feet screaming. A regular certified standing ovation with very good applause, much cheering, standing, but no stomping. I kneel down at the lip of the stage and salute the orchestra on bended knee and with raised fist. This premeditated pandering breach of curtain ritual induces flashbulbs and stomping. Thank you Very Much! I am so dumbfounded that I forget to bring out the librettist. It takes tenor Jon Garrison's excellent diction and operatic vocal power to communicate to me through the hubbub: "GET SUE!"

The curtain comes down and all hell breaks loose onstage. Thick stage makeup is being exchanged all around. *We had them by the throat!*

THERE IS A PERFORMANCE at 10:30 the next morning! The morning after the knight before. The audience is made of school children bused in for "culture." It is an unbelievable event. For the kids it's an alternative to algebra, so they are good-natured but have No Respect. This show also serves as a dress rehearsal for the B cast. Since the piece is long and loud, and will run for five days, we have two of each principal character.

The curtain goes up. The imam comes out raving. The kids burst into laughter. The tenor climbs out of the sea and sings a big number. He is stabbed! The audience cheers!

There is a general hubbub from the massed urchins that obscures almost all sound from the stage. The big percussive orchestral punctuation points that were so dramatic last night produce giggles from these little monsters. The big battle, which actually runs according to plan this time, has them paralyzed in their seats and they light up at the end. They actually stay focused until the second battle, which is a complete failure. By the end of the first act, attention is wandering completely. Fidgeting badly through the finale, the little termites greet the act one curtain with a groan of relief.

For the second act, the kids are again cheerful and curious. When the tenor, who in this cast is the spitting image of Mozart in *Amadeus,* finally greets his long-lost love, there is an audible swoon from the teenage girls. He kisses her and the girls squeal. They sing for a bit and he kisses her again and the girls cheer while the boys hoot. After some more romantic parley, the audience are ready for a third kiss. When they get it, Imre, Mike, and Susan deliver the blow with such dramatic timing that the show must stop. Uproar! Bedlam! Hooting, squealing, and every other noise that human monkeys can make. To their credit neither conductor nor singers bow or break role. They hold their positions until the riot dies down, and the opera continues with new purpose.

We lose some of them during the last scene, but the closing ten-minute denouement has them deep into the plot. The double whammy at the end produces a shriek that turns into wild applause that obliterates the girls' lament, and the curtain is down to thunderous applause, cheering, stomping, standing, and leaving. The curtain calls are brief but ecstatic all around. There is a surprise for young tenor Michael Rees Davis. He takes his first bow to that sudden, happy sound of hysterical teenage girls shrieking. It is a sound that would be familiar to Donny Osmond. An ear-piercing, high-pitched squeal/yell/shriek produced suddenly by a thousand young female voices. It has an almost percussive impact. And young Michael Rees Davis is *loving* it. He deserves it—he literally did have them by the throat of the tender princess.

REASONS TO BE CHEERFUL: THE REVIEWS

> *"A serious undertaking on all counts . . . a valuable addition to the operatic world. . . ."*
> —WALL STREET JOURNAL

Good.

> *"Standing ovation . . . fervent cheers . . . of mild interest. . . ."*
> —NEW YORK TIMES

Hmmm.

> *"A sold-out State Theatre loaded with anticipation and excitement . . . rousing applause and a standing ovation. . . ."*
> —CLEVELAND PLAIN DEALER

Yes.

> *"The audience rose to its collective feet and yelled . . . a magnificent job. . . . This is a story with guts. . . ."*
> —AKRON BEACON JOURNAL

There you go!

"Complete and unredeemed disaster . . .
preposterous twaddle. . . ."
—NEW YORK NEWSDAY

Oh well. . . .

Everything needs yin with its yang. I'll have to make do with mixed reviews, which is not so disastrous when you consider the complexity and subjectivity of the mission. It was predictable that not everyone is going to get my piece any more than I got *Salome.* I'm certainly grateful for all the ink that the press gave us to sell all those tickets. We outsold *Aida, La Bohème,* and *Carmen* in this town (of Philistines?).

All of the preceding fixation with audience and critical response may seem to some like pandering to the punters, but I think it's important. The most intense music cannot be all things to all people, but it must be something specific to someone—namely the punters in the seats. It is communication and needs dialogue, which means the musician speaks and the listeners respond. Hearing and interpreting that response is crucial for ongoing creative enterprise. But even if there is no response and the work falls like pearls before swine, it's the creation that is the fun part. Swinging the mallet and connecting with the ball is worth all the effort, whether or not the shot scores. And, to continue the equine image, I'm very grateful to Cleveland for letting me play on all of those horses.

CHAPTER 13

BAKE-OFF IN FORT WORTH

1990

*H*oly Blood and Crescent Moon is going up again in Fort Worth. Opera is an expensive hobby for any city, and part of the funding comes from gala events at which the burghers, oligarchs, and grand matrons can be snobbed into making larger contributions than one another. To support our production, the opera community is throwing a black-tie bake-off. The contestants are: the mayor; the owner of the football team; one of the players; the director of the Fort Worth Opera; a telegenic quadriplegic kid who has won the heart of the city; and me, the opera composer.

One month earlier, when the event is proposed to me, the organizers are asking about what delicacy I might like to enter into the competition. Well, the most complex items in my repertoire are "bowl de cereal" and "cuppa tea." Fortunately, Fiona, my wife-to-be, has an underutilized flair for following recipe instructions, so we propose a Wolfgang Puck dish that is an angel hair pasta with broccoli.

When we get to Fort Worth, Fiona gets her first exposure to life as Mrs. Composer. She too is press-ganged into events at which her actual title is "Fiancée of the Composer." All unsuspecting, she is lured into a big lunch with the other alpha women of the city. Suddenly a light goes on her and an announcement is being made about her. She must rise from her seat and acknowledge the acknowledgment. It's hard to adequately convey how alien this is to the private and mysterious Fiona. But rise she does and beams beautifully at the bejeweled matrons. With her natural English élan and stylish correctness, she is a big hit with the Texas old money—and the arts are safe for another year.

The Bake-Off is held in a Texas-sized convention hall within which there is a village of extravagantly designed kitchens built on little stages like TV sets. I think each of the little kitchens is the creation of a leading local home designer.

Fiona and I have made some friends among the faster set in Fort Worth, and some of them have stopped by our kitchen, bringing with them a gift of aged tequila. Their Texas hospitality is in perfect tune with my own shine for this spirit, and soon both Fiona and I are singing and carousing as she cooks and I entertain. A mysterious Frenchman appears wearing a sash and medallion. He wants a taste of Fiona's pasta.

Now Fiona has been rummaging around the fake kitchen for the proper ingredients and utensils but has come up with only an approximation of the right stuff for the Wolfgang Puck recipe. The pasta that has been provided is spaghetti, not angel hair. There are no forks. But Fiona is resourceful and has managed to fix up a brew that I'm ready to try myself. The man with the sash and medallion is looking expectant so I find him a plate, tell him he can cut the phony French accent, and then attempt to ladle the pasta using the most efficient utensil that I can find, which is a teaspoon. Most of it ends up spattering his forearm. He's holding a clipboard, which he uses as a kind of shield from my overeager hospitality. By the time I get a pile of noodles mostly on his plate, he's backing away. But he hasn't got any broccoli! He's taking evasive action, but he's not yet out of range, so I lob the perfect broccoli, dripping with

Fiona's perfect sauce, at him. The little blighter is too fast for me and he bats the flying vegetable away with his clipboard and escapes into the throng. Never mind, more for me, I sneer hungrily to myself.

We are having a fine time, but all too soon it's time for the real dinner to begin. We are summoned from our nifty little kitchen party spot to the big dinner tables in the dining hall. This is the dreary part of the evening. Major sponsors of the arts are rewarded with proximity to the artists. It's a symbiotic but not necessarily fond relationship, and it's a fact of life in fine arts. Fiona is ripped from my embrace and seated at the far side of our round table, where she must endure the fawning attentions of those donors who have earned face time with the fiancée of the composer, while I'm stuck on my side with the grandest contributors of all, who get to dine with the composer himself.

You may be wondering what this is all about. For extreme fans of opera (or ballet, or any of the fine arts) who are very wealthy, dinner with your humble correspondent is like dinner with Mozart himself. Since every composer that they know of is a piece of cultural history (or they wouldn't have heard of them), so must also be the composer sitting right now to their left. As I chat with these individuals, I can see them already formulating the tale to bore their grandchildren. It's sort of like rock fandom but in black-tie attire. And they aren't teenage girls, they are ancient plutocrats.

Finally, the dinner drags through dessert and I can't bear another moment without Fiona at my side. I bid extravagant farewells to the opera-loving oligarchs, catch Fiona's eye, and we begin to make our escape. We're almost out of the room when we are caught by my handler, who insists that we return to our seats. I try to reassure her that we've locked in the next ten years of sponsorship with the money folk. My old English boarding school trained me well in the art of brownnosing. But the prizes for the bake-off are about to be given, she persists. By now we have figured out who the French guy was, and I reassure her that there is not the

▲ I married up.

remotest possibility that we will be judged the winner—even though Fiona's pasta was way better than the formal dinner.

"Trust me, we didn't win," I assert confidently.

There is no escape, however, and we must return to our table. As we sit back down, rejoining our dinner companions, a voice is booming over the PA. It's the windup to the prize giving and no sooner do we tune into what the voice is saying, than we hear the announcement:

"And the winner for the Most Interesting Something-Something is . . . Stewart Copeland!"

The name echoes around my head.

"Whaa—?"

Fiona recovers quickly and urges me toward the stage. On my way up, I grab her to my side and mount the stage to boozy applause. I'm still gaping as I take my bows. After years of this sort of thing I'm pretty good at impromptu speeches, so I'm just clearing my throat to thank whoever I can think of when the large voice booms out of the PA again.

"And the winner for the Most Colorful Use of Blah-Blah, is . . . Someone Else!"

And with more applause, we are joined on the stage by another winner, with whom we unexpectedly must share the accolade. Then the voice booms out again, and it finally sinks in. The Last shall be First and the First shall be Last. Everyone gets a prize: the mayor, the manager, the player, the director, and of course the überwinner, to tumultuous applause, the quadriplegic kid. He was probably nice to the French dude.

CHAPTER 14

HORSE OPERA

1992

Channel 4 TV in England has commissioned an opera.

Johnny and I are looking through the smoke down the barrel of a movie camera. He's Billy the Kid, and I'm Jesse James. He wrote the screenplay and I wrote the music for the jig we are about to do. Big Bob Baldwin is over there fussing with the lights—he's the director of this made-for-TV-opera and he's the one who got me into this. It's a good thing he's distracted, because I've got a problem with my big gun.

Over at the armory it seemed an obvious choice to select the longest-barreled handgun to portray the legendary Jesse James. For the scene where I ride into town blazing away from the saddle, waving the big gun is what being in the movies is all about. But now we're in the saloon and the shootin's done. Somehow I have to get the damned eleven-inch barrel back into its holster without looking down. Harder than you'd think. Also at this moment in the movie, I'm bursting into song. Every other part of the action looks cool. My cool hat is pulled down over my weathered brow, my long rustler's coat is swaying with the

motion, and my long arms are magnificently punctuated by the long smoking cannon.

Then comes the dumb, goofy moment. While the smoke from my fusillade swirls around me I have to look down, squint at the holster, and carefully thread the other end of the gun into its leather cleft. All this may sound like a sweaty Freudian romp, but on film it just looks stupid.

Johnny has plumped for a more intentionally comedic persona for his operatic singing debut. As a leading director of stage opera (as opposed to this film version) he could probably see my hassle coming. He's got a little derringer thing that he's handling dangerously with a sort of comedic menace. Baldwin is back on the set.

"Right, Jesse. . . . We'll just pick up from when you've put your gun away then. . . ."

So here we are again, once more singing something daft into the camera. And I'm thinking the same thing as the last time I was here on the mic: I really should spend more time in my bedroom, channeling singers in the mirror. At least it's better than shooting band videos in which I'm *not* the singer. For those I have to twitch sulkily in the background—with no gun in my hand.

We've been having the time of our lives shooting this cowboy opera out here in the built-for-film-production cowboy town of Old Tucson, Arizona. The cast and staff are all Londoners, sweating in the desert sun. The extras and crew are local hard-bitten cowboys from Central Casting, literally.

In opera, every line of dialogue is sung, which makes it all a little more challenging. The backing tracks that I built over in England are coming out of monitors and the actors/singers have to hit exact cues in the music as they move around the set doing exciting cowboy stuff. My job on the set, when not handling my gun, is to conduct the singing. It's the best place to be. The sweet spot in the production is what the camera is pointed at. It's where the lights, scenery, and dressing converge with the talent, and where the magic of movies occurs. Every yard farther from this spot is less and less magical until you get out of the light and the dull boredom of endless waiting sets in.

Right in front of the camera is where we are Making A Movie; ten yards away, time has slowed to a crawl. The actors get short spurts of activity in the Spot and then return to their trailers to wait for their next moment in the sun. The director, the director of photography—and in this case, the conductor—get to play all day in the Spot. As each singer comes before the camera big Bob sorts out their blocking (physical movement) while I give them their vocal cues. Half the time I do this in full Jesse James attire because I have a shot coming up. My gunslinger belt is cool because my conductor's baton fits perfectly into one of the bullet loops. Jesse James is one conducting son of a bitch!

One day my old colleague Andy Summers graciously comes out to play the part of a saloon banjoist. He doesn't have a lot of dialogue. The big moment is when he is summarily, and rather flippantly, dispatched by your humble servant in the role of Jesse James. I've been waiting years for this.

We already have the shot of me firing the big gun; now we need the shot of the target. Since this is opera, we don't need to worry if it's too cliché for the bad guy to shoot the banjo player. Andy is all for it. He's enjoying the costume party and is intrigued by the

little explosive squibs that they're threading into his jacket. Then he notices that a plastic screen is being erected around him, through which there is just a little hole for the camera to poke through. He's beginning to put two and two together as he sees the wires leading away from his coat to a box held by the scar-faced explosives tech.

"Um . . . what are the screens for?" he asks softly.

"For the blood," I reply gently.

PART III
STILL NOT NORMAL

CHAPTER 15

OYSTERHEAD

APRIL 2000

You should be playing your drums," Les Claypool says to me with that strange voice of his. Although I hardly know the man, I'm already tending to believe his sage pronouncements. "And I've got a gig you should play at," he says.

Ten years or so have passed since I last looked at my drums with anything other than reluctance. The Eric Clapton Syndrome has set in. This is when you actually come to fear your instrument. If you touch the sacred staff, miracles are expected of you.

A promoter in New Orleans has asked Les to put a band together for a show. It's some kind of annual jam band thing. He's been talking to Trey Anastasio about it, and between them they have decided to dust me off and drag me back to the stage. We don't need material or anything, he tells me. This is a show where people want to watch you jam. Really? No laborious arranging and rehearsing of songs?

Well, yeah, we'll rehearse, just get to know each other but yup, we'll pretty much make it up as we go along.

It so happens that Les has found me at exactly the right moment. There is a prowling energy that has been building up inside me for a couple of years.

I was once pretty good at whipping up a frenzy with those drums of mine. I could drive the surge of power that you get from a great band and a raging crowd. It's the kind of thrill that sticks in your mind.

Just recently I got a call from Gene Provencio over at Tama Drums. I started playing Tama thirty years ago, and Gene was calling to find out what had become of me. I confessed to a deep lapse in my drumming acumen, but he said he had a remedy for my shame. A gleaming new drum set!

To tell you the truth, I never did get misty-eyed about drum sets. They are too bulky to bond with the way that one does with a guitar (yes, even drummers sleep with their guitars) and when you play in a world-touring band, you never know which of the many identical kits you might be playing. You never share a hotel room with them. You only see them onstage, assembled by other hands. After the show the crew devours them.

Les's band Primus is playing in Burlington, Vermont, next week. This is the hometown of Phish, Trey's group. How about if I fly over there and we meet up at the Phish barn for a jam?

Meanwhile, back in L.A. I'm in the middle of exploring, with The Moody Blues, the idea of conducting their orchestra on their next tour. I have never conducted onstage in front of an audience before, so this is a pretty sexy option for me. I am lucky to have a flair for conducting and this is a chance to develop it into a real skill.

So there is a choice to be made. Do I saddle up my familiar old warhorse or do I go after that untamed stallion in the field? My usual method would be to use the warhorse to catch the stallion. By which I mean that I instinctively say yes to almost any creative endeavor that I'm presented with. The word *no* is alien to me. The problem is, both of these options require massive homework. Even as a naïf you can't mount the podium before a sixty-piece orchestra without full command of the material. And especially if you are a drum god, you can't mount the stage with rubber fingers.

But I've got Les Claypool on the phone and he is a persuasive man.

A couple of weeks later I'm sitting in a Vermont café on a sunny morning, surrounded by bearded granola crunchers, and Trey comes bubbling in. Grinning through his orange beard, he gets straight into grilling me about the ways and wherefores of working with orchestral music, of all things. He's burning up with a symphony that he's writing.

Les saunters in and we head over to Trey's barn. It's a picturesque wooden structure that he bought over there, to put on some land he bought over here. It's a scenic spot at the other end of several miles of dirt road. The old barn is on a promontory overlooking the Vermont mountains, and inside is a recording studio. It's just the kind of place that I used to fantasize about as a kid. The ivory tower where bands go to lose themselves in the magic of music.

Within ten minutes Les, Trey, and I have strapped on instruments and are lost in some far-away magic. We probe the mysteries deeply: soaring, we crest the waves; gliding, we span the universe. Every so often we stop for hysterical laughter. And then we fall back into another groove, another ride, another blazing inferno. Through the day and into the evening we romp around the barn.

Well, I've participated in a few supergroup-type lineups and they are usually disappointing, but this is something else. This is worth coming to the party for.

When I get home, there is a gleam in my eye as I set up my new Tama Starclassic Maple wood kit. The tom-toms come out of the boxes first. The natural wood finish has a luster that is pleasing to the eye and satisfying to the hand. The bass drum is the best. It's too big to hold in my arms, but the large expanse of exposed burl enflames my passion as I search the floor for the position of power on which to land this mighty drum.

Urgently I unbox the maze of chrome stands. The cool metal warms to my touch as I kick the legs open and unfurl the boom arms on which to hang the glittering flotilla of new Paiste Signature Series cymbals.

I am a ten-year-old boy with a large erection of drums and stands that represents the pinnacle of all my youthful desires. To describe this catafalque as the Rolls-Royce of drum sets would be inadequate. The fine tooling, the advanced metallurgy, the sophisticated engineering, the ingenious design all add depth to my growing ardor.

As it takes shape before me my breathing starts to rhythmatize. Sharp patterns are whistling through my teeth by the time I reach for the sticks. I pause to admire, one more time, the virgin beauty of this shining prize.

Top left tom-tom takes the first blow and responds with a joyful boom that travels up my arm and down to my soul. And the monster is released. . . .

The next couple of weeks are consumed by obsessive self-improvement. On the bike path my general physique is strengthening. Deep immersion in mesmerizing rudimental exercises is limbering and strengthening my wrists while tuning the rhythmic engine room in my brain.

In one of the more brightly lit corners of my skull, a team of brain cells is creatively segmenting the passage of time into patterns. These patterns are converted into instructions for my hands and feet. Getting this system to work at high speeds with consistent precision is what practice is all about. The brain is tuned for rhythmic acuity and the hands are balanced for synchronized aggression.

Les is on the phone again. Guess what buddy, the tickets for our show went on sale this morning and were all sold within twelve minutes. Whaa! For a moment my abiding love for my fans wakes from its slumber and the love music is welling up in my heart, until it occurs to me that these ticket buyers must have been huddling over their computers waiting for the sale to open. I happen to know that all three of my fans have jobs. Les is quick to clarify. It's the Phish-heads, a tribe of beyond-loyal fans of Trey and his band. Damn, that cheery little fellow is popular. Maybe that's why he's so happy all the time. A week later Les tells me to look us up on e-Bay, where I see that tickets are selling for $2,000! Now these are my fans, I imagine proudly.

The Primus rehearsal place is a large shed in an industrial park on the waterfront in Sausalito, California. This is where we meet again to get just a little bit organized for our New Orleans show. Since our session in Vermont I've been hacking up the tapes that we made and we listen to the distilled high spots to find nuggets that we can join together to create material. Les and Trey are shouting lyric ideas back and forth and scribbling furiously, but since I'm already blasting around on my drums they mis-hear each other and are writing down intriguing non sequiturs.

These guys amaze me. It's just so how-you're-not-supposed-to-do-it. I come from a world of pop music where improvisation in front of a paying audience is something that has to be surrounded by solid material (songs). The idea of making it up as you go along is plain unprofessional. If you are just screwing around, how does the wardrobe lady backstage know which sequined jacket to bring out and when? How does the guitar tech know which guitar to have ready? Well, it turns out that Trey only uses one guitar for a show, and Les wears the same sequins all night.

Next day we are heading down to New Orleans. I'm getting a real buzz from being in a band with a cool name and I'm ready for mischief. For me this amounts to staying up beyond ten o'clock. My new posse and I are out later than that tonight as we cruise the French Quarter, ripping from joint to joint down Bourbon Street and beyond. When I finally bail, in the wee hours, the youngsters are still raging.

Next day at sound check, Trey isn't smiling so much. This is the other Trey. The one you get every four or five days when the party hits the wall. Sullenly he stares at his foot pedals as we run through our "material" and organize the stage sound. There is an occasional bitter glance in my direction when I crack my snare. Les is only a little more laconic than usual after his night on the town, but he's all business.

Back in the dressing room I'm eager to figure out the set list but get piteous looks from my band. Set lists are for wimps, they tell me, we'll decide as we go along. Now this takes balls! I now realize that I am amongst real men.

Then Brad Sands comes in and gives us the nod. Showtime. When we get to the wings, the stage lights are on. Les and Trey keep walking, and without so much as a "Ladies and Gentlemen . . ." they are onstage plugging in. I stroll on in their wake and strange noises are already coming out of Trey's guitar.

Since we haven't decided what to play first and since the band looks pretty saddled-up, I just start playing something and Les is on it in a heartbeat. There is a buzz from the audience. They know we are faking it and that's what they love! They want to see us think. They want it never to have happened before. They want an uncharted musical adventure.

And that is what they get. For two and a half hours we gloriously indulge ourselves, committing heinous crimes against stagecraft and organized music. Referring to our material only occasionally, we blast here, cruise there, and sometimes drift away completely. Trey has that Andy Summers thing where he can create a whole atmospheric environment with his guitar without even playing it. The focal point of the band though is Les. While Trey gazes into the distance, Les is the one to watch. Between disjointed dance excursions around the stage there are mysterious snatches of storytelling and odd instructions to the audience. His bass is thundering all the while. After the show Trey disappears, and I don't see him again.

When I get home and listen to the tapes, I discover that there were some really inspired moments in there between the train wrecks. As I love to do, I get out my scalpel and once again splice all the best moments together. It's frustrating to get a show together and only play it once, so I like to at least have a listenable recording for my archives.

But it turns out that this is not the end of Oysterhead. A few weeks later the stars are aligned over Las Vegas, where Phish and Les Claypool's Frog Brigade happen to be playing shows on the same night. It's also Trey's birthday.

My brother Ian and I fly over from L.A. in his little airplane, landing in downtown Las Vegas, right next to the flashing lights of The Strip. Phish are just winding up their show as we arrive at the arena. Kid Rock is onstage with them, and Trey is on drums! The show soon finishes and backstage the Phish guys are all hospitality. They really are a fun group to hang with; *very* relaxed. Kid Rock, whose name turns out to be Bob, is back there, still singing snatches of this and that. But across town Les is just about to fire up his band, so we head over to the House of Blues at the Mandalay Bay Hotel.

The Frog Brigade is in full swing when we get there. Les has already told us that he's expecting an Oysterhead moment at the end of his show, so Trey and I are in the wings plotting what song to play and, in a rush of mad enthusiasm, have inducted Kid Rock into Oysterhead. This all evaporates however when Les finishes his show, comes offstage, and gives us our marching orders. They don't include Kid.

Well, it's Les's show, so Trey and I troop onstage and blaze through a couple of Oysterhead songs. It's actually a pretty tight little show. With only twenty minutes to kill (and Trey's birthday party to get to) we curtail our meanderings and cut to the chase. Trey plays a blinder.

Way upstairs in a suite over the city lights, Brad has a party room prepared. There is a set of drums and amps and a well-stocked bar. There are no industry sharks. No local deejays, journalists, or retail bigwigs. No record company promo guys (who are actually usually quite fun). It's just my new Phish buddies and their wives, various odd-looking Frog Brigadiers, and Kid Rock, who now has a little solar system of babes surrounding him. I am delighted to see that young rock stars are still acting the part. Long into the night strange rituals of rock bacchanalia are performed. The floor shakes with misshapen dancing and the walls ring with weird incantations. We are musicians, and in the nighttime after the show, with the door locked, we are even stranger than you think.

ONE YEAR AFTER OUR first meeting, we are back in Trey's barn to record an album. Outside, Vermont is under deep snow. Inside, the three of us are setting up all of our toys. The barn is so big that we have plenty of room to each create our own jungle of (in my case) drums, percussion racks, gong stands, gamelan rows, xylophones, glockenspiels, gran cabassas, and gran falloons.

Trey just uses one electric guitar (made by one of the Phish crew) and one acoustic Martin guitar. Behind him is a collection of vintage amps. At his feet is a carpet of foot pedals. Les has a bunch of basses and a few distant relatives of the bass. Just one big amp drives an imposing array of speaker enclosures far back in the room (bass sound waves like to travel).

At the other end of the barn is a large mixing console, behind which Oz is recording our every move. We are deep in Phishdonia, and we have their briskly upbeat crew around us, led by the ever-resourceful Brad Sands. Brad's day job is to corral the free-ranging spirits of the four happy Phish guys and get them on/off the bus, in/out of their hotels, and to/from the stage. He is the band's interface with terra firma.

We spend the next month working, playing, jamming, overdubbing, lyric writing, singing, and laughing. On a typical day, I get to the barn at 10:00 A.M. The crew don't arrive until noon, so I have a key and let myself in. I have the studio tapes to myself for a solitary morning of examining, editing, organizing, and generally tampering with the tapes of the previous day's wild creativity.

It is art for art's sake, and a real contrast with my day job, which is ultraspecific and very disciplined. The collaboration side of it is refreshing, too. In my film work I collaborate with the director to serve his dramatic needs, but in the music room I am president-for-life. All other musicians on a film score are employees, serving my vision, which in turn serves the director. In a band you share the music: you ride as well as drive. One idea inspires another, and with the right group of conspirators, big things can happen.

THE OTHER SIDE OF band life is the tour. We were never sure that we would make it this far since two of the players are already members of important groups and one of us (me) has a day job. But we manage to push aside other business to make space for a one-month USA national tour with a week of rehearsal in Vermont.

By now it is fall and Vermont is rusty red. Inside the barn we are hard at work figuring out the songs on our record and working up a show. After a week, we are going to do a warm-up show in New York, launch the record (press and stuff), then reconvene a month later in Seattle for the first date of the tour.

One morning, it's nine o'clock and I'm rambling around in my hotel room with the TV on when I notice that there is smoke coming out of a skyscraper. Wait a minute, that's New York! There are flames! Un-muting the sound, I hear a commentator saying something about a plane crash. Maybe terrorists. It's the eleventh of September. My hair is standing on end. "Al-Qaeda!!" I scream at the TV. I've been watching them for some time now. In cahoots with those Taliban crazies in Afghanistan, they have been attacking U.S. targets for years, with increasing audacity. A TV head suggests that it could be some of Timothy McVeigh's buddies. No, this is too smart. Someone suggests Saddam Hussein. Unlikely. Things are going Saddam's way right now. The sanctions against Iraq are withering, the oil embargo is leaking, and America's grip on his throat is loosening. He's keeping his head down. Why poke the Eagle? What the FUCK!!! Another plane crashes into the other tower!! I'm on the phone to L.A. to wake Fiona. Her voice calms me, but she's still fast asleep as I shout down the phone.

"OK, darling," she soothes (she's used to my political excitability). "Turning on the TV now . . . love you . . . bye." I call Les in his room. He's a late riser so I have to keep ringing. TURN! ON! YOUR! TV! RIGHT! NOW!

Later, band and crew are gathered around the TV at the barn. The phone rings. Fiona asks, "Where's Jordan?" A momentary warmth at the thought of my son, then: He's on his way to New York . . . arriving at 5:30 A.M. . . . . for a day of sightseeing!

I'm calculating: off the plane with his bags by 6:30, on a bus to Manhattan by 7:00, getting him to his first site—the Twin Towers—by 8:30. . . .

Mercifully, the dull fear only has a couple of hours to build before Fiona calls again with news that the catastrophe missed my son by about ten blocks. His bus stopped when the first plane hit. He was walking toward the towers when they fell. Unbelievably, my nineteen-year-old thought to call home, even though it took him a couple of hours to get to a phone.

But I digress, and so does Oysterhead. There will be no show in New York. We are glued to the TV like three hundred million other Americans, knowing that the world had suddenly shifted on its axis. Nothing will ever be the same. I fly home through deserted airports. I have the whole plane to myself and it's the easiest day of travel in my life.

A month goes by before we head for Seattle, where we resume our rehearsals. Then, once more, it's showtime for Oysterhead. The first show is in a theater that has been sold-out for months, to Phish-heads of course, who have pretty much gobbled up the tickets for the whole tour.

My brother Miles arrives during the sound check. He finds an empty chair in the wings and waves hello as we finish up. Later, I am reminded of Miles's legendary status in show business when I hear some of the crew describing how Miles Copeland stormed into the hall, glared around the stage, yanked up a chair, and breathed fire upon passersby. A few weeks later I hear the story retold, only now the tale has Miles arriving with a gang of cutthroats, torching the stage, and eating the stage crew. I do love show business.

Brad comes into the dressing room and gives us the nod. And we are ready! We mount the stage with the same cavalier attitude as before, but this time we have done some homework. We still have no set list, but Trey can now call out a song title and we have a solid place to start. The audience is enthusiastic and forgives us for not being Phish. They like it! We like it even more! After the first show we are ecstatic. We really slew us! This is going to be a great tour.

Touring is all different now from when I was a lad. We are using the Phish crew, the Phish sound system, the Phish lights, the Phish trucks, and the Phish tour bus. As an old ex-roadie I'm in awe of the high-tech operation of this crack team. Every day they get this mountain of gear and rigging in and out of these halls and arenas, which is no great miracle—it's the slickness of the system and the coolness of the detail that is so impressive.

A touring band lives in a strange bubble. The real world flashes past inconsequentially as we cross the land in our cocoonlike tour bus. Time passes in a different pattern. We have no connection to any of the cities that we pass through. Food and water is brought to us, as are the hotels and concert halls.

A normal day begins at around three in the afternoon. After an easy shower and breakfast, I grab my overnight bag and slouch down to the bus. It's like walking into my living room. My book-that-I'm-reading, laptop, and other toys are there already. There are two lounges on the bus, separated by the kitchen, bathroom, and sleeping cabins. Each lounge has a TV and entertainment system. As I settle into my coffee and newspaper, Brad, Les, and Trey drift aboard at their leisure. I'm vaguely aware that the cocoon is moving but it doesn't mean much.

Eventually, Brad will tell us that we're at the gig and the stage is ready for sound check. We amble into the hall, greet the crew, and mount the stage. Everything is working perfectly, just like it did last night. The monitors already sound great, the drums are perfectly set up and tuned, and all we gotta do is play. Which we do just to limber up more than anything. We tweak a few show moments, try a few things, and generally polish our chops.

At around six o'clock, we break for lunch. This is a meal served backstage for the three of us and our crew of about twenty guys. Rarely better than K rations, this meal is as close as we ever get to roughing it on the road. In fact, this is the part of the day where things go downhill a bit until showtime. After lunch we go check out the dressing room but usually end up back on the bus, watching a movie as we wait. It feels like early afternoon to us but it's seven o'clock outside.

In the distance we can hear the support band firing up and that starts my internal countdown. I head back to the dressing room and start my finger exercises. Between ten-minute spurts of paradiddles on a folded towel, I play with my luggage. Rather than haul our suitcases in and out of hotel rooms, the crew brings our stuff to the dressing room, where we hand off our laundry and pull out tomorrow's clothes, which we stuff into overnight bags, that go back to the bus. There is a giant, wardrobe-sized flight case with drawers full of clean clothes. In one drawer I have a pile of identical black jeans, socks, and T-shirts, which I now don.

In my youth, bands would put on special stage clothes for the show. Extreme sartorial statements were expected of us. We were supposed to look like normal people cannot look. Since playing drums is extremely hot work, however, I could never wear sequins or plumage, which has always been a disappointment for me. Nowadays bands play in their street clothes and change *after* the show.

At nine o'clock, Brad comes in and gives us the nod. Many bands take this moment to form a love circle and chant something, but in Oysterhead we just give each other goofy grins and head for the lights.

The first few shows are hard work. No matter how fit one gets before the tour, playing in front of an audience burns more fuel. There are times when the frenzy takes hold but the body runs out of gas. An old pro like me knows how to rest while cruising, but the two-hour show is a mountain to climb every night all the same. Every night is an improvement on the last, and every night changes get slicker, the grooves cut deeper, and the surges soar higher.

After the last hurrah, it's straight to the shower for me. This is somewhat of a fetish of mine. The combination of hot water and postshow endorphins is like a heroin bath. Body and soul are rarely happier.

Back in the dressing room, Les and Trey are similarly exhilarated and we enthusiastically applaud ourselves. We are so cool! We really rocked ourselves! We slew us!

As I preen with my friends, the wet heap of my stage gear disappears and my overnight bag is ready to go. On our way out to the bus, we pass the crew who, within an hour of our last note, have cleared the stage and are loading the gear. They are like a Viking gang uttering strange cries as they roll the flight cases into the two Phish tractor-trailers.

On the bus, dinner is waiting for us. Brad times it just right so that there is a hot meal from a fancy restaurant served up as we slip out of town and on down the road. Strangely, the first thing we want to do is watch the show. After two hours of playing it, we now settle down to watch it on TV. We critique the show (rather generously) and spot places where we can add new tricks. In this way our show becomes more developed every night of the tour.

In the dead of night we pull into a distant truck stop. Sometimes Trey will pull out his Rollerblades and flash around the parking lot between the braying eighteen-wheelers. An ancient tradition of the road is the distant truck stop. There is a conspiratorial feel, as if we have escaped from the scene of the crime and have outrun the posse. And we are way out here with the other pirates, spending our booty on trinkets offered by the uncomprehending natives.

Back on the bus things gradually slow down at maybe four o'clock as we finish up a DVD and start to peel off to head for the bunks. We each have our own coffin-shaped cubicle, into which we now climb. With the constant roar of the turbines blocking all sound of continuing revelry in the front and rear lounges, it's actually pretty easy to fall into a deep sleep.

At some point, in the pitch blackness of my coffin, my eyes blink open and I am aware that the bus has been still for some time. Easing out of the bunk, I push aside the curtain and gaze into the sunlit front cabin. It could be ten o'clock in the morning. Time for bed. Brad has checked us all into the hotel, my luggage has already gone up to my room, and my key is sitting on the bus counter. As I waft through the lobby, this is when I most feel the disconnection with the normal world. Everyone is so awake and I am so asleep, at the other edge of the wheel. In my room, I black out the curtains, set the alarm for 3:00 P.M., and resume my slumber. The sheets feel great.

There is an old joke from the film *This Is Spinal Tap* where the band goes onstage and greets the audience with "Hello, Cleveland!" Only it isn't Cleveland. Truth is, it might as well be. To us it feels like the same city night after night. We are hardly aware of our passage through space. The stage looks the same every night, and on it we perform our strange little miracle, which grows more complex every night, more involved. As our journeys onstage become more intense, our journey across the land becomes more immaterial.

For one month we tour down the West Coast, up the heartland and then down the East Coast. Even as we roll down toward Florida on the last leg, we're still tinkering and noodling with the set, still finding new tricks. Then, in Gainesville, it's the last show.

Good-bye Les, Trey, and Brad. Good-bye bus. Good-bye green sparkle drum set. The Green Monster will go home to its storage locker in L.A. while I take up with my maple studio kit.

It's amazing how quickly the bubble pops, the minute you

▲ Sage of the Deep

walk through the home front door. It's like walking out into the street after a movie. Whatever you were laughing or crying about is evaporating by the second as the real world rushes back in. The loving embrace of family and friends and the discipline of work become the meaning of life again. But just occasionally, a little flash of memory of a Claypool aphorism or an Anastasio chuckle will cause a tiny smile and a faraway look.

CHAPTER 16

HALL OF FAME

MARCH 2003

*My old band The Police hasn't crossed
my mind in years.*

Sting's strangely gruff voice is purring down the phone. Congratulations! Our LP is at number one in Germany! And in other news, we're playing the Hall of Fame.

First of all, what LP? We haven't recorded anything in twenty years. But who needs to record anything these days? The record company just repackaged the same old songs and put it in the stores. Stuff still sells, it seems.

I like getting calls out of the blue from Sting. We have discovered that we can be good friends—as long as no one mentions music. Nothing is ever as intense as the first time at anything, and Stingo and I experienced a lot of firsts together.

Second of all, wudda you mean play a show together? You? Andy? Me?

"Yeah, we'll play 'Roxanne,' 'Message,' and 'Every Breath You Take.' We can rehearse here in New York. It'll be fun," he lies seductively.

■

HERE WE ARE IN the biggest and strangely darkest room at the S.I.R. rehearsal facility in New York. Andy is fussing with his pedal board. Jeff, Danny, and Dennis, our principal crew (drums, bass, guitars), are circling the war zone with anxious comity. I'm actually in reasonably good shape after my adventures with Oysterhead and The Doors.

Then planet Sumner arrives. Under a hat, scarf, and greatcoat, suddenly Sting is among us. And look! There are his children! Of which there are many. It's gloomy in here, and I can't really make them out, but an atmosphere of early teendom fills the room.

Immediately Andy and Sting are burrowed down with their interminable faffing over chords and fingering. I completely missed how we got into it but we are now in the classic position B. Position A, rarely experienced, is when we are actually playing music. In position B we discuss. You might think that songs such as these familiar old favorites would roll off the cuff. For me they do, if only we can get through more than four bars without stopping to rethink something. For Andy and Sting there is always some new noodle. But at least we're not in position C, which is All Hands On Throats!

We actually do make it down the short set by the end of the day, and then he's gone. Sting doesn't do farewells, he just vaporizes. Andy is flushed, replete from a day of his favorite stuff: chords and more chords.

WE'RE ALL DRESSED UP and sitting around the sparkly table, but is the party rocking? You would think that it would be, with all this rock and roll in the room. On a table over there is AC/DC. Over here is The Clash. Elvis Costello and The Attractions are having some kind of feud at their table(s) over yonder. For a little gravitas, we even have The Righteous Brothers in the house. We are all being inducted into this newly important address: the Hall of Fame.

But no, the joint is not rocking.

There is not a punter in the house. Instead of staging such an event at, say, Madison Square Garden, with music fans hanging from the rafters to see such a lineup of bands, we are here at the exclusive Waldorf Astoria banquet hall. No one in this room could give a rat's ass about music except for the musicians, and even a few of us might be dubious in this regard. It's all business in here tonight and the aforementioned assets are here to serenade the fat cats who buy and sell us. No matter how glittery we are, these are the people who deliver us unto the world. Tonight we are the dinner and they are the diners. They are the Alpha Insect people, many of whom, by the way, are friends and family. My own kin Miles and Ian are fat cats, although a little rangier than most.

Not to be too grumpy about it though, they do give us a nice award for our trouble. This Hall of Fame thing is relatively newfangled compared with the Grammies or the Oscars. But it's a deviously clever idea. Want The Rolling Stones to play your birthday party? Make 'em feel important. "Hall of Fame" has a very official ring to it in America and it's only surprising how long it took for someone to grab the title and set up his own court of music legitimacy. By the time they get to my generation—artists whose first record came out twenty-five years ago—they already have snared every living artist that I grew up with. I guess when you get a knighthood from the Queen you have to go and do some kneeling. It's odd that in music, our version is that we go and genuflect for the lawyers.

So here we are, the three of us standing in the catering hallway that leads to the banquet hall stage. We're watching a play-on movie roll before we get up there. The little montage on the monitor has our younger selves jumping around in our prime. We were energetic little fuckers, weren't we? We're all smiling now as the film finishes and we mount the stage for speeches and three songs.

Sting speaks for us all with dignity and sagacity, then Andy gets on the mic with his biting wit. The room is waking up. By the time it's my turn for some honest-to-God blubbering on the mic I figure, Screw it, let's just go play these songs!

My job in this band is simple. In fact that's one of the things I like about Police music—the mix of simple and complex. I get the fun part of that, and I appreciate it even more now after a decade of composing and directing music, which is a different kind of fun. All I have to do here is sit on some simple (though satanically ingenious) rhythms as a platform for the guys at the front of the stage. I'm happy with my meager role as omnipotent power dynamo and übergonzo-throb.

Several times during our turn we hit the spot, which is where we land when we know, the three of us, that we are on it, we own it, we *command it*. We like to scare all the other talent. As ever, there are some bumps and grinds, but that's where real music comes from. We push out to the edge, beyond the safety zone. For a couple of moments there is a glimpse of the band that we used to be when we conquered the world, when we played every night together and when we were thirty.

"Message in a Bottle" and "Roxanne" are a breeze. These really are good songs and fun to play. Even the fat cats are lit up in front of us. This feels sort of like a show! And then we break out our biggest hit, "Every Breath You Take." Suddenly it's all very jaunty as the stage fills with what looks like the cast of *American Idol*. There are now several singers clustered around Sting, all crooning away on his sick song. I gather these are all the more recent and upcoming talents and they've been hoisted up to our stage by the bosses for exchange of manna. Then we get to the end of the song and everybody is cheering. The fat cats are lumbering to their feet with the warmhearted glow of vultures applauding a dead zebra.

It's a very low stage, and after a nice bow from the three of us and our new friends, we can walk right off the front of the lip into the crowd. I have to push through the loving, teeming throng to get to my family. The girls grab on to me for dear life. They have had no idea of this aspect of their nerdy dad. Whatever they may have thought of the show, this part does *not* suit them. Who are all these people trying to devour Daddy? He's not your daddy! He's *our* daddy! They're only little, and they're terrified. The boys are older, but they've never seen this, either. I think it's even possible . . . am I imagining it? My hypercool sons . . . are their heads perceptibly an inch farther back on their shoulders? OK, now even I'm impressed. That show had to be some kind of incredible to impress these young Copelands.

After leaving the stage, we are each swallowed up by the crowd. Who knows whatever happened to my bandmates? But I'm here now, deeper into the evening, and I'm chuckling about something with Topper, Paul, and Nick. I'm hanging out with The Clash, which for me is waaaaay cool.

CHAPTER 17

LA NOTTE DELLA TARANTA

AUGUST 2003

*In the summer of 2003 my world music explorations
land me a real live one. I find myself on a stage with
twenty raging brigands locked in a strange ritual with
forty thousand whirling tribespeople surrounding us,
dancing and singing with frenzied abandon.*

The entire city square, and all of the boulevards leading into it,
are jammed with singing, dancing revelers. Forty thousand people
annually congregate on La Notte della Taranta [Night of the Taran-
tula] here in Melpignano, on the southern tip of Italy. Next to the
ancient monastery a giant stage is erected, and the city streets
swell with people dancing to the music of the twenty-piece orchestra. The evening is lit by torches, bonfires, bouzoukis, bagpipes,
accordions, guitars, drums, and tambourines. Everybody is clapping and yelling.

La Notte della Taranta originates in an ancient dance festival of
Dionysian origins (very old) in southern Italy that celebrates the
ecstatic purging of the body that is achieved by wild singing and
dancing to throbbing rhythms. The songs, which are specific to
this event, have been passed down through centuries. The music,
known as the pizzica (a close relative of the tarantella) is flamboy-
antly rhythmic, with soaring melodies driven by raging drums. In

the lost valley of Salento the humble tambourine has evolved into a family of instruments, including some that are monstrous.

The result is an extremely robust form of folk music. The young studs of the region impress the girls with their tambourines rather than with guitars.

The local legend is that the pizzica dance was the best remedy for the bite of the tarantula. Strange pagan rituals whisper of women dancing in a venom-induced hallucinogenic frenzy. In recent centuries the pagan songs have been Christianized, but they still retain a ritualistic Dionysian flavor.

Along for the ride with this crew is me on drums, hanging on for dear life and surfing the surge of energy that this music creates.

Lit up by the joy of this local event I have joined with the city of Melpignano to take the show on the road around Italy and Greece.

 JULY 2004
MILAN

The roar of the show takes about two hours to subside. When I run off the stage back to the dressing room after the last encore, there is still a lot of ritual to perform before the day's work is done. Shower is crucial immediately. Soaking-wet T-shirt turns to ice within seconds of departing the hot stage lights. That's why your correspondent can sometimes be seen sprinting through the halls backstage in a mad dash to the dressing room to yank the clothes off, down to buck-naked.

No sooner do I reach my haven then there is a clamor at the door, which is actually kind of welcome. Depressing are those shows in distant lands where there is no clamor after a grueling set.

The cheerful folk crowding the hall outside my room are usually local backstage-pass holders who are eager to exuberate with me then go home, but they unfortunately will have to wait. Even though I'm feeling pretty exuberant myself, I have to shift my gear and hit the shower to hose off the sweat and lower the body temperature. I'm still squirting fluid out of every pore.

The postconcert shower is one of those sublime creations of our Designer that induces the body to drown itself in endorphins.

Then the wet T-shirt and soaking clothes have to be gathered up into a soggy pile, wrapped in a towel, and stashed. The room needs to be cleared of personal effects right away because those hall folks are getting a little impatient out there, and that door is going to open.

The aftershow meet-and-greet is an extension of the show. You cannot brush off the joy that you have just spent ninety minutes whipping up. So the room fills up, and I spend the next half hour shaking hands, signing tickets, programs, money, T-shirts (often on the hoof), biceps, chests, and sometimes, children. I stand in one spot while everybody gets a turn to get his or her thing signed, have a picture taken, and cop a feel.

There comes a point when there are just goofy smiles and no more bits of paper, so the folks are gently nudged out of the room and finally, I can now power down—or try to.

By now my Salentino band buddies have pretty much finished their own back-slapping, stuff-stowing, and unwinding. When I get to their room they are smoking and joshing. They always give me a cheerful welcome and we exchange show moments such as "Hey, Francesco, you almost exploded during your solo in 'SANTU PAOLU'!"

"I was completely lost in 'Aouli,' and when I looked over at Alessandro for help, he just smiled unhelpfully."

"You think I wasn't lost, too?"

The Ensemble "La Notte della Taranta" is comprised of me and twenty Salento brigands blasting away on tambourines, bouzoukis, and all manner of strange instruments. Sometimes Giancarlo pulls out a bagpipe that is made out of an entire sheep.

We fill up the big stage. Over on the other end is our musical director and bandleader, Vittorio Cosma, on keyboards. At the front, stage right are Enza, Ninfa, and Emanuele, the principal singers. Front stage left (next to me) are three tambourine players. Not your "Kumbaya" variety of tambourines—these are the big, heavy ones.

In the middle of the stage is a thicket of players on bass, guitars, mandolins, violins, and whatnot. We even have an additional drummer on a traps kit.

At the back of the stage, on a huge riser, is a jungle of percussion and mallet instruments with four zany Englishmen (Ensemble Bash) in hot pursuit.

The music that we are playing is made of ancient folk songs in the pizzica style from the Salento region of southern Italy. Once again, these are not your Peter, Paul, and Mary variety of folk songs—these are the big, heavy ones.

The first show of the tour is in Florence. A giant stage has been built right on the edge of a cliff overlooking the old city. As I sit at my drums at the sound check, I can see the famous Ponte Vecchio right behind me down below. All of the shows on this tour are outdoor events and some of them are free—paid for by the city because our show is "cultural."

The sound check was supposed to start at 4:00 but since it's the first gig, the crew are running late and it's not till 8:00 that we can start what was supposed to be a full rehearsal. Doors open at nine. I kind of needed that rehearsal because I only arrived in Italy last night and have never played some of the tunes with the band. I've been rehearsing by myself at home with tapes of the tunes.

So the show is a train wreck, but there is so much random energy among the players and within the material that a great time is had by all and the Florentini go nuts. Our show is all about excitement and dancing—and dance the people do.

Happiness is a day off in the Italian summer. We have the whole day to ease out of the hotel and drive with my buddies Johnny and Mauro down through Tuscany and Umbria to the ancient capital, Rome.

Traveling in a rock band involves five-way committee meetings to decide on important daily matters such as: When do we check out? When do we stop for lunch? Where's the guitarist? On this tour, the ensemble is so large that I'm detached from the group

and travel separately in my own little bus accompanied by chums who come out to visit me on the road.

A meandering pace gets us down to Rome in about three hours. With no show tonight we can keep on meandering and wandering the piazzas, waiting for Fiona to arrive from L.A. At around midnight at the Piazza Navona, right at the moment when the ten-year-old accordion kid bursts into " 'O sole mio," my babe comes around the corner. Rome is like that. Fiona is like that.

DOWN IN MELPIGNANO, BIRTHPLACE of the pizzica, the torches are lit and the stone piazza is alive with laughter and song.

If you imagine a map of Italy shaped like a boot, the Salento region is at the bottom of the heel. It was Sergio Blasi, the mayor of Melpignano, who introduced me to pizzica music when he invited me to be the guest performer (or as they more grandly call it, "maestro concertatore") at La Notte della Taranta.

Who wouldn't accept such an invitation? So I played the show and a year later, for reasons that would require a lengthy tale, the city council has invited me to become an honorary citizen and has offered me the key to the city of Melpignano.

Here I am for my investiture, being led into the town square by the mayor (in full sash and ribbons). There are torches on the stone walls, flags, banners, and of course, tambourines everywhere. The square is full of people shouting "Ciao, Capella!"—which is Salentino dialect for "Copeland." Faces in the crowd resolve into people I remember, such as the waiter at the restaurant where we spent a wild evening in Otranto, or the duchess at whose palazzo Fiona and I met Gorbachev. And the bandsters are here! They used their day off to drive down from Rome and welcome me into their tribe.

When all are seated, the speeches begin. The city officials are assembled at a long table on the front steps of the city hall. For an eternity, my qualities as a humanitarian are extolled by numerous soaring testimonials. No virtue goes unpraised, and many vices are overlooked. Fiona is radiant at my side. In spite of a slight queasiness it's actually quite moving. I must be one helluva guy! If it weren't for the mischievous twinkle in Fiona's eye, I'd be blubbering. It feels sort of like a wedding or baptism into the warm heart of the Salento people.

Finally it's time for me to stand up and accept the key to the city, which is silver, about six inches long, and very ornate. I mumble a few words of humble gratitude and then, just like that, it's done. Suddenly the tambourines strike up and we are all dancing to the Pizzica. Ich bin ein Salentino! I can't wait to get back to L.A. and start kissing all my buddies on both cheeks the way I'm now culturally obliged to do as a newly minted southern Italian.

But these things fade. By the next morning Stewart Copeland, the great humanitarian, can be overheard at the hotel breakfast grumping about the shower and scowling at passersby. Too much yin causes yang.

ABOUT THREE HOURS WEST of Athens is this ancient amphitheater in Patra. It was built in 200 B.C. and makes even Italy seem young! The acoustics in this sixteen-hundred-year-old structure are perfect and at the sound check, without much help from the monitors, I can clearly hear each of the twenty players. Makes me wonder about all of the noisy clattering or dead, muffled stages that I have been playing for forty years. Acoustic architecture has been regressing all this time.

The tiers of seats are banked very steeply, which makes standing (or dancing) dangerous; so the audience must remain seated. This is a concert for listeners, and in this case that includes us. We can all hear one another beautifully, and we really swing together through the nuances of the show. It's hard to describe the feeling of joy/energy/ecstasy/power that derives from locking

together with a large ensemble in this way. It's the best show of the tour.

Even after we quit the stage the rites of Taranta continue on into the night with the tambourine guys hammering and the women taunting. When I get out of the shower they're still blazing and we pretty much kanga our way down into the town, ending up at an empty disco. We are all on such a high from the concert that we're soon crowding the dance floor, gyrating absurdly and shouting our own pizzica songs over the disco beats. In this manner we rave until dawn.

"HAPPY BIRTHDAY, STEWART!" CHORTLES Derek Power down the phone from L.A. He's rattling my cage about advancing decrepitude, seeing how far he can push it before getting to his punch line. "You've been nominated for an Emmy! Your score [for the TV series *Dead Like Me*] is deemed to be one of the best five scores this year."

Well, this is good news indeed, even though I have no chance of winning because the competition this year is stiff—kind of a blessing, really, because I can enjoy the whole process right through the crushing defeat that would be felt if I had a better shot at winning. To have written one of the top five scores in TV-land is fine with me.

As soon as I hang up the phone, I'm back in Naples, Italy, heading down to the piazza for dinner with my Salentino gang. The glittering recognition of my work back home seems vague and insubstantial as we stroll the Naples waterfront. After a week on the road we are all pretty comfortable grooving along the corniche at 4:00 in the morning.

The Naples show is different from all the others. For one thing, it's set in the middle of an old industrial park that has been turned into a museum. It's quite scenic in an *Eraserhead* sort of way: huge smokestacks and monstrous rusting machinery.

The folks in Naples curl their lips a bit at the neighboring Salentino tribe. In fact they have their own tarantella music that is a close cousin to the pizzica and they see cool tambourine players all the time. For the Salentini their local culture is alive—teenagers do it. For the Napolitani the music and the dialect are for grandmothers. I have arrived in Shark country with the Jets. I'm here in Hatfield country . . . with the Real McCoys.

So the show doesn't go over that well. We start out with gusto, but I can feel that we are losing the crowd with each passing song. I also have my own problems and am having a hard time finding the groove. No matter how much I try to shake it off and listen to the band, I still feel like the drummer at the Korea-Vision song contest: not groovy.

At the end of the set we leave the stage to meager applause—which has died to silence by the time I hit the ground. For the first time in thirty years it looks like there will be no encore. But as I pull out my earplugs and head for the shower, the crowd starts up again and actually start to make a noise. Fuck 'em. I'm not going back out there unless they start a riot. But maybe the shower can hold for just a minute. Sure enough, the noise builds to a chant, and the folks are stomping and screaming so OK, we'll give them some more.

But I forgot to put my earplugs back in, and when we start up the volume almost knocks me senseless. Damn, it's loud up here! I'm howling with pain as we romp through our most energetic song (traditionally saved by most bands for the encore—you *always* expect to play an encore) and I'm trying to blast the rhythm while gesticulating wildly to Fabio to turn my monitors down. There must be blood coming out of my eyeballs. Even unamplified, my drums are very loud, especially my snare drum—which I tune so sharp as to be able to bring a bird down from the sky. It adds up to a lot of noise, and when you factor in the perspex box that they build around my kit (so that I don't bleed onto the bouzouki microphones) it is a hell pit.

WE ARE FINALLY DOWN TO OUR LAST SHOW. After touring the most scenic parts of Italy it's time to get serious, in Milan. It's the most important night of the tour since this city is where most of the media are based. Most of the national impact of the tour will be made here.

The stage is built in front of a magnificent palazzo surrounded by hundreds of acres of ornate gardens and parkland. The dressing rooms are in the massive drawing rooms of the palace itself, with wood-paneled walls and painted ceilings. A very cool place to play a show. Even the shower is perfect!

But Raiz is in trouble again. He had a show at a festival in Genoa and is racing back to Milan, but he is going to be late. Since the place is packed and ready by 9:00 we send out the singers Ninfa and Enza, with Emanuele on guitar and Antonio on tambourine to play some pizzica songs in the traditional acoustic style. Then Ensemble Bash will come out and do fifteen minutes of their stuff. Hopefully, by then Raiz will have arrived and we can do our show.

▲ Vittorio with the tambourines of doom

Cities like Milan are usually hard to impress because they get to see any show that passes through Italy. For a band touring Europe, Milan is often the only gig they will do in Italy. It's the same problem with London or New York. The critics get to see your show in front of the least impressible audience.

But tonight, for some reason, it's different. This crowd is like a vat of gasoline. Emanuele just has to go out there with a lighter (his acoustic guitar) and the place is immediately ablaze! The folks are already clapping, hollering, and dancing to the bare-bones pizzica—so much that I'm worried about how my Bash buddies are going to follow up.

But it's not a problem. Chris, Andrew, Joby, and Steve (Ensemble Bash) are four eccentric English percussionists who are my hit squad whenever I do stuff in Europe. They have a strange act that is hard to describe—kind of Blue Man Group meets Debussy by way of Steve Reich. They have been accepted into the band of Salentini, but I'm the only one who has ever seen their show. So it's fun to see our Italian chums gasping at the antics of their strange English friends. And the audience is still going nuts. Will there be any cheers left for the main event?

By the time Bash have finished their turn all the Salentini are at the side of the stage to watch them. As the stage crew re-rig the gear for the full ensemble, we find ourselves singing Christmas carols for some reason. I don't know who started it, but we're all singing "Silent Night" in Italian, even though we are sure tonight will not be silent. Halfway through "Jingle Bells" Reno the stage manager gives the signal, and it's time for the show.

We start our set with "Ucci," a fast, splashy tune to wake up the crowd. But these folks are already awake. They are already so whipped up that the energy invades the stage and this sprightly tune becomes a devil's thrill ride. We are playing so fast, infused with such superhuman energy, that I swear the stage is revolving, bucking, and heaving to the music and the crowd is swirling around us in a frenzy. And this is just the first song. BAMP! We hit the last hit of the song and go straight into the midtempo "Mena-menamò." Now this is usually a solid heavy number that loosens people up after the flashy intro, but tonight the folks are stomping and whirling already.

Pacing is a very important aspect of live performance—and not just for artistic reasons. My instrument is demanding physically, but different types of rhythm use different energies. So after the hundred-yard sprint of the first tune, the easy lope of "Mename-namò" is supposed to be a breather, with Mauro, Antonio, and Canaglia (the Rascal) doing most of the work with their tambourines.

But tonight there is no stopping for rest. The crowd immediately pick up the new beat and we just have to feed the monster. We rage through the song and hit the end trick like a daisy cutter bomb. The crowd is screaming and whistling and onstage we are all laughing and shaking and hollering at one another. This is the last show of the tour and we're going to soak up every minute.

Usually, after a song finishes, you wait for the applause to die away before starting the next tune, but tonight there is no dying away, just a continuous whistling and cheering.

Our next tune is a cheerful dance, kind of a light moment usually but no sooner do the tambourines hint at the rhythm than the crowd is on it. By now we have regained our professional composure and manage to keep the groove light and bouncy even though the audience is providing a driving rhythm of its own. The stomp of the crowd is so strong that we lay right back on our instruments, riding the wave. We're holding our fire because we know that it's time for the secret weapon.

Halfway through "Stornelli," a large sound is heard and suddenly Raiz is in the house. He oozes onto the stage and we kick into a new gear behind him as he gets into some kind of spoken anthem. God only knows what he's growling about in that strange dialect, but he whips himself, the audience, and the band into a wild fury as we break into a chorus that the crowd picks up on and it's a sea of upraised arms shouting with Raiz.

We crash to another big song end and the crowd roars—which is fine, but we have to shut them up now. We have been onstage for maybe twenty minutes, pretty much raging all the way, so now a change of pace is needed.

The next tune starts quietly with voices and wafting sheep/bagpipe. When Giancarlo leans into a few wailing notes, the crowd gets the hint and the hubbub dies down. While the singers hold the spotlight, I nip offstage to grab a dry T-shirt from a pile next to the monitor desk. Heaven right now is a dry towel and a jug of Gatorade as I watch Ninfa and Enza beguile the crowd. A minute ago the joint was rockin', but now it's a still atmosphere. From the monitor desk in the wings I can see that the women are completely enveloped in the music, concentrating intensely. Their voices rise into the night air.

It's a storybook concert, one of those rare times when the artist, the audience, the venue, the moon, and probably some voodoo all come together. The thrill of a great show is a two-way current that energizes an audience but positively electrifies the performers.

It would be interesting to analyze the brain chemistry at such times.

▲ La Notte della Taranta in Melpignano

Leaving the stage after a show like this is kind of bittersweet. It's the last show of the tour, the last cheer, the last pizzica groove, and the last event requiring focus, energy, or health. No more hand maintenance will be required. No show moments to fix, no point tweaking the kit, it's over. Burn the stage and everything on it. I probably won't see my drums again for months.

As I lope from the stage to the palace dressing rooms my heart is full of joy. I'm not religious but usually the thought in my head is one of gratitude. Thank you Lord for this gift, this body, this life.

CHAPTER 18

INCUBUS

THE HYBRID

DECEMBER 2004
LOS ANGELES

Out of the blue comes an e-mail from brother Miles saying:

> **All confirmed. Rehearsals are next Friday, and your show with Andy Summers and Incubus at the KROQ shindig will be on Sunday.**

Whaaaat? I dimly remember Miles mentioning something about this, months ago. At the time I said, "Wow, cool," and then forgot about it.

So I'm thinking about it now (a little panicked) and figure, What the heck? They're a cool group, they were nice to my boy Jordan when he interviewed them for his belly dancing documentary, so why not?

Of course I had better dig out my drums and try to get some life into my wrists. After a long layoff I can still play, but the tiny little muscles that provide the finesse, that enable the cool persnickety stuff that the folks like, are only good for a few squirts before they quit. Actually, it's nice to have an excuse to blast away on my long-suffering tom-toms.

I get a phone number and call up Mike, Incubus's guitarist, to see what they have in mind. He proposes that we play "Roxanne" and "Message in a Bottle" (from The Police) and "Pardon Me" and "Megalomaniac" (from Incubus).

Mike suggests that we meet up for dinner the following night at a fancy restaurant in Santa Monica. When I get there at the appointed hour, I find Andy regaling the Incubus guys with his vast repertoire of road stories. They are a fun crew and we have a riotous evening trading notes and tales. We haven't met their singer, Brandon, yet, since he is off with the flu but the rest of this cheerful gang seems to be led by Mike, who has an easy, confident air that relaxes me. Ben, Jose, and Chris each have their own vibe, though. In fact they are like the United Colors of Benetton. Black scratcher, Latin drummer, Jewish guitarist, Mulatto bassist, and Scottish/Native American/Mexican singer. They seem very close. Maybe because they have been playing together for fifteen years!

After dinner, as we climb into our cars everybody admires my brand-new conveyance, which is the newly modeled Jeep Grand Cherokee. Since I suspect that I may be among liberals, I tell them all that it's the new Jeep hybrid.

Next day we meet again for rehearsals way over in Glendale. I get there early to tinker with my kit. I've got my boy Scott in tow and he is very impressed to be hanging out with a band that many of his friends are into. His ol' Hall of Famer dad is just a dad, but Incubus, like, *wow!*

Andy arrives at the crack of 2:00 (the agreed-upon downbeat) but there is no sign of our new friends for another hour. While we wait we remember with joy the glorious anarchy of young players.

We also get a chance to inspect their gear. The first thing that an old seventies' rocker like me notices is how small it is. Speaker cabinets are now so efficient that no one needs the huge stacks that I used to fantasize about as a kid. Mike just has a couple of small two-speaker enclosures with a classic Marshall amp and Ben's bass rig is similarly unintimidating. What they do have a lot of is effect pedals. Andy walks straight over to Mike's collection clustered on the floor next to his mic stand. He is muttering: "Got that one and that one, sold that, and . . . what's that?"

Even the drums are small and oddly shaped. Jose has every-body's (except mine) new favorite brand of kit called DW. He has them tuned way tight like a jazz kit (so do I, but neither of us play jazz). Kids these days have it all figured out. I used to be the only drummer who knew how to get a heavy sound from high-pitched drums. Kids today start out knowing everything that we had to learn.

The most elaborate corner is the deejay rig. It's a row of turn-tables, rack-mounted FX boxes, and odd retro synthesizers. He even has a theremin, that strange, squeaky instrument of the sixties.

When the band shows up they are all business. We go straight into "Roxanne" and everybody seems to get it pretty quickly, so with time to fool around, Ben suggests that we could go into the Marley song "War" during the bridge. Veerrry cool idea.

By six o'clock we have knocked some semblance of order into the material and call it a day.

Walking out into the parking lot I see Chris climbing into an enormous, tricked-out black Cadillac Escalade SUV. Thing must weigh three tons. He looks over his shoulder at me, flicks a dread-lock out of his face, says, "It's the new hybrid," and then roars off into the night.

■

THE GIG IS ACTUALLY called "The KROQ Almost Acoustic Christmas" and there are eleven bands playing tonight. At the sound check this afternoon, eleven drum sets and a hundred tons of amplification are being hustled around the stage by black-clad gangs of tattooed roadies. It's all very professional and good-natured but I still want to run home, rifle through the kids' toys, and see if I can find me some tattoos. Maybe some Polly Pockets or a big Sponge Bob right over my jugular.

The drums and amps are all set up on rolling platforms, and it's a revolving stage so the pace is brisk. As one band runs through its sound check another is setting up behind it. The stage revolves, the gear is wheeled off in a twinkling, and the next crew rolls their stuff on.

When it's our turn to bat, we go straight through two of our songs and are trying to cram in just one more, but the stage is turning. We're still blazing as we rotate out of the hall and into the sunshine outside the Universal Amphitheatre.

When I arrive back at the gig after an afternoon lounge at home, the rock-and-roll party is in full swing. There is a large backstage area separated into layers of access to the booze, bands, and stage. Everybody backstage gets the booze. It's a mob of carousing fun lovers with crazy hairdos and loud clothing.

One layer deeper is where the dressing rooms are. Some are large suites; others are small. Once you get into this area, most of the people you see are rock stars. Down the hall, the early-playing bands (in the small rooms) are full of aftershow swagger. Their doors are open and they are slouching in and out of one another's rooms exchanging manna. Closer up are the bands who are still getting ready, and the atmosphere is a little more sober.

When I get to our room, Incubus are all there. They seem pretty relaxed as we goof around, with about ninety minutes to kill before our moment. There's a TV monitor in the room so we can watch the show onstage and rate the competition. Sum 41 are there one minute and next it's a guy with a lot of tattoos. Then it's us.

Or rather, then it's Incubus. They depart for the stage to do their own show. We'll be joining them after a few songs. They look great onstage and have a lot more going on musically than anyone else I've seen today. They are an excellent combination of power and poetry.

There is a tunnel under the backstage party area so we can get up to the stage without having to run the gauntlet. After a short wait in the wings, the crew pulls the drapes off my drums and out we walk. As soon as I'm sitting down my hands take over and my horse is charging through the bit and over the fields. Somewhere I can hear Andy and Mike start up the *Doo doo doo* riff and I try to rein it in a little so that Brandon can sing the song.

Next up is "Message in a Bottle" then "Roxanne" and then just like that, in a flash, it's done. Sure, there were a few fender benders. OK, so I played too loud, too fast, and too much, but shows like this are such a rare treat that I feel no remorse. Catch me at a real concert, on a real tour, and you may see some finesse, but this was something else. So shoot me if I had too much fun.

As Andy and I leave the stage and head back, we pass Velvet Revolver coming up the tunnel. For some reason we studiously ignore one another. Maybe because Andy and I have postshow swagger and they have preshow tension. I've actually met Duff and Scott at various times in the past and they are good guys.

By the time I get out of the shower the rest of the band are all whooping it up in the dressing room. Everybody is happy. It was a good show and the crowd obviously liked it, too. The room quickly fills up with friends and family. On the TV monitor, the show goes on with Velvet Revolver in full swing. The sound is down so I can't hear them, but they are raging away. Pity about that hat that Scott is wearing. It gives them kind of a Village People vibe.

The band that I really want to see is Green Day. I lost a bet that I made ten years ago with my niece Ashley that they would vaporize after one hit. I had them figured as a McPunk band (which I didn't hold against them because that's pretty much what The

Police was at first). Well, I was wrong. They are still here and I want to know why. So I drag myself away from the party and head out to the auditorium to catch their show from the front. Here's why they are still here: they write hits, keep it simple, and they connect with the audience. They are tight, professional, confident, and energized. I'm not about to rush out and buy all their CDs, but I respect this band and I owe Ashley one dollar.

Life is full of rewards and miseries, but I'm very happy that shows like this come along every once in a while. To some it may look like Andy and I are clutching on to past glories by playing old hits rather than doing something new. Fact is we are both doing much new stuff. Heck, I have a whole new and unrelated career as a film composer.

The Devil may take me, but every now and then I will reach into the cookie jar. . . .

CHAPTER 19

DANCING WITH THE (POLL)STARS

FEBRUARY 2004

*A typical night out in sparkling Hollywood
with the glitterati.*

Haven't checked Sting's pulse in a while, so I pick up the phone. He's somewhere down the beach, but Kathy Schenker quickly returns my call. "Are you coming tonight?" she asks.

Well, no, I hadn't heard about it, but it turns out that tonight is a big night for Stingo. It's one of those Man of the Year evenings where he will be surrounded by the glitterati of Los Angeles as he endures speeches about his virtues and performances of his songs by esteemed artists. Well, it ain't the keys to Melpignano, but it's a big honor nonetheless. By some mix-up, we didn't get the invite, but Kathy is urgent on the phone now.

Problem is, I've already got a gig tonight handing out an award to someone else. My brother Ian has twisted my arm to attend the Pollstar Awards ceremony, and further, to be an award presenter. This event is the Grammies of concert promotion. The winners are not just agents, promoters and performers; the venues and trucking companies are also honored.

It's also my buddy Henry's birthday party night. After handing

▲ Ian, Miles, me

out the brass, our plan was to meet up later for further hilarity at a fetish club in West Hollywood.

But Stingo is Man of the Year tonight and I absolutely cannot but add my voice to the accolades that will be sung. It will be a busy evening, so we set off into the golden L.A. dusk with the intention of hitting every base.

Over in Hollywood at the Kodak Theatre is a cheerful throng of faces from my old touring days. They are all suited up and shiny for their big awards night. And there's my brother Ian! A particularly warm glow lights me up as he shouts a big hello. Ian has a way of energizing any gathering. In his company, everybody and anybody becomes vital, interesting, and amusing. In the Ian zone everybody is relaxed and chuckling about something. We spot Miles and we three musketeers toast the blessing of our nest. Miles has his Bellydance Superstars along to wow the assembled promoters in the show tonight so he is all business, which actually isn't much different from his vibe at Sunday lunch.

Downstairs in the dressing rooms, there is a minor constellation of celebrity award presenters. Alice Cooper is there, and Don Was. Sharon Osborne is there. Alice, Don, and I soon have our heads together, exchanging war stories and comparing notes about the different eras in which we worked. Alice is the coolest guy, quick laugh and droll comportment. This is a man who has been around the block a few times.

The show has started so we wander up to the wings, marveling at the obscurity of the awards that we will be handing out. Don is doing "Christian Music Booker of the Year."

I am handed a nominations list and a sealed winner's envelope with the title "Arena of the Year." I check the list, and sure enough, the nominees are buildings: concrete and cement. I look around to see if my old friend Shea Stadium is fretting hopefully somewhere in the audience.

When my turn comes, I stride importantly to the microphone and intone the nominees. There is a flourish of music, then, "And the winner is . . . Madison Square Garden of New York!"

There is a heartwarming applause from the audience of agents and promoters for this storied concert hall. I accept the award on behalf of the building, and after a few modest words of thanks (on behalf of the building) to all the Pollstar voters, my work here is done.

Soon we are sailing over to Culver City to cheer on my old buddy Sting. At the Sony Studios, the parking lot is full of the slickest, longest, and blackest limousines in town. Our car drops us outside one of the huge aircraft hangar–sized soundstages and immediately we can smell the rarefied scent of show business royalty. This is a much higher caste than the lowly carnies and hawkers back at Pollstar.

We have missed the start of the festivities and there is a woman onstage singing one of Sting's songs. Could be Alanis—or a Dixie Chick for all I know. It's a pretty tame rendering of "Walking on the Moon." In the middle of the song she stops singing and addresses Sting directly at his table in front of her. She's gushing with soaring eloquence, and there is hardly a dry eye in the house as she picks the song back up and finishes the tune to tumultuous standing applause. Useful. Now I at least know where his crew is sitting.

Fiona has been scrutinizing the table plan and doesn't see us anywhere. I grab her by the hand and thread her through the applauding throng to the Sumner tables.

It's a wonderful moment. The band has struck up, the glitter ball is swirling, and the royalty are ringing with joy.

My Main Man has risen to the stage and is basking in the adoration of his peers. This is when we are spotted by Kathy and Trudie, who light up.

Trudie Sumner is unique. Not one for half measures, she always greets family with full Latin embrace. No pecks on the cheek for Trudie—she inspires and demands full mouth-to-mouth resuscitation. She can turn the most Nordic of dweebs into Antonio Banderas.

Just as she is sweeping into my arms for our customary operatic greeting, I can see out of the corner of my eye that The Man of the Evening—her husband—has reached the microphone and is about to speak. People are now sitting down, to reveal the Wife and the Nemesis, right there at table number one, performing our reenactment of *Il Trovatore* in front of the entire gathering. Fiona, with her instinct for invisibility, is long gone. At the sound of his voice, Trudie turns, and I am vapor. Sheeeezus!

"Dahling," says Fiona when I catch up with her, "did I lose you there for a moment?" She twinkles.

CHAPTER 20

SCORING WITH ANJELICA

MARCH 2005

This gig had the added unstated threat that if I didn't get it right Anjelica would turn me into a rat. Anyone remember The Witches?

It was a gig that arrived very quickly. At about four o'clock in the afternoon my manager, Derek Power, tells me about a movie produced by Larry Sanitsky, an old friend of his, and directed by Anjelica Huston. Sounds cool. I once sat next to Anjelica on a transatlantic flight and we got along famously.

First thing next morning Derek is on the phone again. Have I watched the movie? Um, it just arrived by FedEx. So I watch the movie.

It is a three-hanky tearjerker starring Rosie O'Donnell as the retarded sister of a sleek power bitch played by Andie MacDowell. It is a very emotional piece and O'Donnell eats up the screen. At the end of the film, just as the end credits begin, and as I'm reaching for my fourth hanky, the phone rings again. It's Larry Sanitsky, the producer. Can we meet at my place in, say, half an hour? "Sure," I sob.

Anjelica and Larry soon arrive and we all yuck over how Anjelica and I have both been dining out on how we slept together (well, in adjacent seats) over the ocean. Does this make us members of the Mile High Club?

We get down to business and spot the movie. This is when we map out where the music will be and what it's going to say. We talk at length about the meaning and sub-meaning of each scene how the music can impart, imply, illuminate or even obscure the different threads of the story.

Anjelica is leaving town for ten days so I'll have the score pretty much completed by the time I show her anything. This is good because I can really tweak it before the first show-and-tell but bad because I may go down a wrong path and waste effort. Usually, I like to do about a third of the score and then get some feedback earlier in the process. This is a new client and music can hit people in unpredictable ways.

Well, I have a terrific week. Scoring is fun and this is a good film. I've been doing a lot of comedy lately and this deep emotional stuff makes a change. When actors direct, you know the performances will sing. Actually, very little music is needed. Rosie and Andie don't need much help from me.

After the composing phase I call up my favorite players and start recording. For this score I call Michael Thompson for guitar; a small string ensemble, led by Charlie Bisharat; and my all-round Swiss Army knife of music, Judd Miller.

On the appointed day Larry and Anjelica arrive for the first show-and-tell. It's time to face the music. I sit them down and ply them with coffee and cakes (blood sugar saturation is good for business).

The first thing they hear is the main title music. It's an upbeat piece, and I can see that their toes are tapping and they have assumed appreciative body postures. This is good.

Soon however, as we get into the movie, a cold chill has entered the room. I normally play all of the music cues in a row so that the director can get the overall picture before going back to discuss each cue individually. By the time we get to the end of the first pass, the temperature has dropped thirty degrees. There is silence in the room, but the body language is growling. Uh-oh. I have already mentally rearranged my upcoming week since I know that I'll be rescoring this movie. Or not.

Tempting as it may be to meet unlove with outraged indignation at the nonappreciation of my work, it is actually smarter to be suave. There are just a couple of things wrong but since they apply to cue after cue, by the end of the presentation these faults have the curse of Magog upon them.

One offender is the rack of cymbals and crotales that I like to use for an atmosphere of magic nostalgia. I probably mixed them a little hot, but if you decide not to like them, they cut through everything. Cue after cue. The biggest surprise is Larry's reaction to all of Judd's stuff. He spots the sampleness of it instantly. I have *never* been busted for Judd's work before. I rely heavily in all of my scores on Judd's ability to give me rich woodwinds and brass (as well as all other kinds of weird drones and wails), which he plays with great sensitivity. Although I congratulate Larry on his eagle ears, I silently suspect him of having peeked behind my curtain. For cue after cue Larry is like a Puritan fingering witches. Out, Fake Instruments! Out! And just to rub it in he keeps referring to Judd's lovingly recorded, crafted, and performed samples as "synthesizers."

Anjelica has just one problem. It's the fundamental approach of the composition. Since the actors on the screen are creating much of their own music, I have just given them wafts of atmosphere (the accursed crotales and woodwinds) with unconnected pangs from a solo acoustic guitar. Wrong. Being Irish, Anjelica needs actual melody. A waft here and a sprangle there would work well for many directors, but not if they are Celts.

To their credit, neither Larry nor Anjelica appears to be panicked by this parade of dud cues, and they leave the studio mollified by the remedies that I have smoothly proposed. I award myself a D– for the presentation and then start rescoring the entire movie. Whole new composing concept, whole new sound palette.

Meanwhile, there is the issue of a song that is required for one scene in the movie. It's a three-minute scene of the two sisters frolicking by the lake and rediscovering their love for each other. It is the emotional center of the movie. My job is to commission a songwriter, find a singer, and record an original track. There is a process for this. Pro songwriters will normally work on spec for this kind of thing since a good song can have many uses (if we don't use it) and having one appear on network TV in an Emmy-potential movie is good enough bait to get several guys across town competing for the gig. A couple of the guys stabbing at it have won awards and had big hits. This ought to be easy.

Well, I have a productive week. Scoring can be challenging work; I'm not as fresh as I was the first time around, but at least I'm better educated as to the proclivities of the client. I write some actual melodies and get my players back. As I work, songs are beginning to arrive via e-mail. One of them is hand-delivered by the most unlikely contestant of all, a slightly scraggly and darkly mysterious young woman. Very young, very nonindustry.

After completing the second pass at the score I collect up the four songs that have arrived and lay them against the scene. Two of them just plain suck, one of them is right on the money, and one of them has a mysterious, haunting charm that works not with picture. Pity, it's got a kind of charisma to it. All of the other three, written by flinty-eyed professionals, follow the contours of the scene perfectly. Even the ones that suck soar when the scene lifts and duck when the scene goes to dialogue. The haunting one just sits there.

Now it's time for round two with the director and producer. They are in good cheer as they arrive and I briskly caffeinate and seat them. Then I hit Play on my keypad.

I run down the cues, one after another, without stopping for comment. The body language is not bad. Every now and then Larry's head jerks to a forty-five-degree angle (skeptical) but mostly, he's relaxed. Anjelica is leaning forward intensely (engaged). I figure, anything less than major improvement would be reflected by morose hunching of the shoulders, brooding forward tilt of the head, ugly sideways glances.

When we get to the song scene, none of the submissions pass muster. They are just too straight, too perfect. Except for the strange one, which is kind of cool but just sits there.

With the score, Anjelica declares herself pleased. She likes the tunes and the sounds and looks very relieved to have something to work with. Most directors leave the studio happy at this point. Anjelica is just getting started. We spend the rest of the afternoon microscoping each cue. She is fixed like a laser on the pace and nuance of every line of dialogue. Although she likes the music I wrote, she likes even more to move it around like paint on a palette. She cheerfully moves cues around, switching them, mixing and nixing them. After mashing down the entire length of the movie, she and Larry leave, exhausted but happy.

All I have to do now is tidy up after the carnage. Wherever we grabbed phrases and pasted them here and there, I have to smoosh the seams and make beautiful the new transitions.

On the song front, two more wrong songs have arrived and I'm starting to worry. Meanwhile the hippy tune is reappearing in my head. I give Jesca Hoop a call and she comes right over. I put her song against the picture and try to explain the dynamic of music and movies. When the scene goes up the music needs to go *up,* I gesticulate. Lift, rise, swell, release, grow, *up*. Although it appears that the words coming out of my mouth are Chinese to her, she nods vaguely and offers to take another stab. It needs to go *up*.

Next day she comes back with a new version. I put it to picture. At the place where it should go up, it becomes more beautiful. Very beautiful, in fact, but not UP.

Over the course of the next week Larry and Anjelica come over several more times. I think they like my place. My studio, situated on a leafy knoll, is a large square tower with windows on all sides. Facing the ample screen and terrifying array of speakers is a large couch, from which directors love to play with music. Who wouldn't?

Most of the score is done by now, but there is one scene that evades us. Anjelica has the idea of using an ancient Irish air (melodies that are ancient are always bankable) so I find a version of "She Moves Through the Fair." Michael comes back and plays it like a leprechaun. Just one mournful solo acoustic guitar with long reverb. Everybody in the room is weeping. How about if we try laying it over some of those other scenes?

For the song there is only one way forward. I strap Jesca's demo (which is just her voice and an acoustic guitar) on to my computer, figure out the tempo, analyze her fingerpicking guitar part, and insert a section of my own device that goes *up*. I build up the backing track with drums, bass, electric guitar, and whatever else I can throw into the pot. I give her the track, which has a piano tune indicating a melodic line for the new section, and she goes away to write some more lyrics.

By the time she comes back and sings all her stuff into my fancy microphones, this song is beginning to really pop. She has a great voice, and her pitch is good enough for her to stack up some pretty oblique harmonies. Time for the Huston/Sanitsky shredder. Actually the bosses are pretty happy with the song, but how about if we take that cool part which goes "Yeah, Yeeaah" and put it over this shot? And that second verse sounds a bit vocally light. How about if we get a big black voice to sing the song? OoooK. . . .

Damn, at three o'clock, the day before the dub (which is the giant mixing session for all of the music, sound effects, and dialogue) I have to find a black lady singer. Vicki Randle, my favorite, is out of town, so I have to take a chance on a stranger. Actually, two of them, since the first sounds like Ethel Merman and we have to find another. Finally, Alex Brown comes over and is able to match Jesca's exotic phrasing, adding that rich black timbre to the vocals.

On the morning of the dub, the bosses swing past my studio to check out the song. Eureka! Huzzah! It's good! How about if we take the Yeah Yeeaahs and put them over the end section? No problemo. With a trifling flick of sound editing we are at the finish line! With bittersweet hugs and kisses I bid them Godspeed at the dub and they leave. Aaaaaaaaaghhh. Jeff Seitz staggers off to pick up the threads of his life. I quit the applications; decouple the crevulators, and power down the hard drives.

For the first time in weeks I notice that the birds are singing outside my window. The sunshine is dappling gently through the trees on a gorgeous California morning. I drift down to my Jeep and glide down the valley to Venice Beach for coffee and a newspaper. Lunch by the pier stretches into a meandering afternoon of idleness and light contemplation. I've got a hot date with Fiona tonight, so I eventually head home, but on the way, I stop by the studio. There are six messages for me. Larry and Anjelica want to know if we could. . . .

CHAPTER 21

FOO FLYING WITH THE FLY FOOS

JUNE 2005

I feel like the winner of an MTV prize. Here is my itinerary: Whisked by limousine from my home to an airport in Van Nuys, where I will meet the Foo Fighters. We board their Gulf Stream IV jet, which will take us to San Francisco to attend a concert there before flying to New York to participate in an MTV special event. Duration of adventure: thirty hours. Professional obligations: none (almost).

Now look at the itinerary of these young professionals who are my hosts. They just returned from a trip to Japan and Australia. Last night they played the *Tonight Show*. Tonight is the gig in San Francisco (for twelve thousand fans). Within an hour of the last note of the show, they are airborne for New York. Arriving at 9:00 A.M., pretty much sleepless, they get half an hour in their hotel rooms before going live in front of the cameras to host MTV for twenty-four hours! The event is called "24 Hours of Foo." For them it will be fifty hours without sleep. For the last twenty-four of those hours, they will be holding the attention of worldwide

MTV viewers, pretty much with only their charisma and what's left of their vitality. A long day, even for soldiers like these guys.

But I'm whistling a happy tune as my car pulls up to the plane. Charter jets are not just about lavish leather-lined luxury. The main deal is the pulling-up-to-the-plane part—dispensing completely with the airport terminal. Ten yards from car door to plane door.

Dave and Jordyn Grohl are the first Foo Fighters to arrive. As bandleader, Dave sets the example. But always one step ahead is the band's tour manager, the bearlike Gus Brandt, and his black-clad assistant, Nick Flynn—who ushers me on board.

As the bandsters show up, we luxuriate in the rarefied atmosphere of Million Air. No shit, that's what the charter company is called. Things wake up when Taylor and Alison Hawkins arrive. As in many bands, the drummer is the life of the party. As in many bands, Nate Mendel, the bass player, is the mysterious one. Chris Shiflett, the guitar player, is already at the gig—he's playing earlier in the day with his side project band. As an hors d'oeuvre to the MTV marathon, Chris is playing two shows today, with two different bands! This rock star thing can sometimes look just like hard work.

For me it's a vicarious thrill to ride along with this team. Back in the day, when this was my life, I didn't enjoy it so much because even for a hardened pro, there is constant preshow tension that dampens any day-of-show activity, no matter how exotic.

Flying up to Frisco is a breeze and soon we are arriving at the gig. It's an all-day radio station–sponsored affair (kind of like the KROQ/Incubus thing) with bands playing all day and the Foos headlining.

As the van pulls into the backstage enclosure, the huge stage is booming and the crowd is roaring. There is the usual horde of tattooed stage crew heaving gear around, and the scaffolding reaches right up to Rock Heaven.

The band zone is a cluster of trailers/dressing rooms like circled wagons. It is populated by a happy throng of strangely clad, unnaturally hued musos, and their (often weirder-looking) friends. The Foos have many chums among the other bands and our arrival is greeted with fraternal warmth and intricate handshakes all around. The last person anyone expects to see trailing in the Foos' wake is me. But these are all muso types back here and I feel the love of my kind, even though they're all strangers and I haven't heard of a single other band on the bill.

There are two bands to go before showtime, so Taylor and I wander over to inspect his drums, which are set up on his riser backstage. By now he has persuaded me to join them for one song during their set, so I had better check out his sticks and kit to see how dented my knuckles are going to get.

Every drum set is different. Unlike guitars, which are pretty standard, drum sets are very personalized for the height, arm length, and physical style of each drummer. Playing someone else's kit isn't like driving someone else's car; it's more like wearing someone else's clothes. But you don't just look funny; you dent your knuckles.

I'm kind of long-armed; I sit back on a high seat and flail most comfortably at distantly placed cymbals and drums. Since I play orthodox grip, my snare is tilted away from me. Matched grip players tilt the snare toward themselves. Taylor is a matched grip forward-leaner on a low stool.

But I hate to be precious about these things. I always respect the musicians who just plug and play so I try to shun public tweakage. I spend hours at home tweaking my kit but this is Taylor's gig, and the guy whose name is on the ticket is the one who has to shine. So, despite my misgivings about how close his cymbals are, I declare the kit to be playable and we head back to the dressing room.

Pre-gig tension. Almost every performer of every kind suffers from it. Everyone in the dressing room is upbeat but there is a shortness to the laughter and a distraction to the banter. Everyone is twanging their instruments, warming up their fingers. Dave is reminding them about recent adjustments to the arrangements. He has decided to start the set with the first song on their new CD, a song that they haven't rehearsed or played live before, so now they run through the tune acoustically just to tune it up.

The lads have got it into their heads to play an old Police song called "Next to You." It's probably the most scorching Police track that they could have chosen. It was an epic even when I was twenty-four. I darkly suspect Taylor of thinking, "Here's one the old bastard can't play anymore." But it turns out that he knows the words to this one and he's going out to the front of the stage to sing it while I hit his drums. So we run this song down one time, with me clacking sticks on the table and them strangely able to play the whole song from memory. They remember it better than I do.

Gus gives them the nod, and it's showtime.

There is always an excited thrill in the wings as a band emerges from its trailer and mounts the stage. It's dark but there is enough light for the players to plug in and find their spots. Actually, most bands these days don't plug in with wires anymore. They have radio connection from axe to amp and they could play the show from the dressing room if they chose.

The band starts up with a mysterious wind of noise, Dave is shouting something, and the crowd is roaring. The band kicks in, the lights flare up, and the show is on. This band has the most gigantic array of back line speaker cabinets that I've ever seen. The amp stacks tower over the players, rising to at least twenty feet. It's an iron curtain of sound. These stage speakers are very directional, so from the wings, the volume is not too extreme, but it's kind of muffled. They run through their set briskly with hardly any gap between the songs. They keep the pace up and the crowd rages along with them.

Then I see Taylor jump off his riser and go downstage to the mic, and he's looking over his shoulder at me. It is a mere three

▲ The drummer prepares.

feet from the darkness of the wings to the blazing light of the stage, and it's now time for me to jump in.

> *Brat-un, Brat-un, Brat-un, Brat-un, Brat-un, Brat*
> *da Dada Dada*
> *Chug, chug, chug, chug . . .*

Ouch! Fuck!

My left knuckle slices the hi-hat on its way to the front tom. My right stick snags the ride cymbal on its way to the floor tom. I can hardly hear the band through the din of the house monitor system. The seat is so low that my right ankle is at an uncomfortable angle on the bass drum pedal. This all seemed comfy enough tapping around earlier backstage, but now that there are twelve thousand people in front of me who have been revved up by an energetic band, larger gestures are required.

"Plug and play," I mutter to myself as I shake off the adversities and put up as much of a fight as I can. I just have to unleash the hounds, even if they're going to crash into things. At least I've been in training for my upcoming summer shows, so I've got enough juice to bluster through the song with enough energy to drive the band. I'm actually beginning to enjoy the show when suddenly we're at the end of the tune. I've got four Foo Fighters staring at me with an urgent look that says, "Oh Sun God of the Immaculate Rock Valhalla, you idiot, we're at the end of the song!" So we hit the grand washing-up and crunch to an orderly halt. "Thank you very much!" And I'm headed back to the dressing room. Well it wasn't a performance worthy of legend, but if I worried about that, I wouldn't ever play.

We get five minutes to yuck it up in the dressing room. The lads are bitching about the house monitors, but with postshow

▼ Stage full of Foo

endorphins kicking in, they are laughing as they bitch. Of course they all tell me how great I was (what else are they going to say?) and I razz Taylor about his potential as a front man (I was actually too deep into my private Idaho to notice how he did on the mic). This is on the bus back to the plane; Gus has us moving pretty briskly along the itinerary. We're on our way to New York.

On the Foo jet, dinner is served as we rise out of the Bay Area and head east. The conversation among the band, as it ever has been among bands, is about other bands. You can tell how well things are going by the attitude toward the competition. The Foos talk mostly about bands they like; struggling bands gripe about bands they hate.

One by one the travelers peel out of the conversation to get some sleep. Problem is, there's nowhere to peel off to. The seats are way luxury-lined, but they aren't beds. The cabin goes dark and quiet. It's one of those nights when you're forever trying to get to sleep, and then you wake up and think great, I slept! But your watch reveals that only five minutes have passed.

Finally, I see a gray light sneaking into the cabin from cracks in the shades. It's dawn over New Jersey, and we are going down. Everyone rises from our slumber party to nibble some breakfast as we taxi up to the vans. By the time we get to Manhattan the sun is blazing and it's rush hour.

The Mandarin Oriental Hotel is a supercalifragilistically deluxe wedge of skyscraper that is poised like an axe over Central Park. Gus has put me in a corner suite with living room, dining room, and bathroom complex. These fancy hotels can be ridiculous. In the bathroom suite, there is a coffee-table book called *The Art of Shaving*. Call room service and a Vassar-accented voice says "Thank you for calling In-Room Dining, my name is Kimberly, and I'm your dining communication liaison. How may I make your day special?" OK, I'm exaggerating a little, but the obsequiousness does make you want to shout, "Fuck you Kimberly, send me some eggs!"

Still, it's a pity that I only get to spend two and a half hours in this Xanadu. A few dark snarls would abbreviate Kimberly. There is a TV in every room and the view is terrific.

Two hours later, there is a soft ringing in my ear. It's Kenneth, welcoming me to a Mandarin morning on the occasion of my 12:00 P.M. wake-up call. Would I like breakfast, newspaper, a shoe-shine, taxi, or string quartet?

The Foos have already been on the job for a couple of hours when I get to the MTV studios in Times Square. Actually, they are down at street level in the MTV store, hamming it up for the cameras and throwing swag to "fans" from Central Casting. Actually, these are real MTV prizewinners.

And now for the reason they flew me all this way. Dave and Taylor and I are going to engage in a drum-off with some street drummers. Out on the sidewalk are the local heroes and a cluster of Tupperware. They are already blasting, so us white boys sit down, grab sticks, and pick up the groove. In a heartbeat, we are woven together in a tapestry of rhythm. The guys on my left and right are as culturally removed from me as Egyptian sailors, but we are soon reaching into one another's souls as we respond to the pulse. It's a dialogue that's clear and deep. Each of us is a spoke in a spinning wheel. We give and take. We support and challenge. We are one.

I know this sounds like hippy shit, but banging these plastic buckets on a grimy New York sidewalk really has got us all completely enthralled. My sticks are a blur, and my heart is soaring with joy. Never mind the heat and sweat; all of my being is just a vehicle for this gift of rhythm.

Eventually, there is an MTV producer with headset and clipboard shouting, "We are clear!" which means that the eye of MTV has shifted to scan other horizons and we are off the air. This is only momentary for the Foos. They are immediately hustled off to the next location, with a brief backward "Yo!" to our new drummer dude brethren.

MTV is a fortress. We have the heavy heavy "Artist" laminate passes so we are rushed past the many layers of security by men with walkie-talkies. Trailing along is I, going, "fuck, Fuck, *fuck!*" My hands are shredded. In all the time-honored locations, the skin is shaved down to the pink.

The penalty is that from now until August, my hands will be the focus of constant and tedious attention. Working up the calluses is a careful process, and this blows it completely. I won't be able to look at a drumstick without strapping up with full armor plating, and the next few months are full of drums for me. Why didn't I wear my FUCKING gloves?!

The cameras are on the other band members, Chris and Nate, now. They're doing a barbeque on the roof. They officiate spring break–type competitions while cooking burgers. It's just like a real roof party, but with cameras and flinty-eyed production crew prowling through the throng. The throng itself is curiously pleasing to the eye. The idea is that MTV throws the boys a twenty-four-hour party and provides them with sets and toys. It is hoped that the boys will partake thereof and enjoy it all as photogenically as possible. Doesn't sound like too much of a Dark Deal with the Devil, does it? Roll the cameras, let's party!

Downstairs is a soundstage rigged for fun. As well as drums, amps, and music toys, there is Ping-Pong, foosball, pinball, videos, and all the very latest in indoor entertainment. A team of professionals has spent weeks dreaming up party tricks to keep the lads and their audience entertained. The coolness of it all hits me at the point where I'm goofing off with Taylor; he's laughing about something when I look over his shoulder and out the picture window across Times Square to see him goofing off and laughing on a huge screen that covers the entire face of the opposite building. I give him a poke and he youches live around the world.

Just as this Midsummer Night's Foo is getting started, it's time for me to bail. Gus gives me the nod for my 7:00 P.M. flight back to L.A. After tearful embraces with Chris, Dave, Taylor, Nate, and Gus, Nick guides me through the layers down to the sidewalk. Just like that, I'm out of the band bubble and on the streets of New York City. Times Square, in fact.

But the limousine door is open and I'm on my way home.

CHAPTER 22

GIZMO

SUMMER 2005

Able was I ere I saw Elba.

This mysterious Napoleonic palindrome rattles around my head as I gaze out from the terrace overlooking the harbor of Portoferraio. Jutting out into the bay is the castle where we will play our concert, and behind me is the Teatro dei Vigilanti, in which my new band, Gizmo, will be rehearsing for the next ten days. When Napoleon was first defeated and given this Mediterranean island in exchange for Europe, he noisily put down roots and engaged in public works, giving every impression that he intended to retire here. Secretly he was plotting his escape. He built this jewel of an opera theater, in which Vittorio and I are plotting Gizmo.

It is a tiny dollhouse opera theater in the classic horseshoe form, with about a hundred seats on the floor and three stories of ornate boxes around the rim. Our gear is nested on the stage. From my drums I can look straight through the theater, out the front door, across the piazza, and over the terrace to the bay, where fishing and pleasure craft are wafting past.

It's just another fine mess that my friend Titti Santini has landed

me in. Titti is the impresario who first brought me to Italy four years ago to play the Orchestralli tour and then introduced me to La Notte della Taranta festival. He's rare among southern Europeans for his brisk organization and rare among promoters for his zeal for unusual music. This time he has hired me some very slick musicians to create a new band called Gizmo.

Rehearsals start with just keyboards, guitar, and me. In the absence of bass, percussion, and vocals, the most logical place to start turns out to be the Klark Kent songs that I will be singing—which takes us straight to the most intriguing plot point of the project. I have almost never done this before. Remember *Top of the Pops*? I earned my crust riding my drums, but as a singing guitarist at the front of the stage, I'm just about to open the first door as a rank amateur.

Leaving aside that I forgot to bring my instrument (verrrry professional!), the first challenge is that I have to walk up to the microphone, with (borrowed) guitar loaded—in front of the crew, local promoter, and some serious pro musicians—and sing. Showing them the parts and groove are easy—I've been playing guitar all my life—but approaching the mic is like walking up to the precipice and thoughtlessly leaping into the void.

So I start singing and my dull baritone reverberates around the hall. In fact, it sounds magnificent! Every utterance into the mic sounds grand and important. It's not a hard tune to carry, so pretty soon I'm channeling Elvis and putting full attitude into the song. I always suspected that the singing thing would be easy, and it is! Fun, too. Problem is, my guitar chops have disappeared completely. Guitar, vocal, and vibe—I get two out of three. I can play the guitar and sing while staring at my fingers, or play the guitar and dance around without singing, or sing and dance around while only pretending to play the guitar. Clearly the latter course is the only way forward. It's odd that, after all these years, my big Guitar Hero moment is subsumed by the supremacy of the song. As I tell all of the youngsters: Everybody is working for the singer. Even when the guitarist *is* the singer.

Is my enthusiastic debut as cool as it feels, or does it suck? There is an absence of comment from band and crew. If it weren't my band, this would have been a debut swan song. But it is my band, so even if it does suck, we're doing it. It's in the show. With practice, I'll get better at it. For the moment, from the people around me the clues point to suck.

The next issue is the matter of the extra bass player. I have managed to entice my old friend, the legendary Armand Sabal-Lecco, Prince of the Deep, to join me on this tour, but there are a few dates that he will have to miss, due to prior commitments. Fortunately there is an eager sub, by the name of Max Gazzè, Prince of Italian Pop. From his ivory palazzo in Rome, Max has heard rumors of Gizmo and has instructed his agents and managers to offer his services. Although known mostly as the singer of a substantial string of hits in Italy, he's actually a pretty slick bass player. He is excited to be "just the bass player" on this tour and go nowhere near the mic. The plan is for Max to attend the last couple of days of rehearsal, once we have the material worked out, and then Armand will show him the parts.

▲ Armand, Lord of the Low

But Max can't wait. He bursts into the theater on day one, having learned all the parts from the CD that I had sent to all the players. He is completely prepared, and with not only the bass parts. He can sing the guitar solos, too. Since Armand hasn't arrived yet, Max gets to work with a zeal that is infectious.

Then Armand arrives. After our exuberant African greeting with hugs and elaborate handshakes, I pull him aside and explain what's up with the unexpected early arrival of the other bass player. Musicians can be touchy about these things. From the inky blackness that is Armand, there is a brilliant flash of his smile, fully six inches wide and three inches deep. Benignly, he draws his bass and plugs in. He hasn't done any homework because he just Knows What To Play.

Max is unsinkable. Over dinner we are entertained by his quick-fire zany humor and for the rest of the week, he is into everything. He plugs earphones into his amp rig and learns his parts silently. Then he's into the percussion, then some backing vocals (very careful to not step on Raiz's turf), then he's fussing over the monitors, then the lights. With his restless energy, he's into every possible thing that can advance the cause of Gizmo. A man after my own heart.

Vittorio Cosma, my Taranta buddy, is our keyboard player and music director. As music director he has analyzed all of the material, figured out the parts and form of each song, and is ready to direct the rehearsals for efficient assimilation by the players. Having written the material (with Vittorio), I can now just play my drums while Vitto runs the band.

I'm amazed by his flying fingers. With the Taranta ensemble he mostly directs the twenty players to play the parts, but in Gizmo he's doing it all. He immediately bonds with Armand. Our singer, Raiz (a.k.a. Rino Della Volpe) sits on a chair at the front of the stage, intently organizing a plethora of lyrics. He keeps another chair nearby, which he occasionally trashes, when the word/rhyme/tune puzzles tax him too severely. Dave "Fuze" Fiuczynski from New York is the guitarist and master minister of the chart. While the rest of us thrash and weave, he meticulously notates every wrinkle of the arrangement. Four bars of this, two bars of that, guitar tune, then break down until the signal from Raiz, and so on. At least someone knows what happens next at any given moment in any given song. Over on the percussion rack, Mauro Refosco doesn't need much organization for his parts. He's Brazilian—he just grooves.

Right next door to our lair is Marco's little café, where we refresh, eat, and plot. For lunch, we lean over there and Fuze heads off for a sea plunge. Refosco climbs onto his rented Vespa and grooves off into the town. The rest of us languorously lunch and lounge, while taking in the view and general Italian vibe. Sometimes the ladies join us. The little girls run around the theater balconies while Fiona, Lian, and Txell regale us with the splendors of Elba that we are missing.

Armand is usually the life of the party, but periodically he goes dark. For several hours, as the lava flows, the tour managers and stage crew keep their distance—in fear for their lives. I have learned not even to inquire as to the cause of any eruption. Whatever it is, it always blows over and the big grin is back, and soon the crew emerge from their bolt-holes. Everyone has learned to keep his helmet ready.

At around seven in the evening, I run out of gas and head for the shower. As I soak away the day's exertions I can hear the band continue to jam. During rehearsals, anything that sounds like jazz receives a curt reprimand from me, but as soon as I leave the room, the players degrade into those fetid figures of harmonic Hades. Fact is, virtuosity is fun; and jazz, a music that elevates dexterity over spirit, is an evil temptation that lurks around the highest-caliber players. My immunity to the stuff comes from childhood immersion in it. My daddy raised and trained me to be a jazz musician, which is why it holds no mystery for me. It reminds me of those dreary drum lessons with old Max Abrams. Professor Fuze likes to rattle my cage by pointing out jazz chords

▲ Raiz, Max, Vitto, Fuze, Mauro, Armand, me

in my music, but no one would mistake my stuff for jazz. Well, maybe some would, but that's just because it ain't exactly rock music, either.

All too soon, our idyll is interrupted by work. It's time for our first show. We have been given full accommodation and the use of the theater by the city of Portoferraio in return for one concert, to be played in the castle that sits at the mouth of the harbor. It's an unbelievably atmospheric venue for a show, even though it's a tad on the small side, with a capacity for just five hundred seated people. We have been hiding out here on Elba, but now the press arrive with their cameras and microphones. We now have to explain what we are up to, and why.

So, while Sergio and Matteo break down and shift the gear, we have the day to spend with the microphones, concocting a verbal logic for our endeavor. We also have to line up against the wall to have our picture taken as a band. It's actually the first time we get a look at ourselves. None of these players were chosen for their pretty faces but, if I say so myself, what the hell, we are Gizmo.

 WATERLOO

Where's the band? I'm pacing around a very cool circular dressing room, occupying one floor of the fat defensive tower of this castle, in the lee of which we are going to play for our supper. It's the first Gizmo gig, and I'm alone in the dressing room. There are drinks, couches, garment rails, and towels, but no band. Colombo comes in and gives me the nod. It's showtime and the band are down there, ready to go. I come down from the tower and out into the starry night. I get a glimpse of the audience sitting primly in their seats as I head for the side passage that takes me backstage.

When I get there, the lads are mooching around behind the stage waiting for me. "There's a dressing room?" Armand is asking as we walk on.

I mount the stage, stride to the front, grab the mic, and enthusiastically yell to the people of Portoferraio: "Ciao, Porto Ferino!"

I have completely mispronounced the name of the town. It's a classic "Hello, Cleveland."

There is a weak ripple from the sophisticated-looking crowd. To the drums I march, count in the band, and we're on.

Immediately, there are two problems. One of them is serious. For the first time since my high school band, the bass drum beater is stuck inside my trouser leg. I can shake it loose, but it immediately gets caught again. My war chariot is severely hobbled. I'm blazing away with my top kit, trying to drive the pulse while shaking my pant leg. Right about now the sweatband across my brow starts to creep up my forehead. It's creeping up the back of my head, too, and soon I will have a hairdo.

With an imperious rake of my left hand, I yank the headband free without losing a beat. Problem is, my microphone headset is tangled with the headband and now it's stuck hanging off the side of my head. I'm not fully into the music at this point. With a wave, Vittorio conducts the band into that section of the song in which I'm supposed to explode with drum fireworks. It's my name on the ticket, and this is where I'm supposed to show 'em what they paid for.

One hand drumming furiously is what they get until I can get myself untangled. There is a break in the music where the rhythm stops and Fuzy wafts into space with some sprangly guitar effects. Pretty quickly I recover the headset, jam my trouser leg into my sock, cyclist style, and peer out of the foxhole. Vittorio looks like he's watching a funeral. I kick back in, fully operational. But there is still something wrong. The sound onstage (now that I can think about it) is thin and unimportant. It's a midrange clatter with no warmth. The drums go *bink* not BOOM. Even Armand sounds muffled and indistinct. His grin is down to four inches. At the front of the stage, Raiz is in his own private spotlit hell. The band sound has too much volume and not enough power. He's screaming into the mic to fill the void. In the same fashion, I'm trying to get more sound out of my drums by killing them—which makes them sound even thinner.

Some stages are like that. They just reverberate all the wrong frequencies so that the sound is a jumble. After all, this castle was built for war, not music. For the band it's the Alamo. We are cut off from one another by the noise. Fuze is hitting the power chords, but his amp just squeaks. Most of the band have their heads down, working to find the pocket, but Refosco the Brazilian looks like he's sunbathing. He's grooving.

As we work our way down the set, the audience is slowly picking up momentum. After a few songs, we are all professional enough to pull ourselves together and play the arrangements that we have worked out. All the parts that sounded magnificent in our little theater sound small and dumb on this stage, but we just have to trust that Taketo Gohara, our front-house mixer, is delivering something better to the audience than what we are hearing.

So we're slogging through the set, slowly working up the crowd but there are still glitches. We get to one of the new songs that I'm supposed to kick off. But my mind is blank and I have no recollection of the tune. I just have to start playing something and see what the band comes up with. The carefully worked out song endings (very important for sparking crowd response) are hit and miss. Even when we do all end together, we can't help looking sheepishly relieved, when we're supposed to look triumphant. The songs that I count in are too fast and the ones that Vitto starts are too slow. But ever so gradually, things are improving. Every now and then are moments of actual music.

We get to a Raiz song that he does alone, accompanied only by some clouds of abstract guitar. He's so relieved for the clattering to have stopped that he really wails into the song. It really is beautiful. The night seems to come down from the sky and blow through us. Then Armand and I do our improvised duet thing. This is always an easy score. Our entire preparation for this moment in the set was comprised of a few words over dinner.

"Will you be releasing upon our grateful listeners the blessing of your bass solo, Armand?"

"If you desire it."

"Let the people hear *all* the music."

So Armand starts off softly and tunefully and pretty soon has the crowd enthralled by some serious African magic. I start stabbing him with little flashes and bursts from my toms. He responds with sharp ripostes, and then we are blazing, hurling insults with our drums and bass. It doesn't really matter what we play, as long as there is lots of it. After about a minute of raw, random, raging aggression, we suddenly stop. The crowd goes bananas. They always do. Armand and I have been doing this for years. Easiest score in show business. Of course it only works with towering bass players—Stanley Clarke taught us this trick.

By the end of the show, the crowd is actually sounding pretty enthusiastic. We put on a brave face as we take our bows and limp off the stage. The people are still howling as I sprint along the side passage, across the courtyard and over to an administrative building that has a shower. My dry clothes are already there. The shower is problematic, but I cast off my soaking wet gear and slump under the cool water. This is the signal for the endorphins to kick in with a sudden burst. My day's work is done, and it's all good. . . .

Or would be, if the audience would stop howling. I can still hear them. The time-honored signal to the crowd that Elvis has left the building is for the house lights to come up and the deejay starts spinning tunes. But this hasn't happened, and the folks out there are still yelling for more. When they have worked this hard they should get more. But Elvis is in the shower. It's great to leave people wanting more, but it's a drag to leave them pissed off about it. I add this to page thirteen of my things-to-fix list and turn the water to maximum cold as the yelling petulantly dies off.

My shower cheers me up terrifically, and when I burst into the dressing room I'm ready to hit the guys with a jocular "Well, that wasn't so bad. . . ." I haven't talked to the band since dinner. But the dressing room is still deserted. Where the hell is the fucking band?

I quickly roll up my soggy jeans, shirt, socks, boxers, belt, sweat band, and sneakers. I gather up my earplugs, headset, gloves, and show glasses (wire-rimmed, light, and bombproof). With a last glance around the room for forgotten articles, I'm out of there and heading back to the stage. I'm now suffering from band separation anxiety.

When I come out of the tower, the well-wishers are waiting, but I brush past them. The bandsters are where I last saw them, mooching around behind the stage. Titti and Mauro are pouring wine down them. Everybody has his own litany of miseries to share. Pretty soon we are chuckling over it all. It's only a show, and nobody died (physically).

There is a solemn absence of comment from our crack management team. Derek has a sage look that says, "We'll talk about this in the morning." The journalist from the Italian *Rolling Stone* is looking blank. Even Giovanni and Eugenio are looking mournful.

We can hardly hear Taketo telling us that the front sound was actually pretty good. Mostly, the clues are pointing to suck.

Well, we needed waking up after our all too idyllic sojourn on Mount Olympus. Now we are in Valhalla (where the fallen heroes rise again).

IT IS GOOD TO be back in Rome. We are playing on an island at the center of an ornamental lake, at the center of a giant villa estate. Crammed onto the island with us are four thousand music lovers. Across the water are another four thousand or so souls, spreading over the park. It's a beautiful evening and the air is thick with anticipation for our show. Since I first came here a few years ago with Orchestralli, playing for eight hundred people, I have been back a few times, with different ensembles, each time playing to bigger crowds. This is going to be great.

In my trailer, I'm twirling my drumsticks and tweaking my ratamacues on a practice pad as my little girls flirt coyly with Max's suave Italian progeny. Armand is in Barcelona so tonight we have Max on bass. We are all straining at the leash, waiting for the nod. Over the PA there is an announcement requesting that the seats not be trashed. The crowd roars as we get the nod, climb the steps up to the big stage, and hit the lights with horse, foot, and cannon.

"Ciao, Roma!" I pronounce correctly into the mic, and the din surges.

"One! *two!*—"

BOOM! The band sounds huge. I love these big outdoor stages. All the right frequencies resonate perfectly. We are laughing as we rage through the first few bars. Everything sounds great. We are locked together in rhythm. Then, with a crack of the whip, we cut down to an underlying groove and Raiz takes over. And Raiz is hot tonight. He soars, he roars. He cajoles, consoles, and controls. Max seems to be enjoying watching another singer work while he pumps the bass. Fuze is leaning into it, and Vitto's face is all crinkled up with joy. Refosco the Brazilian still looks like he's sunbathing. He's just grooving.

All of our cool points of music are working out just like we planned, only with that extra drama that you get from a hot crowd. When we get to my guitar/singing moment, I feel like I've been doing it for years. We rip through "Strange Things Happen." I manage to fit "Roma" into the lyric and the folks lap it up. Tonight I'm channeling James Brown as I improvise a sobbing dramatic conclusion to the song. The folks go wild. Then, after rising up and taking a bow, I'm backing away toward my drums, and suddenly I'm upended! I have been tripped by a monitor cabinet and, mid-triumph, am flying backward into the percussion riser. I hit the deck with an impressively amplified crunch from the guitar that I'm clutching, and the crowd goes even wilder. Somewhat dazed, I crawl to my feet, recover my poise, and with guitar held aloft stride up to the mic. "I rise again!" And a great time is had by all.

All too soon the music is over and Colombo is maneuvering me through the backstage throng to a car, which is going to take me to my shower in a hotel nearby. As the car threads its way out of the park through the departing revelers there is a real crackle in the air. The punters are buzzing as they leave the show. But they're not as excited as I am. This is going to be a fun tour.

The next few dates pass by very quickly. After a night of self-congratulatory celebration in Rome, Max and I pile into a car with Vitto and drag ourselves up to Urbania for a show, then over to Asti. As we wind down out of the mountains and across the Italian heartland, we are serenaded by Max's new Greatest Hits CD. Actually it's a double CD. Vittorio grips the wheel and drives like the wind.

Along the way, I learn a new Italian expression, an expression of such power that it will make the most decadent Italian recoil in horrified hilarity. It doesn't sound like much when given in English, but observant Catholics please skip the next sentence because I am going to translate: "Pig God." There, that ain't so bad, is it? In English, it doesn't sound like much at all. In Italian it has excellent phonetic impact (Italian speakers skip this): *Porrrko Dio!*

This term is most effective when used utterly gratuitously, as in, "Where is the post office? . . . PIG GOD!"

My first opportunity to deploy this monstrosity comes after the Asti show. Emerging from a blissful postshow shower I remark to Colombo, "Ahh that was great . . . PIG GOD!"

He almost jumps out of his skin. This hardened tour manager is suddenly hyperventilating, sweating profusely, and then falls to the floor laughing hysterically. We sadly lack any such expression in English. Our term for the act of love, most frequently used to celebrate sudden adversity, has nothing like the nuclear effect of this Italian bomb.

Vitto and I are driving up to Senigallia. We are on our way to two days of rehearsal with the Taranta ensemble, in preparation for a string of Notte della Taranta dates. As we drive we are listening to tapes of last year's show. Listening with mounting dread to the quantity of parts that the Gizmo guys have to learn. This is a completely different set of material. The horde of Salentini that we will be meeting up with all know the show, but our guys will be very busy.

 PIZZICA ROCK

Senigallia is a beach town on the Italian east coast. The band is staying at a place right on the coastal boulevard. Armand is back! Which poses again the question of too much bass. Armand is Prince of the Deep, but Silvio, the Taranta bass player, is the social focal point of the Salentini. Sort of like an informal tribal chieftain. And he knows all the parts. I offer Armand my Fender guitar instead, but there is only a low, growling sound from The Deep.

The rehearsal space is an enormous theater with a stage that must be half an acre wide. There is enough room for the twenty or so players and then more space around the edges for goofing off.

And then my brethren arrive! The fathers of Salento, who adopted me as one of their own, have sent their finest sons to perform the brave pizzica music of their tribe, with your humble correspondent as their maestro concertatore, for a short tour of an evening known as: La Notte della Taranta.

Antonio, Enza, Francesco, they are all here! There are a couple of new singers, but it's good to be back with this familiar posse. The new singer, Clara, is causing great excitement among the younger players. They are brisk and alert when she is on the mic. She sings like an angel.

Spread across the stage we have violin, accordion, bouzouki, keyboards, Silvio on bass, as well as a tangle of tambourines and singers. We have Antonio on traps drums and Giancarlo, who plays an inflated sheep. Add a layer of Gizmo and it's a very busy stage. And then for the really big moments, we have Raiz.

The players are eager to assemble themselves and soon we are blazing through the familiar songs. Piece of cake! The homeboys completely have their parts. With great patience, they indulgently introduce Fuze and Refosco to the mysteries of the pizzica. There is a lot to learn and the Brazilian ain't sunbathing now. In fact, he reveals a hitherto undisclosed talent for mallets as he tackles the quite vicious xylophone and marimba parts that Vitto and I have concocted.

At one point Vitto is explaining to the ensemble the required attitude for a certain show moment. His lengthy direction in Italian ends with the recognizable word *atmospheric*. I have sneaked up behind Silvio, and I whisper "Atmospheric . . . PIG GOD!" Silvio explodes. With a crunch, his bass hits the floor and bedlam breaks out among the Salentini. A good twenty minutes of rehearsal are lost to shocked, guilty hilarity. The women are hiding their blushed faces and their shoulders are quivering. The guys are

▲ **Your average Italian venue**

wide-eyed, slack-jawed, and suddenly unsteady on their feet. The crew is howling like a pack of hyenas. Fuck-damn! We need something like this in English!

After our two days of polish, we play the first concert. This one is a free show, set in a large circular piazza, so there is a very large and cheerful crowd. With the power of the pizzica it is no problem at all to light the place up. Toward the end of the show, the tambourine players and I are doing a little improvised dueling when there is a dark and mysterious sound welling up from The Deep. Armand has arrived on the stage like Emperor Bokassa. We do the bass and drum thing, but I just hang back and let him duke it out with the three Salento boys and their big war drums. They all break out like the plague and when the band comes back in the piazza is shaking under the stomping feet of what seems like the entire population of Senigallia. This pizzica music never fails.

■

A PERFECT SHOW FOLLOWED by a perfect shower has me in extremely good cheer as we hit the seaside restaurant for the post-gig dinner and hang. At this late hour we have the place to ourselves. The Salentini have enjoyed their week of music and are returning tomorrow to their lives as farmers, smugglers, postmen, and pirates. Long into the night we talk, laugh, and sing.

I'm making a list of things I like about this country and it's running many, many pages. Just a few of the things are: the monasteries that hang up into the sky like earrings, the microscopic espressos (for which the Italians have learned to tune out the cosmos for the duration of the two exquisite sips), the habitations that are not blots on the landscape, the absence of plywood, the perfect table settings, the cultural envelope of an ancient and great civilization (no need for plastic patriotism), the unregimented minds, the optimistic maybe-can-do attitude, the natural inclination toward an aesthetically pleasing world, and the impossibility of finishing dinner before 2:00 A.M.

CHAPTER 23

JUDGE HARD PLACE AND THE BBC

(NICE VERSION)

2006

I have been appointed by Her Majesty the BBC to cast aspersions upon my fellow artists. With relish I become a turncoat.

Today's mission is a trip to London to be a judge for the BBC on one of those *Pop Idol*–type TV shows. Life often throws up strange opportunities like this. Many are the invitations that I get to participate in media events of one kind or another, some of which are naff and some cool. Some are cool but onerous. Some are naff but fun. This one is very much the latter. To partake of some kinetic ritual of this kind, in the company of millions of TV viewers, is irresistible—no matter how daft.

Twelve hours out of L.A., my plane touches down at Heathrow airport at 11:00 A.M. Three hours later, after a shower and a dash across my old home town, I'm deep in the bowels of the BBC Television Centre, getting briefed on the nature of the show and meeting my fellow judges. I'm sharing the judicial bench with Trevor Nelson, a flash radio jock; CeCe Sammy, a vocal coach; and the sixties icon, Lulu. Trevor is a real live wire, Lulu is a dear, and

CeCe totally looks like a pop star to me. I wonder why she hasn't got a record deal of her own.

Our boss (producer) is the formidable and heavily pregnant Noleen. It turns out that we have many bosses, some of whom we never meet. We are surrounded by identical BBC babes, all with perfect skin, posh accents, and clipboards. I'll never be able to tell which is which, but I'm sure that if I call out "Penelope!" one or more of them will respond.

The game show is comprised of competing duets performed by one pro singer and one celebrity nonsinger. I've never followed this kind of show before, but to see these couples come out and sweat bullets as they lay it on for live TV, with an audience of millions, is actually damned compelling. I totally get it.

After each turn, the cameras turn to us, the judges, and we lay into the brave fools. I am ever mindful that these artists do a far braver thing than us who sit in judgment upon them.

But we have a job to do. We have been appointed by Her Majesty the BBC to add jeopardy to the show. Our judgments are hurdles that they must overcome. This isn't "We Are the World," it's *Gladiators*. Each duet has a different drama, and by the end of the first rehearsal, I can see why tens of millions of people tune in. I've got the best seat in the house.

HURRY UP AND WAIT! Today is the first show and it's going to be way live. My car collects me at 1:00 P.M.; today's Beebster is called Carly. She shows me to my dressing room—where I sit until my first actual duty, which is makeup at three o'clock. This takes about twenty minutes, then I go back to my dressing room.

4:00—Wardrobe check. Every day they give me a different shirt to wear under my black jacket. They color-coordinate everything, even the judges. I'm a little disappointed that they haven't got us in magisterial robes and wigs. Anyway, the whole transaction takes three minutes, and then I'm back in my dressing room for the rest of the hour.

5:00—Solo briefing. Two junior producers, Sharon and Debbie, come into my dressing room with their clipboards and notes. They tell me a little about tonight's show and tip me into some of the plotlines that they want to develop. This singer had a shouting match with her partner, or that singer has his mum in the audience, and might (hopefully) burst into tears. Their mission is to nudge this "reality show" into factual dramas that are stranger than fiction.

6:00—Judges meeting. We go up to a conference room and meet with producer Richard and the clipboard ladies. We start with the video clips that they have concocted of all the duet teams throughout their rehearsals. They are always looking for a little backstage drama to share with the viewers during the show. If there isn't any drama, they employ a technique that is known in the trade as "Frankenbite."

ON AMERICAN SHOWS OF this kind, they film all kinds of interaction among the contestants, and then cut up the footage to create stories that don't exist. With skillful editing of comments taken out of context, they can create, for instance, sexual tension within the duo (always a favorite), or animosity, jealousy, or pretty much anything they like. The BBC version is harmless enough. They aren't taking any huge liberties, just nudging and suggesting plotlines. As a judge I think I'm pretty safe, but I know that they are looking for stories wherever they can find them and that I had better watch my step.

In our upstairs room, we also watch the previous night's show and critique ourselves. With three BBC producers riding herd, we scrutinize our own performances. They tell us what they like and don't like. The main thing that they don't like is when we ramble.

We're supposed to keep our spiel down to fifteen seconds. If we run over, we are cutting into some other part of the show. Remember, it's a live national broadcast. They generally like my offbeat expostulations but point out some of the Americanisms that the British folks won't understand.

Then we watch the dress rehearsal that's going on downstairs. The contestants don't know this, but we are already starting to work out the scores. It's actually for the benefit of the singers that we don't force two full-on, judged performances out of them in one day. They can relax through their dress rehearsal—as they should—and then lay it on for the show. We factor this in. This double look at the performance helps us to be more fair and considered in our judgment at showtime, when the lights are flashing and the band is playing into our faces. Or so we tell ourselves.

Downstairs on the set, it's a rehearsal for not just the artists, but also for the crew, the presenters, the cameras, the band—and us. Stand-in judges make innocuous comments and give generous scores, while upstairs, we are forming and trading opinions. We're confirming our shared observations and sharpening our differences. Sure, this is a breach of spontaneity, but at showtime, the audience and the performers get better analysis—and, more important, better gags.

We also divide up the areas of judgment. CeCe is the singing expert, so she does the technical stuff—breathing, passaggio, and whatnot. Trevor has an encyclopedic knowledge of every song ever recorded, so he does the comparisons to the original versions. Lulu, with her decades of experience on the stage, deals with the stagecraft and body language. As the resident ex–rock star/drummer, I'm in charge of bullshit wisecracks.

One of the hazards is that the singing sounds great in the room, on the night. But on the video next day we can hear all the imperfections loud and clear. Performances that we applauded on the night are riddled with tuning problems and garbled lyrics. So we resolve to listen more closely during the show and assume that the slightest whiff that we can detect will be far worse for the folks watching their TVs at home.

IT'S ALL FLASHING LIGHTS and razzamatazz in Studio 1. There is a huge band with several guitarists, two keyboards, drums, strings and backing singers. The sound is big and the room is sparkling with energy. Schmaltzy music never sounded so good!

Everybody survives the first show. It's just a warm-up, to get the folks at home voting, so there's not much jeopardy. But the drama is there all the same because everybody is nervous. Especially the Radio 1 DJ Nicky Campbell. He comes on first, with an intensity that has me completely riveted. He can't sing worth a damn, but you just can't take your eyes off of this hurtling train. Amazingly, he gets through the track with his pants on. The rest of the competing duos run through their numbers, which we critique and score. Not all of us judges have mastered the pungent sound bite so we overrun our time slots, the show runs long, and they have to cut us down to two judges per turn. There are plenty of first-night snafus in every department, but like on any first night, the general excitement carries the show through with a manic energy.

After the show I overhear Siân, one of the contestants, spitting with fury about her partner, Russell "the Voice" Watson. I hope the Beebsters are getting this.

THE HEART-PALPITATING STORY SO far is that Martin Fry and Gabby Roslin are the first team to be heaved overboard. They were weak and deserved to go. The big surprise was last night, when Fiona Bruce and Alexander O'Neal got the heave-ho. He's a great singer and I thought she was quite adequate, and pleasing to the eye in a frosty Princess Diana kind of way. She reminds me of my Fiona. I am a sucker for the long English girls, but mine is the best of them. Nicky came out last night with a rock song that saved his bacon. He had been looking a bit vulnerable after his thin ballad performance the night before. Not much of a storyline yet with Mark Moraghan and Natasha Hamilton. They're pretty steady every night and are loved by my colleagues on the bench. They could win. Chris Fountain and Jo O'Meara are the frothy golden couple. I hate their kind of act, but I have to confess that the little brat boy can sing. The kid is just eighteen!

The runaway favorite for me though, is Matt Allwright and Jocelyn Brown. The big soul mama and the skinny white boy. He's got all the moves and she is just drinking that boy up like a glass of champagne.

They Frankenbite me with Siân Reeves and Russell Watson. He's an opera singer much be-hated by all of my fine arts friends— probably because of the zillion records that he has sold. He's pissed me off a little with his air of snoot and has sensed it. So they cut together shots of him lamenting that I've got it in for him, with shots of my harshest comments from the bench. Nothing inaccurate here. The producers have sniffed out a story and they are on it. So the story is: Stewart hates Russell. Oh well, I wonder what happened to Siân hates Russell? After some argy-bargy on-air, we bump into each other in the hallway backstage and have a laugh about it. He's OK, he can take it—but I will still go after him if he doesn't lose the ponce.

The strongest storyline is Penny Smith and Curtis Stigers. The woman cannot sing. At all. But she has three big assets. Curtis is a great singer, Penny has an engagingly warm personality, and most important of all, she has her own morning TV show—watched by millions. Every morning during her show, she has the voting telephone number at the bottom of the screen, with the message SAVE PENNY! VOTE NOW! So she is judge-proof. We cannot get rid of her. Which is no tragedy because she's so likable.

■

ONE STRANGE THING IS that we interact with the contestants all day—in makeup, backstage, and in the green room after the show. That should make it hard to be cruel, but oddly, it doesn't. The contestants have been (mostly) good sports about it. The main hang is in the makeup room. While sitting in our bibs the judges and contestants josh one another, and I pretend that I don't have The Whole Story about their upcoming performances. One or two of them are a little frosty.

A few days into the show, a new element appears in my afternoon solo briefings. Before the upstairs judges' meeting, there are private conferences down in my dressing room with two clipboard ladies. I am given the clear instruction to cause trouble on the bench. They like it when I throw bombs, and they want more. Well, I never! I debate whether or not to share this dirt with my newly bonded judge buddies but am quickly shushed.

"Blindside them!" I am commanded.

A dark smile crosses my face. . . .

The shows really are fun. About twenty minutes before showtime the contestants, presenters, and judges gather in the wings of the big soundstage. When the audience is seated we amble to our positions.

My spot is on the bench, which is a raised platform directly overlooking the stage. There is a bank of audience seated behind us and a desk in front of us, from which we have been engaged to helpfully harass the singers. This is some kind of serious drummer's revenge.

Before we go on air, there are a few rituals to perform. First, two of the pro singers mount the stage. The band strikes up and the pros hurl into a song together. This performance will be slugged into the live broadcast, as a way of keeping the action moving along while the public vote is tallied, when the competition singing is done.

They are usually quite good. Unhitched from the celebrity amateur baggage, the erstwhile competitors can really rip. The Nicky

Campbell traumas have been so riveting that I never noticed his partner, the incredible Beverley Knight. Put her on the stage with Jocelyn Brown, a raging big band, and a classic R&B tune, and we get a ninety-second blast of hair-raising actual music ecstasy.

This wakes up the three hundred punters in their seats, who are then further aroused by the preshow teaser, a comedian who comes onto the stage and plays with the audience. His job is to rowdy up the crowd so that, during the show, the music will be wildly applauded and the jokes will get hysterical laughs. He gets this side of the room to shout louder than that side of the room. He gets punters onto the stage to perform dumb tricks. He exhorts booing for mean judge's comments and cheers for happy ones. It's all about limbering up the punters, who enjoy this unexpected preshow entertainment.

Then it's time for Tess and Vernon to bound onto the stage. They are the show hosts and as a newly married alpha couple, they are the very latest in dazzling copresenters.

They are good together. She may look like just a stunning blond, but she handles the trickiest links and rides herd on the judges while Vernon keeps up the cheerful banter. For his part, he's not only good at making all the scripted gags sound spontaneous, but is pretty sparkly at the rare improvised moments.

Then there is the ten-second countdown to showtime. Just like New Year's Eve. The band kicks up and we are live with seven million TV viewers.

Most elements of the show are what they call "branded," which means that they are ritualized and repeated in every show. The contestants are introduced the same way every night, even though there are fewer and fewer of them. Each performance is preceded by a video clip of the tribulations suffered during the team's journey to this point (my harangues are a popular tribulation). The same ritual follows each turn, with Tess leading the defendants over to the judges like lambs to the slaughter. Criticism is always greeted by ritual boos. Sometimes the punters are not sure how to take my more esoteric comments and they do a kind of BOOoo-YYAAAaahh-Hunh?

Then they move down to the fake green room, decorated like a pink sixties' fairy bar. Here they meet Vernon, who riffs with them about the judges' comments. Then the dramatic prerecorded music swells and the judges deliver their scores. The cheers/boos are relative. If the first judge gives a six than the second judge will be cheered for a seven. If the first judge gives an eight, then a seven will be booed. At first CeCe is appalled to get booed—such a sweet girl—but we soon come to enjoy it all. The producers want to hear a big noise—up or down.

During the show, Sharon and Debbie are hiding in a trench behind us. They have headsets and are getting directions from somewhere mysterious upstairs. They poke us in the back and hand us notes. Mostly they are innocuous enough things like "Running long—three words only" or "More technical" (or less). But sometimes I get "more hostile" or "pick a fight."

A keen-eyed audient close to the judges' stand would observe that the judges are checking—not writing—notes about the performances. We have already prepared our shtick and tentative scores. Most nights, the singers sound way better in the room than they did upstairs on the screen during the rehearsal. Which does cause just a smidgen of unwelcome spontaneity to insert itself into the proceedings. We try not to look too surprised when they get it right instead of wrong.

ONE NIGHT, AFTER THE show, I cruise the Internet to check the vibe out there.

There is one site that contains a long list of hostile posts. Man, they hate the show! Strange thing is that there are a lot of them. Why are they online chatting about a show that they hate? I think that they are reality competition show regulars who care deeply about any manifestation of the genre. For these aficionados, our show looks scrappy and thrown-together. Jeez! If they could only see the huge resources that the BBC has thrown into this show! I'm not an expert, but it all looks pretty slick to me. They also complain about the lack of spontaneity. Well, they got that right. The only thing that is actually scripted is the hosts' patter, but all other aspects of the show are closely managed to get a desired result. In my humble opinion, this is show business, not the Olympics. The bullets that the singers sweat are real. Only the jeopardy is fake.

There is another site, with an equally long list of posts, that is much more congenial. These people aren't commenting on the quality of the show, but rather, are concerned with the competition itself. They love some singers and hate others. They occasionally refer to the judging, and this is the interesting part. Most of my artistic endeavors are received by people who know something of my history. I'm kind of a niche guy. This show is in the big mainstream. Most of those millions of people who watch the show, have never heard of my investiture as a Hero of the Pizzica—nor of The Police, for that matter. On this site there is the occasional post asking: "Who is that American guy with the glasses?" They think I'm nuts, but they're laughing. . . .

On my own site, members are confused at first. What is their tortured artist doing on such a schlocky show? A few words of explanation from me quickly dispels their concern and they get into the cheerful frivolity of the mission. A few of them even get into caring who wins!

In show six, we finally get rid of Penny. I'm sure she could have held on for a couple more shows, but Siân and Russell "the Voice" have pulled a fast one. After an excruciating performance that has surely earned the wrath of the judges, Siân bursts into tears. I'm the first judge up and my meat cleaver is raised in a righteous fury when the waterworks hit. For an instant, I'm stunned. She is blubbering, and I'm stammering. So I switch over to my preplanned Russell abuse. Which, under the circumstances, just sounds mean. The other judges, thankful for the chance to regroup, offer loving support to the poor distressed contestant. Hearts are breaking for her all over the country. As she straggles off to the pink fairy green room, Trevor leans over.

"Wait a minute, she's an actress!"

I have a sudden new respect for Siân's game.

In almost every sport that I know of, semifinals are always ugly, and this game is no different. We are down to three couples. The frothy golden couple whom I have dubbed "Barbie and Ken," Siân/Russell "the Voice"; and my favorites, the bricklayer Mark and pop diva Natasha. With a churlish disregard for impartiality, I want to get rid of Siân. Although she's a plucky soul and works hard to carry the tune, the screeching sound that comes out of her throat is just painful. I have actually come to like her partner Russell, who has been through a personal voyage of self-discovery during this show. He may be an odd kind of opera singer who has never sung in an actual opera, but he does have a pretty incredible God-given voice. It's just that I want to see a final where the two ex-girl-band-babes square off, accompanied by the Golden Kid versus the Bricklayer.

Mark the Brick is a character actor on British TV and has a kind of lowbrow charm as he hefts his heavy self around the stage. As an actor, he knows how to adopt the role of a singer. He's also got a pretty good voice. His partner, Natasha, was the main singer of a girl band called Atomic Kitten. She's pretty good, too, and has the edge on the frothy golden girl, Jo/Barbie.

The other team's Jo/Barbie is an almost stunning blond, with an evil Swiss sado-masseuse vibe. Her singing is in trouble though, since she had her tonsils out three weeks before starting rehearsals. The good thing about her team is the frothy golden boy, Chris/Ken. The kid is amazing. Like Mark, his day job is acting, and he too has adopted the role of singer with professional ease. He has been choreographed and wardrobed like a piece of dancing candy. A real Back Street Boy. I have been haranguing this team for their plastic presentation, all the while marveling at the kid's chops. Of all the contestants, his gifts are the most startling. Probably hasn't got an original thought in his head, but he takes direction well and hits all his marks with panache. He sure looks and sounds the part.

Since Siân has survived her performance tonight without tears, the judges can now slash and burn. In fact we get a little carried away, so you know what happens next. Barbie and Ken are out! The voters at home have once again overruled the learned but somewhat mean judges to bring us to a final between the Screecher and the Bricklayer.

Well, it's the first time I slink home after the show in a slump. For just a minute, the competition has actually got me under its spell. For a fleeting moment, winning or losing this clash of the Titans has meaning.

By the next day, however, my equilibrium has returned. There are no losers on this show and I'm not even sure what the prize is for winning.

For the final showdown, the two teams have to sing four songs each. In this desperate race for the finish, I'm all paternal sagacity, supportive to both teams, but I get a poke in the back from Penelope's clipboard: "Be hostile—DRAW BLOOD!" Ha-ha! I love the BBC!

So, playing for gasps, I rip into my pet team and lavish praise on Screech. Then I turn about again and erratically heap praise and scorn in the most capricious fashion as the teams take their alternate turns. All the while my scores are working out dead even. I have already decided to call it a draw and let the public choose their winner. What would I know about this kind of schlock music anyway? Finally we get to the drumroll of destiny . . . the nation is holding its breath. . . the lights are somber . . . the judges are stern. . . .

And the winner is . . . Screecher and the Voice!

Now comes the final comedy. After the dramatic victory moment, after the winning duo has been presented with the coveted perspex slab trophy, it's time for the victory performance of the winning song. "Great Balls of Fire" is the unlucky tune.

The band kicks in, the lights are twirling, and the special effects are flaming. The choreography for this number is very strenuous. Russell has to throw the girl around in that old rockabilly style and at the end she has to jump into his arms for the final pose. After a pretty tough week of competition, Siân and Russell are tired. Their moves don't quite work out as planned, and her singing is pretty much reduced to grunts and yelps.

When the moment comes for the big leap, she just hasn't got the gas. Her rubbery legs only launch her about as high as his knees, and she almost bowls him completely over. The crazy lights are swirling; confetti is ejaculating everywhere. The final pose finds them locked in a weird embrace, with her legs scissoring his thighs and him trying to gather her up, clutching at any and every protuberance. But everybody can kiss their ass—they won!

I love this TV gig. I ought to give up music and take this up full-time.

CHAPTER 24

THE GRATEFUL DAD

2007

The all-star band from hell strikes up for the Wildwood School fund-raiser.

And you, and you, and you, and You, and *you*. . . ."

We're all sitting cross-legged in the school assembly hall, glowing with morning virtue and singing this song, pointing to each of the children around us.

Fiona, Eve, Grace, and I are here to cheer on our smallest girl, Celeste, who is going to be performing in one of the opaque class productions that are presented every Friday morning. The parents and siblings around us are the most pleasant folk imaginable. Wife beaters and Satanists behind closed doors I'm sure, but damned mellow to hang with at school functions.

These nice folks are dressed down, and there is very little bling on display, but they're masters of the universe nonetheless. *Tout le monde* of Los Angeles is spread out among three or four schools, including this one. Since our town is the world capital of the entertainment industry, the parent body has a concentration of the most acute creators of film and song.

These great minds are now absorbed with rapt delight in the

worst catastrophe of stagecraft imaginable. Script, pace, execution, talent—it's hard to imagine a more cheerfully chaotic parody of what these parents do. All except for Celeste of course, who comes on the stage beaming and utters her non sequitur uncomprehendingly but with unmistakable charisma. We too are rapt in delight.

"HELLO, STEWART, THIS IS Gene Simmons . . . you know, the guy with the tongue, ahm . . . can you call me back about the school concert? I'm at—"

I wish there was some way that I could easily save and file some of the messages that have been left on my answering machine over the years. This is one of my favorites. Gene, it seems, is the dad who has been snared to organize the music for the school fundraiser party this year. So far, the school dad band is comprised of Gene Simmons, Stephen Stills, and Solomon Burke. Bob Dylan is going to get back to us. Put me on drums and we can call ourselves The Grateful Dad.

DOWN A LONG LEAFY lane off Mulholland Drive lives the legendary Stephen Stills. It's the perfect spot for a California crooner. The south wing of the house is devoted to a charming analogue studio. The walls are clad from floor to ceiling with vintage guitars. Jeff is in the drum booth setting up a stripped-down version of my drum set, and eying me suspiciously are two hoary old geezers on bass and Hammond organ. They have no idea who I am, although they may have heard distantly of The Police (one o' them short-hair punk bands). It doesn't matter to these old bastards how many teenage hearts have been broken by my teenybopper band, I might as well be a Jonas brother.

This is how the hierarchy works. We piss on those who come after us. It's not a matter of who sold more records or tickets, it's about who hit first. These guys hit when I was in college, so even a major patriarch of fifty-six years like me is just a pissant.

Stephen arrives after everyone else has convened, including his son Chris on guitar and his daughter Eleanor on vocals. He's all genial hospitality and we get straight to work. The first song up is "Proud Mary," sung by Eleanor, which is a no-brainer for everyone. There's hardly a living American who can't play "Proud Mary." Stephen counts it off, and after the distinctive introduction we lock down into a groove for the song.

For the first verse I go into a kind of hybrid reggae thing that takes the old bastards by surprise. But they can't deny the motion and the sound we're making is right in the pocket. I had forgotten how fat a real Hammond can sound through real Leslie cabinets (don't ask). I've been making do with samples of Hammonds for years, but Mike is the real thing. He has the drawbars tweaked just so . . . and I can swear that we're in an Alabama tabernacle. This feels great! Everybody is smiling now. The Mount Rushmore dudes are beaming. Stephen is beaming at his little girl on the mic. There is something deep about playing music with people who have been doing it for decades, like soft old leather. Mary was never so Proud.

And then Stephen starts to sing. It's one of those quiet acoustic guitar songs, "Teach Your Children," for which normally I'd be the wrong drummer. It's the kind of song that is so gentle that the drums must be played with brushes. I know this song only too well. In college this music was surefire for melting the girls, and with Stephen singing it now in the room with us I'm pretty darn transported myself.

"OK, EVERYBODY, MY BASS is tuned down a half step so everybody tune your stuff . . . down a half step."

So commands Gene, our music director. Onstage with us at the last rehearsal and sound check before the show, are a dozen Wildwood teenage guitar gods. Each one of the students has his own little amp and they are all piled up in an impressive stack on the Wadsworth Theatre stage. Down a half step? First one kid, then the others start to tune their guitars down to the required pitch. It sounds like a fleet of B-52s all running out of gas at the same time. The old Stills cats are gaping in disbelief. Did he say . . . down a half step? That's insane!

Just as the cacophony is reaching its most deranged pitch, it dawns on the music director that these kids are a little sketchy on tuning at any level and they're peering blankly into their electronic tuners while detuning their instruments to God knows what.

"OK . . . bad idea . . . everybody back to concert pitch. I'll just tune my bass up a half step."

Now it sounds like a fleet of kamikazes starting up their engines. Cool, since we now have everybody completely out of tune, let's rock. Moving quietly through the kids is my Foo buddy Chris

Shiflett. He's helping them tune and organize. We actually get a couple of songs into workable shape, with little spots for each of the kids to shine.

Gene is also going to do a song with his own side band, a hairy gang of tattooed rocksters who will surely cause palpitations among the alpha moms. They're probably going to do some Satan worship right in front of everybody. We all clear off and leave the stage so they can do their sound check. Gene counts in his band.

"Hunt, Two, fee, *fah!*"

CRUNGAKLANGACRUNGAKLANG—

"Stop, stop!" calls Gene. And he shouts to the sound guy at the back of the hall for more drums and less guitar in his monitors.

"OK . . . Hunt, Two, fee, *fah!*"

CRUNGAKLANGA—

"Stop, STOP!" cries Gene, and calls again to the sound guy at the back of the hall with more instructions for what he wants in his monitors. The Stills cats are still gaping. We're all thinking the same thing. Each of us wants to shout "Yo, Gene . . . the sound guy at the back of the hall isn't fixing your monitors. The monitor guy is over here in the wings!" Personally I'm way impressed that a guy can have such a lengthy and prosperous career as a stage performer and not know where the monitor guy is.

But all this is nickel and dime. Gene Simmons is a motherfucker. The Stills cats can snicker about the musicianship, but there is no denying the raw animal charisma and cunning of the man. By the end of the evening he's got my vote.

During the long evening of speeches and music, Gene and I get to talking backstage about a subject that fascinates both of us. It seems that we're both Bible-thumpers, students of Mosaic literature. Well, it is a beautiful concept, isn't it? The Kiss bassist and The Police drummer arguing Old Testament theology is just what you would expect at a Westside school function. Mostly us two eminent scholars are just trying to one-up each other, glad to find listening ears for our dusty hobby. We're two slum-dog million-aires who just happen to know some of this stuff.

What I really like is how all of the alpha moms are scandalized by the Neanderthal lowbrow vibe and just can't stop twittering about it. Sure, they're swooning over the gentle beauty of the old California ballads, but it's the big guy in leather who has got their pulses racing and bosoms heaving. Ha-*ha!* The age of chauvinism is not dead!

CHAPTER 25

SUNDANCE

NOVEMBER 2005

It was the Night Before Thanksgiving, I'm deep in the studio making music for someone else's film.

The phone rings right as I'm deep in the middle of a problem cue. Usually I'm pretty bombproof, but right now I'm not in any mood to be disturbed. Soon, however, I'm glad I picked up the phone. The caller identifies himself as Trevor Groth and he's telling me that my little movie, which I've been working on in my spare time, has been selected for the Sundance Film Festival. Holy shit!

LAST YEAR I FINALLY got around to digitizing all the old Super 8 films that I shot back in The Police era, and have been snatching moments between work to cut it all up into the ultimate home movie. I love to tinker away on my computer at various creative enterprises and this has been one of my more consuming exercises.

I never really thought anyone but my friends would ever see it because anything to do with The Police is so fraught with legal constraints. My local chums, of course, were full of enthusiasm, urging me to release it out unto the world. For this, the first stop must be Universal, who own the rights to the recorded Police music. It took several weeks to get a meeting. They were mildly interested and reasonably supportive but said (truthfully) that nothing could happen without Sting's permission to use his compositions. Never mind the band, the guy who wrote the songs holds the key.

So after dithering for a couple of months, I sent him and Andy DVDs. They both responded immediately. They don't mind it! I'm all warm and glowy from this uncharacteristically warm response.

At this point the film was my sole creation—untouched by professional hands. I told Universal that I had the necessary blessings, and could I have some money to redigitize at a higher standard and hire professionals to complete the movie? They offered less than I asked for, but at least I was now in business.

The fateful moment came when I was talking to my buddy and sage, Les Claypool. You should send it to Sundance, he said, and he guided me right then and there on the phone to the online application site. It took a couple of minutes to complete, I sent my $35, and then forgot about it. The legal work with the bosses dragged on and I got back to work, earning a living.

Then comes the call.

Suddenly, I have to seriously finish the movie. Starting with a title. I had been calling it "Behind Andy's Camel," knowing full well that such a name (lacking the words "The Police") would never survive the first marketing meeting. Now I have a nice lady from the festival telling me that they need the definitive title by close of business—today!

Thinking up names for bands, albums, and children is something that takes time. The most brilliant ideas often sound utterly lame twenty-four hours later. You have to try them out on people, consider unintended connotations, say them aloud, and check how they look in print. You are going to be stuck with this name forever.

I had tentatively landed on Miles's suggestion: "I of The Police," which seemed clever because of the pun with *I* and *eye*. In print there is also the visual pun with *I* and *1*. Actually, quite ingenious. Problem is, I just don't like saying it. It doesn't sound so bad for other people to say, but coming out of my mouth, it sounds a little solipsistic. I need to be able to speak the name of my own movie.

So now, on a Tuesday afternoon with Miles in France, Derek unfindable, and Fiona's cell turned off, I must come up with something for tomorrow's press release. Feverishly, I go online to my fan site with a plea for help. Suggestions start coming in immediately. I had already been toying with the idea of *Everyone Stares,* which follows the established tradition of using a song title, but I've still got to get "The Police" in there.

A mysterious person called Lady P comes up with "The Police Inside Out." Not bad. I get on the phone to Andy and he approves. I call Les Claypool and another chum, Taylor Hawkins, and they both concur. I'm striding around my studio, saying it over and over. Still sounds good: *Everyone Stares: The Police Inside Out.* I count to ten and say it again. Yup. I exhale and call the lady in Utah with three minutes to spare. She even likes it. The die is cast.

Next thing I know, my e-mail is jammed with messages from strangers offering to sell my movie to the world. Their résumés include every independent film you have ever seen. The guys who sold *Super Size Me, Fahrenheit 9/11,* and *My Big Fat Greek Wedding* are now interested in my little film. And the people they sell to are on to me. One morning I find three messages in a row from Sony Pictures Classics, Focus Features, and Miramax.

My next meeting at Universal is a little different from the first. I walk into a huge conference room containing at least twenty vice presidents, all with their chests out, arms raised, and their voices singing in unison about their zeal for my movie.

There is a gravitas to this Sundance thing that slowly blows my mind. It has more impact than last year's Emmy nomination, more even than the Hall of Fame thing. This is *really* big. My

head is spinning, I'm hyperventilating. I'm having trouble string-
ing sentences together. But there are suddenly a million loose
ends to tie up.

JANUARY 2006

Man, this is the best breakfast that I've ever had. The vending
machine has delivered an omelet with sausage that I am eating in
my rental car at the Salt Lake City airport. I've been dreaming
about this meal since rising at 4:00 this morning (in L.A.) to get
here for the Sundance Film Festival.

Eastbound on I-80. The sun is reflecting off the snow and I'm squinting as I sing and laugh, driving up the mountains. The last month has been a tornado of exertion and excitement to bring me to this moment. The movie is finished and I have this moment of mental freedom on the highway as the snowy mountains draw me up to the frenzy of promotion that will be my mission for the next week.

Fiona and I pull up to Park City, Utah, in the nick of time for my first interview. Amy, the publicist, has fixed up a hotel suite for me to sell from. Her two accomplices, Katie and Kim, are unloading boxes of postcards, posters, T-shirts, and other promotion materials. Two journalists are settling down and placing their recorders on the table, and the hawking is ready to begin.

I have already been doing this over the phone for the last week, so by now I have the basic sound bites down pat. The rest of the day goes by, talking, talking, talking.

It's not all in my own room. Amy and I spend the freezing cold days trudging up and down Main Street, hitting the TV crews and news pools while Derek and Cassian, my new William Morris rep, work the buyers.

After a photo shoot for *People* magazine, I'm taken to the swag mall. This is a suite of rooms where purveyors of high-end articles like $5,000 watches and $300 jeans shower the celebrities with their products. It's called "gifting." Most of the stuff is way out of my style but, after a while, moving from stall to stall, it gets easier and easier to just say yes. A nice person holding a logo-splattered holdall follows me. No sooner is the word "cool" out of my mouth, than the article plonks into the bag. I barely notice the photographer.

"Cool."

Plonk.

Click.

Each of the major promotion points has such a mall, and by the end of the festival I will have picked up three ski jackets, two pairs of boots, an iPod, an mp3 player, a digital camera (does movies, too) a telephone/camera/movie player/communication device and several thousand dollars' worth of watches, jeans, and handbags for the girls. And a slightly soiled feeling.

(A couple of days later, Fiona is mortified to see shots of herself holding wrong stuff on offer to tabloids. I'm only partly able to calm her down by showing her shots of *tout le monde* similarly busted. On Wire Images there are shots of all the cool people holding uncool—but free—products.) We end up giving most of the stuff away.

Getting into any of the parties on Main Street requires shoving to the front of a mob and shouting names through a half-opened door. Even your own party. This evening the *Everyone Stares* crew is participating in an event called Chef Dance. It's a cook-off by the most famous chefs in the land who will provide dinner for me and twenty chums. There are several filmmaker groups in this large, busy restaurant. Andy has shown up, as well as a few of my favorite L.A. chuckle buddies. There is a bottle of tequila making brisk rounds of the table. My young postproduction crew, Brit Marling and Mike Cahill, are swaying to the beat of a great party. The room is alive with laughter and song. Andy is in fine fettle and we are carousing uproariously when I look up, gaping. Sting is here! In a moment he is among us, and the three of us are hugging and knocking over drinks. I always get a warm glow when the old band gathers up together. We go straight back into the old repartee, cooing and jabbing at one another. Across the table from us, a swarm of flashbulbs are going off as we grin idiotically. It's a strange kind of friendship that the three of us have. It feels different this time.

IT'S TIME FOR THE big premiere. In the bright snow outside the stage door, Andy and I are hamming it up for the cameras. I have been hammering away at the press for days, but this is the first glimpse they have had of Andy. He is on a roll and has the news teams lit up. Inside, the theater is packed and there is a distinct crackle of preconcert buzz. When Andy and I enter the big room and take our seats, there are hoots and whistles from the crowd. The hubbub dies down as Trevor Groth takes the stage. He says a few kind words about my little film and then summons me to the mic. I have a gag planned for this moment (suggested by the ever creative Doreen Ringer Ross). Halfway up the podium, I stop, reach into my pocket, and pull out my new T-Mobile camera phone. Swag, of course—this is why they give us the stuff. I put it into Record, raise it up, and film the crowd as I continue my progress up to the lectern. The crowd gets the gag and their hollering follows me to the mic. When I get there and I'm just about to hit the punch line ("My next film . . ."), I notice that I had the camera back to front. Aww, damn.

"I just got a great shot of myself," I confess. Then I turn the camera around.

"Could you do all that again?"

And they do! The place goes nuts as I hose them down again with my telephone-cam. This is going to be a fun evening.

After a brief introduction to the film, I return to my seat and the lights go down. The film comes up. The first discernible dialogue is Sting saying to a concert crowd, "Say hello to Stewart's camera!" and he looks over his shoulder at the camera. There is a cheer from the concert audience and a yell from the movie crowd. This could be described as a sympathetic audience, and as the movie picks up speed, the crowd is rippling, chuckling, and empathizing. Anything that could be construed as a gag gets a laugh. All of the little moments and nuances, and the subtle wry twists of phrase in the narration get ripples of approval. Scenes that seemed interminable on my computer screen flash past all too briefly. Sting looks way suave in the film, but Andy has turned out to be a real resource. His scenes get all of the big laughs.

In no time at all, we're at the end of the movie. There is a big noise from the house, the lights come up, and I'm on my way back to the stage for Q & A. Well, at this point it's not too hard to face an audience like this. Love is in the air. One guy asks where all the fights are. I reply that I honestly don't have any film of band strife. All fifty hours of my old footage show us enjoying one another's company. Another lady wants to know about the short shorts that I wore. I remind her that self-respecting basketball players wore them back then. Then comes the question, "What's that music? Are you going to release a soundtrack?"

I like this question because it allows me to recount the excellent adventure that I had a couple of years before making this movie. I was cutting up and lobotomizing Police music to create new tracks. But the tale had an unhappy ending. After making these tracks, which I called "derangements," my bandmates nixed them for release to the public. Until the movie came along they were orphan tracks, moldering in my vault. Unblessed. You could say that my brethren had put out the red light.

"So how about it, folks?" I ask the crowd.

"Andy is with us here tonight. You want to tell him what you think about these tracks?"

There is bedlam in the house as Andy rises from his seat and faces the audience. Like a Roman emperor, he extends an arm, thumb of judgment outstretched. To cheers and laughter, the thumb goes up.

"Two out of three!" I declare into the mic.

PART IV
ABNORMAL AGAIN
EVERYTHING IS DIFFERENT; NOTHING HAS CHANGED

CHAPTER 26

LOCK UP YOUR MOTHERS: WE'RE BACK

FEBRUARY 2007

*I had intended to post this message
on my little fan-site but. . . .*

As I hit Send on this message I'm walking out the door of my studio. There is a car outside to pick me up and take me to a press conference with Sting and Andy. We're on our way to announce a five-month world tour as The Police.

It all started, I think, on the night Sting unexpectedly showed up at the *Everyone Stares* party at the Sundance Festival. Suddenly there were the three of us head-to-head, laughing and joshing and carousing. There is always a buzz that we get when the three of us are together, but this time was different. Can't even say how, but the bond between us felt like a current that had been switched on. The wires had been there for twenty years, but now there was electricity running through them. More than just a reunion of old friends, we felt like a band.

Then Andy's book came out, then Sting's lute CD. In October, there were three of us crisscrossing Europe hawking something. Actually four when you count Henry Padovani, with his book and CD. My BlackBerry was full of messages from my old buddies. I

missed Sting in Paris by a day and in Berlin by about twenty minutes. Andy and Sting crossed paths in New York and London.

In my head, everything to do with The Police has been in a lockbox for two decades. Making the movie about the band didn't change that. In fact, emotionally it was like house cleaning. Making the movie tidied it all up so that the lockbox could take up less space in my garage.

So just when I'm about to resume my life as a film composer, Sting is on the phone.

"The time is right," he growls. "Let's do it."

We make a plan to rehearse in May and then tour from June through October.

It takes a few days to sink in. We are already talking about schedules and personnel, but it hasn't occurred to me to pull out the lockbox and open it up. When Sting e-mails me a set list and I look at those song titles as something for my future rather than my past, the dam finally breaks. I'm laughing and shouting as I dance around my studio. We are going to burn it up! I'm in a band! I love being in a band, always have, but this is *my* band. This is *the* band. The Police has been so removed from my present life that it almost feels like Led Zeppelin called up and invited me to play drums with them. Odd enough that they should call a humble film composer for the gig, but here's the kicker—I get to actually be the original guy! The icon is clean and I'm a part of it. The Police is me again rather than an accolade on the shelf.

But there's a snag. We have a lot to do before word gets out. For twenty different reasons we have to keep totally quiet about it. It's November, and we have to stay mum until mid-February. And it's not just about restraining exuberance. I have a life and career that involves many commitments to all kinds of people. I'm supposed to be producing a TV series, directing a film, and planning my summer concerts. But now I must be evasive and flaky. The people with whom I'm making all of these plans are wondering what's wrong with me.

After my few moments of hysteria, I bottle it up again. I tell Fiona but not the kids. To my friends I'm just abnormally cheerful. Funny thing, though. In my world, a part of conversation is the question "So what have you got coming up?"

It's a polite but loaded question. Due to the capriciousness of the art game, you never know if the person you are talking to is unemployed and dead in the water, or on the verge of something hot that they can't wait to talk about. My own response to this banter now has all the marks of a belly-up film composer. The *Everyone Stares* cycle is done and dusted. I'm not taking any meetings nor reading any scripts. Nor do I appear to be on to any good scheme. "Going on holiday for six months" won't cut it for anyone who knows me at all. And "Working on my solo album" is as good as asking to borrow money. Film composers do not do solo albums. If they are employable. I suffer the pitying looks with an idiot grin.

■

MEANWHILE WE ARE E-MAILING back and forth, reassembling the machine for the big tour. Right about now some roadie in Ireland is claiming to have been hired for the 2007 Police Reunion Tour. Right on my Web site the speculation begins, and then spreads out across the land. The first tabloid past the post is the London *Mail on Sunday.* They only have vague quotes from the record company, but it's enough for a page-three spread with color photograph. POLICE FANS MAY SOON BE WALKING ON THE MOON AGAIN is the rather poetic headline. Pretty soon the news is everywhere. It's hard to keep a secret when you can see it in *Rolling Stone and Billboard,* and on CNN.

"So, Stewart, what have you got coming up?"

"Um . . . long holiday." Idiot grin.

Back in L.A., Sting has a lute show down at the Disney Center. We haven't actually seen one another since before we hatched our plot. So Andy and I hire a car and take Kate and Fiona out for the show. Waiting to greet us is the multitentacled organization that is Sting World. We are slickly ushered into the best seats in the house. Trudie is there with two fully adult Stinglets. Jake and Mickey Sumner, in all their adult glory, stand before me . . . as complete strangers. Literally a lifetime has gone by.

Onstage Sting reaches the furthest point in his trajectory away from our band with a commanding rendition of Elizabethan music and storytelling. He uses everything he has—his voice, his fingers, his stagecraft, his charisma—in the most extremely alien environment that can be imagined for a rock star. The Elizabethan singing style is very specific and rigorous. The lute strings are tuned upside down and backward. He walks out to an audience who are accustomed to amplified music and familiar songs, and has to craft an atmosphere of concentration and stillness. In classical music, the performer ranks a little lower than the composer. Sting must, on this night, serve someone else's compositions—which is a new kind of body language for my old friend. But none of this is a problem. Piece of cake for Stingo.

Back in the dressing room, the three of us are together in a room again for the first time since Sundance, almost a year ago. But this is not a big Police moment. Sting has just played a lute show, and the room is full of people who are attached to the lute. It's a lute moment. We put our heads together only long enough to mutter "next week" and "jam" and "new" and then Sting is swept away by the celebration of his lute CD—which is the biggest-selling classical CD of the year. If he gets a Grammy for the fucking thing, I'm going to have to steal it.

A couple of days later at Trudie's birthday party we get a little more time to chat, but really, we are all waiting to get to Vancouver, where we will say what we really have to say, which is our music. I, for one, don't feel the band vibe yet. I'm toying with the thought process of "I'm in a band," but it still isn't me yet.

In two weeks we will meet up in Vancouver to rehearse for a surprise (hopefully) appearance at the Grammy Awards. I get down to working up my technique and muscling up my game. The Police songs are all lined up on my iPod Shuffle, and I blaze through them for a couple of days before realizing that they are all still hardwired onto my brain.

Doesn't seem like further attention is required, so I load up the headset with random music of every kind. Anything with an infectious rhythm has me bopping along in some way. Sometimes I use the music as a metronome while I work on myself. This is all about tweaking, training, streamlining, and calibrating the synapses. Actually it's the only time, in the dark of my practice room, where I permit myself to listen to myself as I play.

It is my music religion to immerse my mind in the combined effect of all of the players in an ensemble, and not to think at all about what I'm doing. It's my job to harness all of the players to the rhythm, so as to provide a solid context for the focal point of the music. Listening to myself would be like a bartender serving only himself.

Actually the mundane job of getting my biological tools (hands) up to scratch is the only part of the job where I have to use self-discipline. Forgetting myself and listening to the band is much more fun. Sometimes I'm deep in the pocket and sometimes I'm out riding on a parallel groove, but it's always about listening to the music while my hands do what they do, driven by some deeply buried primal lobe of the brain.

I'm counting down the hours until the black car comes to take me to my flight to Vancouver. Andy and I fly up to Canada to meet up with our charismatic singer and start cutting up the old tunes. He's held up for an extra day in Cuba, so it's just guitar and drums at first, with our old crew around us. Billy gets us to the sound-stage, just like two decades ago; Tam Fairgrieve meets us at the stage, where we find Danny and Jeff. Just like two decades ago. Andy's "new" tech, Dennis, has been with Andy for fifteen years.

Everything is different and nothing has changed.

On the first morning in Vancouver, I go down to breakfast and right on the front of the newspaper, taking up the entire page, is a picture of the three blond heads and a two-inch headline: POLICE SIGHTING. Just as I'm chuckling about this, Sting shows up, and here we are again. No lute, no birthday girl, nobody but us—and we're in a band together again after many years. This is the reunion, right here, over coffee in the Four Seasons café. We're still not sure what to say to one another, but the vibe is warm. We have a very strange relationship. Very deeply affection-ate but very guarded. In spite of our intense adoration we are capable of hurting one another, which we do almost as often as we snuggle.

CHAPTER 27

WILL THIS FLY?

2007

VANCOUVER

Police rehearsals are like bathing in razor sharp diamonds, then toweling down with barbed roses before donning a Prada hair suit. Quite beautiful but there is blood.

A little silvery bell just went off in my head, you fucking toad," I'm muttering to myself as he swings away from the drum riser back to his microphone.

"And do you want to know what that means, you *prick?*"

It means I've hit the limit, beyond which I can take not one more word from you about anything. Do not even make eye contact with me, let alone make another suggestion about how I should play my drums . . . you *fucking piece of shit!*

Jeff hits the click and we start up the tune. Sting himself is rigid with frustration. He has explained, in as many ways as he can, that the blindingly obvious approach to the required stick technique is this, this and *this*. All afternoon we have faced each other with courteous masks, seeking to achieve musical unity in spite of drastically divergent musical philosophies.

The morning started out quite cheerfully. I got to the soundstage early so that I could limber up with some groovy tunes in my player. Turned out that Sting was an even earlier worm and he's

already here, engaged in his strange rituals and tortures. He's curious about the odd collection of ecclection that I'm grooving to.

When Andy arrives, it's time to work. We don't play, we work.
After twenty years of not playing together, we don't jam or groove,
we go straight to work. Before I've had a chance to play eight bars
of music with my long-lost brothers, we are in classic Police attitude B. Now, I have a lot of patience for position B. When Andy
and Sting put their heads together and start noodling, wonderful
things happen. As they noodle over chords and fingering, I take
my ease on the drum riser, silently conceiving a rhythmic envelope for what they're doing. In olden times, they would reach a
conclusion, and then we'd play the figure together. The addition of
rhythm to the equation would light them up, and we would groove
together, loving ourselves. Clever bastards, were we!

When the stringsters come out of their huddle and turn up the
volume to play with me, I kick up a groove and we're about to start
swinging . . . but no, we're stopping. At this point Andy is still getting to grips with his own mission, so his mind is on his fingers—
which are *very* busy. Sting, with a yeomanlike zeal for the job at
hand is headed my way with what turns out to be a fully conceived
plan for every aspect of my participation in the music. He's very
generous in this regard—he has *plenty* of time to help me play my
drums. Any rogue instinct that might lurk in my timid heart is affably ignored. My own desire is to follow my beloved leader and to
bring a glint of pleasure to his heavy brow.

Remember that Sting has been arranging rock bands for almost
forty years. He knows every aspect of how to use drums. Believe it
or not, there are many ways to hit a drum and many different effects that can be achieved. Sting is fully conversant with all of
them; different sticking techniques, different cymbal and hi-hat
effects, bass drum techniques, and so on. He's actually a proven
genius at it. My measured response to all of this inspired expertise
is: Fuck OFF out of my FACE!!! Sting and I got along much better
when he didn't have any idea of what I should be doing—and

when I wasn't so sure myself. Now I've been playing drums for fifty years and although there is still room for improvement, that little silvery bell just tinkled in my head. It told me that, after a day of badgering and scolding, one more word from Stingo will take us to Code C.

It's been twenty years since I've had to put up with this, so maybe I'm a little stuffy and cranky, but his obsessive creativity has evolved into a monster. He hasn't heard the umpire's whistle in thirty years. Back in the day we clashed, but the struggle made us better. There was a mutual respect that fueled the debate and we always ended up with a result that we were all proud of. This isn't that.

The great musical mind that brought so much joy into our lives has veered off into a style that confounds me. Maybe our prophet is onto something that will surprise the world—starting with us. It's always worth listening to Stingo, he's had at least of couple of good ideas in his time. That's why I've been listening all day. But now he can shut the fuck up.

He does know when to stop though—right at the moment before we hit Code C. The threshold is way past my comfort zone, but I'm sure he can hear my silvery little bell, too. It's the sound that you hear in a Hitchcock film just before something very bad happens. Right at the moment when my hackles are up, my knuckles are swelling with murderous desire, and a feral snarl is rising up my gorge, he swings away and the heat is off. We coast blankly until the end of the day. Sometimes the back of his head is better than the front.

CHAPTER 28

EBERHARD SETS US FREE

1978
GERMANY

*Flashback: We found our band sound
almost by accident.*

O K. . . . Komplete Dunkel!" commands Eberhard Schoener, eminent composer and conceptualist. The giant aircraft hangar–sized soundstage falls dark. Andy, Sting, and I are three hired guns, ready at our stations. Andy, the triple-scale alpha session guitarist, has managed to get Sting and me hired as bass and drums on this fat German tour. There are other players and performers around us in the shadows.

Above our heads, on a giant screen, brilliant geometric shapes begin to flicker and dance. It's this new thing called Laserium. I start up a tickling hi-hat thing and my companions kick into gear. Starting with little stabs and thrusts, a rhythm starts to build. Inspired by the dazzling display above us, we gather momentum and soon are flying down the groove. We've never played like this before. Back in London we have our own band but it's constrained by punk dogma. In our own band we abhor sophistication or anything comfortable or introspective. London rules are very strict.

But we are flying now. Eberhard, like Francis Coppola, values instinct above all in his players. After explaining his dramatic needs for the opening of the show he cuts us loose. There aren't any London cognoscenti in earshot so we get grooving in ways that would kill us back home. We're actually pleasantly surprised by ourselves. After the discipline of the punk straitjacket, we're concise in our playing; but now we're free to blow like the wind. When I first met Andy I valued him for his edgy command of the riffs, but now he's coming out with stuff that has Sting and me lit up like a laser show.

Olaf Kübler leans into his saxophone with a sound that we had forgotten existed. The German players are old-school, which is to say that they play with sophistication and depth. We look a little strange among them with our spiky white hair and hostile attire, but they are all over our groove. With Olaf we surge to a raging gallop at a tempo that astonishes everyone, and then fall back to a canter. This, unfortunately, is the lame part.

The "jazz" element to our ensemble is represented at one extreme by Olaf, all smoke-filled soul, and at the other by this young American jazz singer. The most jazz thing about her is the attitude. Perfectly nice girl offstage, when she gets on the mic she slouches into a jazz pout and sings out of tune—and *likes* it that way. She's the official singer of the tour.

Still, we do our best to support her turn in the focal point. She conjures up an arty attitude with her jazz babbling, and then we all decrescendo gradually down to a whispering thread of rhythm and mysterious lights. At a signal from Eberhard, stationed at his keyboards, we hit the end of the line, and there is a sudden silence in the dunkel.

Lights go up; the promoter and his guests are applauding wildly. The big room is echoing with their cheers. We're looking at one another in amazement. We've never heard anything like that before. Did we just play that?

Eberhard shoos off the guests and we get back to work with some urgency. We're creating a show that involves as many disparate elements as Eberhard can assemble. Every time we start to make some progress, the promoter arrives with sponsors or journalists or TV crews. And then it's "OK . . . Komplete Dunkel!" and we play the opening tune again, which gets more and more amazing each time we play it. Problem is, the first show is coming up and we haven't gotten as far as rehearsing the end of the set. Our leader has verbally walked us down the length of his concept and we have actually worked up some terrific stuff, but we're not at the finish line.

The tour begins and the first sound check is when we finally get to address the finale—or we are intending to, but there are all kinds of technical problems for the sound crew to deal with. By the time the stage is clear for us to work, it's time for the doors to open. It's showtime, but our finale is just something that we've only talked about. Never mind. . . .

This time, when we start up the show with our well-honed opening ride, there is an audience, which provides a whole new propulsion. When we get to Olaf's solo the train is screaming down the tracks at four hundred miles per hour and he soars, incandescent overhead. Even the lame jazz chick almost doesn't suck. And then, when she is spent, something unexpected happens.

One long, clear note of golden purity rises in the eastern sky. It's a man's voice of such power and beauty that every heart is breaking as it rises up, pauses, sucking in the concentration of emotion, and surges through the entire evening of sound and light.

On the dark stage beside him, under the laser-lit galaxies, Andy and I are hearing for the first time the sound that is going to take us to the promised land. Right before our eyes, our prophet ignites, lighting up our future with a keening wail of intense beauty. Every heart will be broken. . . .

CHAPTER 29

A MIGHTY WIND IN THE MAGIC STINGDOM

MAY 2007

After a murderous day and a baronial dinner at the Palazzo. . . .

■ ■ ■ **d**isbelief spreads across his face and he looks helplessly at Andy before dissolving into wild laughter.

"Rox-ha-ha-ha-an-an! You don't have to . . ."

But it's all over. Andy still has the riff going, but we've lost Sting. He's gasping for mercy, leaning forward, agape, as I murder the bass line to his classic song. Every wrong note that I hit on his 1955 Fender Precision bass sinks him deeper and he's howling.

> *"You know my . . ."*
> Wrong note
> *"Is made up . . ."*
> Wrong note
> *"So put away . . ."*
> Wrong note

We are at the foot of a huge staircase that sweeps up into the dark. Scattered around us is a collection of stringed instruments.

It's a baronial hall with stone walls, and the sound that we make wells up around us.

This whole bass thing is his idea. Andy and Sting have taken to pulling out acoustic guitars after dinner and most nights we end up here in the stairwell sounding like The New Seekers crossed with The Gypsy Kings. It's actually kind of impressive to hear them dueling away with the twanging strings reverberating off the ancient walls. Couple of frustrated Manitas de Platas, the pair of them, blazing away there by candlelight.

To stop me from going to grab some bongos, Sting put this venerable antique bass into my hand. Andy shouts out key changes to me and the two of them are head-to-head, exchanging phrases and trying to extravagantly outnoodle each other. I plod along on the bass, mostly keeping up, except for this verse in "Roxanne."

I'm a little giddy about my promotion to bass player in the band. Of course it's just a power grab by Sting, who wants to upgrade to six strings, but I'm happy because now that my new instrument produces actual pitched notes (as opposed to the banging and clattering of my previous rank) it makes me officially one of the musicians. I can join the huddle. The best part is that the notes on a bass are so low that it doesn't really matter what notes you hit—except to Sting, whom I can now demolish with hearty wrongness on his own axe. And then Andy pulls out an . . .

CHAPTER 30

THE DISASTER GIG

MAY 2007

*This is the blog posting that everyone took too seriously
and which got me into trouble with my band. In
hindsight, some of the language is unfortunate, but I
swear I was chuckling fondly as I wrote it.*

Mr. Copeland, at your leisure," says Charlie, the tour production
director, as two crew members hold aside the giant gong, creating
just enough space for me to slither onto my percussion stage,
which is down in its pit. I leap on board, but my foot catches something and I sprawl into the arena in a jumble as the little stage
starts to rise into view. Never mind. The audience is screaming
with anticipation as I collect myself in the dark and start to warm
up the gong with a few gentle taps. But I'm overdoing it. It's reso-
nating and reaching its crescendo before the stage has fully reached
its position. Sort of like a premature ejaculation. There's nothing
for it so I take a big swing for the big hit. Problem is, I'm just frac-
tionally too far away and the beater misses the sweet spot and the
big pompous opening to the show is a damp squib. Never mind.

I stride manfully to my drums. Andy has started the opening
guitar riff to "Message in a Bottle" and the crowd is going nuts.
Problem is, I missed hearing him start. Is he on the first time
around or the second? I look over at Sting and he's not much

help—his cue is me, and I'm lost. Never mind. *Crack!* on the snare and I'm in, so Sting starts singing. Problem is, he heard my crack as two in the bar, but it was actually four—so we are half a bar out of sync with each other. Andy is in Idaho.

Well, we are professionals so we soon get sorted, but the groove is eluding us. We crash through "Message" and then go straight into "Synchronicity." But there is something wrong. We just can't get on the good foot. We shamble through the song and hit the big ending. Last night Sting did a big leap for the cutoff hit, and he makes the same move tonight, but he gets the footwork just a little bit wrong and doesn't quite achieve liftoff. The mighty Sting momentarily looks like a petulant pansy instead of the god of rock. Never mind. Next song is going to be great. . . .

But it isn't. We get to the end of the first verse and I snap into the chorus groove—and Sting doesn't. He's still in the verse. We'll have to listen to the tapes tomorrow to see who screwed up, but we are so off-kilter that Sting counts us in to begin the song again.

This is unbelievably lame. We are the mighty Police and we are totally at sea.

And so it goes, for song after song. All I can think about is how Dietmar is going to string us up. In rehearsal this afternoon we changed the keys of "Every Little Thing" and "Don't Stand So Close," so, needless to say, Andy and Sting are now onstage in front of twenty thousand fans playing avant-garde twelve-tone hodgepodges of both tunes. Lost, lost, lost. I also changed my part for "Don't Stand" and it's actually working quite well, but there is a dissonant noise coming from my two colleagues. In "Walking/ Footsteps," I worked out a cool rhythm change for the rockabilly guitar solo, but now I make a complete hash of it by playing it in the wrong part of the song. It's not sounding so cool.

It usually takes about four or five shows in a tour before you get to the disaster gig. But we're The Police, so we are a little ahead of schedule. It's only the second show (not counting the fan gig— four thousand people doesn't count as a gig in The Police scale of things).

When we meet up backstage for the first time after the set and before the encores, we fall into one another's arms laughing hysterically. Above our heads, the crowd is making so much noise that we can't talk. We just shake our heads ruefully and head back up the stairs to the stage. Funny thing is, we are enjoying ourselves anyway. Screw it, it's only music. What are you gonna do? But maybe it's time to get out of Vancouver.

CHAPTER 31

ANGRY IN EDMONTON

JUNE 2007

A couple of days later.

I'm storming around my dressing room and I'm very angry. At myself, at the world, and at my band. I haven't been this kind of angry in twenty years. I'm angry at my band because they're angry at me. For one thing, they didn't love my blog posting. They probably haven't even read it, but they've heard the clamor. Apart from a couple of regrettable choices of word it was a cheerful little glimpse behind the curtain for the few denizens of my tiny Web site. I don't even know how that crafty AP reporter even found the piece on my site, but he wasn't shy about adding a few pejoratives and turning it into headline news.

DRUMMER PANS HIS OWN GROUP! may not seem like much of a banner, so it must have been a very slow news day. Suddenly all the happy news about the big heroic comeback band gets a new round of attention as dirt, and I'm in the doghouse again.

This all broke out yesterday in Vancouver, about an hour before lobby call for the flight to Edmonton. My profuse apologies to the band were grudgingly accepted, but the atmosphere in the van to the jet was cold and nervous.

It should have been glorious. The first shows in Vancouver had been a smash. All the reviews were good (except mine) and this was the first day of actual touring. Our first ride on the band jet. The sun was shining, the birds were singing, but The Police was a cold dark cavern. Three grumpy millionaires in a bus. I'm expecting an ambush.

Sound check is hideous. Any other band would be swaggering around our cool new stage, enjoying the big Tonka toys. The stadium rig really is quite spectacular. It's a huge set that wraps around our arena rig—which is already verrry fly. The colossal scale of the stage, screens, lights, and amplification would normally gladden the heart of any performer. Right at the heart of this behemoth is us, with our back line. Two amps and a drum set. We get to play right in the focal point of all this technology. We are the eye of the storm.

But our hearts are not glad and we're not swaggering. There is a layer of cold dank hostility on the stage. We run through some songs. The Police riffs rattle around the empty stadium as each of us selects an area of empty sky to glare at. All the crew is hunkered down. Almost all of the crew. Billy Francis, our tour manager and chief of staff from back in the day, is smirking wickedly. He knows that band brawls fuel the hottest shows. He and Brad will be snickering about this later.

Big Mike Keating, who runs the front-of-house sound, gives us a wave from way down at his end of the stadium and sound check is over. I can withdraw to my own sanctuary, to the quiet of my own opulent dressing room.

This is all so alien to me. It's still very early in the tour and there is a lot of preshow tension to deal with, but I've only ever felt this way in this band. I'm the problem—the weak link. Just a few months ago I was a happy patriarch, but now in this band I'm nothing, no one. They are muttering darkly to one another about

me. As I sweat in my room I'm exaggerating everything to myself, replaying the tapes of our band discourse, attaching sinister significance to every word, gesture, and glance. Then Brad gets a message on his unit. Band meeting at eight. Oh great.

After twenty years of a good life, rich with family, laughter, and accomplishment, I'm back here again. Back *here* again! I glower around the room with its silk drapes and mood lighting. There is an army of wardrobe assistants, chefs, therapists, ambience coordinators, and talent wranglers deployed right now to coddle every moment between now and showtime. There is another army of crew, with eighty trucks' worth of gear assembled to project my show. OK, I get it. Maybe I'm worth a little more than nothing.

When did I ever look to Sting or Andy for adoration or support? In this band we torture one another. We poke and prod. When Sting sears the masses with his yearning melodies, his pain is real.

Now I'm prowling and stretching. After snarling down an ambush by my playmates, I'm going to walk out there on that big stage with two giant musicians to face forty thousand emotional Police fans and burn every calorie of energy that I possess. When I was a kid this band was all that I knew. It could crush me. But now I know better.

CHAPTER 32

CONQUERING HEROES

INSIDE THE EXPLOSION

JUNE 2007

A week or two goes by. Every show is different.

Mr. Copeland, at your leisure," says Charlie Hernandez, the tour production director. The two guys holding aside the giant gong are smirking wickedly. It has been our running gag of the tour that I'm liable to trip on my way up to the little percussion stage as it rises from its pit into the arena. Tonight I'm lithe as a leopard as I leap aboard and a shriek goes up from the closest seats behind the stage. In the darkened arena there is an ocean of anticipation, but right behind the stage there are thirty or forty people who can see me and they know, before everyone else does, that the show is starting. "Stewwwaaaaaarrrt!!!" they are shouting wildly as I begin to warm up the huge gong. This thing is so huge that even as it begins to rumble my innards are vibrating. The deep sound is filling the arena; the roar of the audience is deafening on every frequency, washing over the people behind the stage. My arm goes back for a full swing. Twenty years of waiting for this moment has pumped so much energy into my shoulder that the heavy mallet is propelled like the hammer of Thor into the heart of the gong.

WHHHOOOOOMMMMMMMMMMMMMMM!

It's perfect. My hair is standing on end. But we're just getting started. Andy is mounting the stage and is still walking when he hits the opening riff to "Message in a Bottle." The shriek of the crowd goes up an octave. Andy has them by the throat. I stride manfully to my drums. The room is already throbbing in time with the guitar riff, but I can just add a little four-on-the-floor with my bass drum to focus the twenty thousand pairs of feet into a stomping pulse that will surely weaken the structure of the building . . . and then, CRACK!

And Sting is on the mic. *Sting is in the house!*

"Just a cast—" he begins. . . .

"AWAY! . . . AN ISLAND LOST AT SEA-OH!" scream the tumult of voices as if their lives depend on it.

It's perfect. We are the mighty Police and for the next two hours we are going to play our music as if our lives depend on it. We are The Police and we are *back!*

"Message" is the perfect way into our show. The song is like a diamond. It has resisted all our attempts to resculpt it, so we've been playing it in almost exactly this form through four months of rehearsal. The response from the audience is perfect. They may have been wondering, When are they going to play "Message"? and the answer is: Right Now.

In the front row heads are bobbing, arms are waving, and there are a few people who are sobbing. I'm pretty excited, too.

Sting is at the helm like the Flying Dutchman, with his 1957 Fender Precision outthrust and his voice gliding over the waves of singing people. Over on my left Andy is an orchestra of sound. He has the most detailed job in the band. While my sweat comes from physical labor and Sting's comes from emotional commitment, Andy sweats over some of the most complex guitar parts in show business.

"Message" pays off with a tight little turnaround at the end and a solid thump so the crowd knows we're done. But we're not done; we're straight into "Synchronicity II." Once again Andy starts us off, this time with a vaguely familiar fragment of a familiar riff and then we kick into Sting's tribal yell, and we're blazing away in another heavy one. It's going well; for the first time this tour I actually remember the push into the second verse that we've rehearsed a hundred times. Andy looks surprised, the rotter!

On stage right, the Lion of Judah is on the prowl. Sting has so much physical energy that any instrument less robust than a bass would crumple in his hands when he plays this kind of music. All of that power goes into those four heavy bass strings that lay the rhythmic and harmonic foundations of our music.

At the end of the chorus, going into the guitar solo, it's all so damned exciting that I loose the hounds before Sting has finished his song. He whips around from his mic and comes charging up to me full of fire and brimstone. For a moment I'm raising the shield because Captain Queeg is coming for me. But he's not glaring at me personally tonight.

He's on a new bass riff that has just popped into his hands, a kind of an upside-down version of what he's supposed to be playing. I like it when this happens. He kicks off from the drum riser and then goes to harass the front rows while Andy rips up his solo.

And so it goes, for song after song. We have an almost perfect mix of well-greased moments and seat-of the-pants challenges to keep us alert as the waves of passion from the heaving crowd sweep over us. Some of the time we're so on target that we throw one another little curve balls and trick shots. Other times we're skating with urgent concentration through thinly rehearsed recent music changes.

Both of my buddies have new tricks. Andy used to obsess with Sting over the parts so much that he hardly soloed in the old days. He's burning it up now. He has a command of his instrument that allows him to develop his classic parts into abstractions that catch fire as searing wild lead lines. Old-school blazing guitar. And then he snaps back into the delicate and precise fingering of classic Police arpeggio ostinatos ("Message," "Every Breath," "Magic," etc.). And it's not just his fingers that change gears. At his feet is an array of guitar sound gadgets. Like Fred Astaire, Andy dances on his pedals, switching textures with huge contrast as the band powers through the sections of the songs.

And yes, there are many unintended departures from the plan (behind locked doors we call them mistakes), but the trick is to make them work. We have an epoch of stagecraft experience between us and we could write the encyclopedia of swaggering through mistakes. That's the great thing about music. If you played it, it's correct. The worst musical train wreck hurts absolutely no one. It's all part of the show. In fact it's how we get to the great stuff. There is no penalty for skating on the edge or throwing ourselves off the cliff. So we do.

I'm told that our set runs over two hours. It seems to me like twenty minutes have gone by before we're at "Roxanne." This song is the easiest/hardest, simplest/most complicated in our oeuvre. It is our own curse of Macbeth. All three of us have equally besmirched form cards on this one, and tonight it's my turn. After the first bridge, I go to the chorus instead of the next verse. Since this has happened so often over the decades at this spot in this song, the solution is an extra flourish that snaps right off and the moment is cured while Andy and Sting share a smirk. Songs of this caliber are bulletproof.

Cool thing is, when you miss a shot, you get all fired up with renewed commitment. You play your way out of a hole. So when we get to the jam, I'm full of a homicidal rage and go hurtling off the chorus riff into outer space. This is when I really experience the thrill of this band. I'm with two players who can ride anything.

They know I'm a little excitable and are now dusting off their years of experience with my tantrums. They are well armed for dealing with the clattering tirade coming from the drum riser. Sting rides the surge for a while, occasionally pouring fuel into the flames, and he then goes into some call-and-response with the crowd. That always shuts me up because I like to hear the folks singing. A big crowd in a big space, singing a big tune, is worth stepping aside for, so . . . BOMP! I stop dead, and the audience can hear itself. The folks are responding to their own power, and rising with Sting's exhortations.

Roxaaaaaahnnoooooooooooooohhhhh!

We have done our work. The room is alive with its own swelling momentum. The joint is rocking and we can dance along silently while the good folks carry the rhythm and the tune up through the roof. The front row is foaming with the babes who were sixteen back in the day and are now forty-something. They look great! As they pulsate to the mating dance of our species and ogle Sting, their husbands are behind them with happy faces because they know that they are going to score tonight. Aahhh . . . we're hardwired for music and this is what it's for.

Well, the next half hour is what all of us musicians live for. When you come back onstage for the encores the body has caught up with the mind and there is a different atmosphere to the rest of the show. Even though the ritual audience/band etiquette guarantees that the encores are fully included in the ticket price, there is a just-for-fun casual joy in the "extra" music. This is when we really own every moment of every bar. We have fought the waves, climbed the mountains, and now it's all ride.

When there are no more songs to play, I climb off of the drums and go to the front of the stage for the corny traditional band bow. I take out my in-ear monitors and am bowled over by the volume of the howling cheers. It's hard to be at the focal point of so much joy and not lapse into goofy body language. Hard to imagine a more ideal moment, really. Can't say I can think of a more euphoric circumstance for a musician.

Well, thank *you!*

It's getting better with every show.

▲ **Much more like it . . .**

CHAPTER 33

MALIBU

JUNE 2007

"Let's get a male choir. . . ."

We're staring out to sea, the three of us, with Kathy Schenker intently examining the wooden deck beneath us. Behind us is a chamber full of singers and some worried-looking executives. This ain't working. I had high hopes, but now I'm shaking my head. Sometimes in art things aren't as obvious as they ought to be. The idea of texturing the proposed Unplugged MTV deal with a choir of male voices grabbed me immediately, but as Jordan asked me later, what did I *think* they were going to sound like?

"This is the only thing that has excited me, that has got me thinking," says the gravelly voice. "If not this, then maybe nothing at all."

A little eye contact with Andy has confirmed that we both are thinking that "nothing at all" is looking like a better option. This is a shark that we are reluctant to jump.

I long to just get on the piano, ask Andy to help me out—tell me how many sharps we're working, and build some modal textures that would take us closer to Barber and away from Streisand. But I haven't got the nerve. It would be like one of the crew leaping forward with a suggestion. After decades of being the boss of everything in music I'm back in this movie, in which it's just not my role.

Much more strange is the abdication of the leader whom we're here to serve. The reason that I'm content with my role as noise-maker is that my buddies have it covered. Sting's pretty good at this stuff, Andy, too, but he's just sitting there while a genial professional arranger is painting fey stuff over our music.

The singers are an extremely tight choir. Even these milque-toast charts have them individually singing oblique lines. They are right on the money, so none of this is their fault and we're trying to give them a good vibe—but we're not a Broadway musical. Jordan and his fiancée, Ami, are filming everything, but this is one scene that probably won't make it in to the documentary.

As usually happens when danders are raised, ultimatums are made, and Danubes are crossed, life in The Police becomes suddenly bearable. As the sun follows the rain, love follows the hatchets. Sting and I lack emotional stamina; we lose our taste for righteous anger within the hour. Andy exacts a higher price. Piss him off and he goes dark for days. Today he's happy, though, and we're soon chuckling at his dry wit as we finish the session. The mighty Police sounding like a wedding band for Freddie Mercury is actually pretty damned funny. These two eight-hundred-pound gorillas of mine can be vexatious at times, but it's never boring in this band.

CHAPTER 34

HOW BIG IS MY AMP!

JUNE 2007

How heavy is my truck!

The Police is an army on tour. 100+ trucks and eleven crew buses. At the heart of all of this is the team of Billy, Phil, and Brad, whose job is to herd Sting, Andy, and me, respectively, in and out of our hotels, on and off the band jet, and to and from the gigs. There is a huge industrial complex for whom the staff must deliver the three "principals"—in mental and physical working order—to the stage.

OK, everybody, switch to show channel number 16."

Dug's voice is squawking out of Brad's unit. While I wrap my fingers down in my room, the army of Police crew are swinging into gear. Fiction Plane has just finished their set; it's time to clear their gear off the stage and rig for the main event.

There are two bands on tour but just the one giant stage. Within the horde are actually several crews. Way out there, probably asleep right now, are the truckers and drivers. After they drop off the gear and crew, they hit the sack. They'll wake up again when it's all over, and then load back up and drive through the night.

▲ Big Mike at far right.

When we arrive at a gig in the afternoon we pass though acres of parked sixteen-wheelers and tour buses. Man we are *large!*

Mostly the trucks are full of steel. The stage shell is made out of thousands of bars and clamps. There are several buses just to carry the swarm of unnamed riggers. We hardly ever see these guys; their work is done long before we arrive.

Our arena stage is an oval plateau, upon which we strut with our two amps and drum set. It's actually a living, breathing mechanism, a separate animal from the lighting and video towers. The huge structure that looms over the field is a shell into which our stage fits. They actually build it separately and roll it into position.

Above deck is the world of music, lights, and joy; belowdecks, our Nibelungen toil. With only three of us in the band, we're kind of shorthanded when it comes to switching sounds or instruments. Each one of us requires maintenance during the show. Our principal crew—Jeff Seitz, Danny Quatrochi, and Dennis Smith—have been with us since back in the day. It's like a submarine down there, with about a dozen crew inside the stage operating the lifts, monitors, video cameras, and blinking technology.

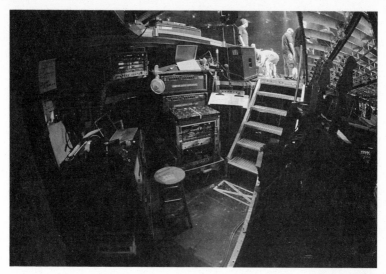
▲ Sting's hatch.

Deep in my casbah of pipe and drape I can hear the increased bustle in the halls outside. Even though we do this every day, we have to do it right. From this moment until midnight, when the trucks are rolling away with our tents and camels, every move by every member of the show crew is tightly choreographed, including us three musicians.

By now I've got my armor on and my blood circulating. Jeff pokes his head in for drum report, Ian checks the batteries on my radio packs, Karen Nicholson runs a lint brush over my black threads.

The units squawk. "We are . . . Ready On Deck."

"Thank you, Dug," squawks Billy.

If Billy has done his job today, by planes, trains, and automobiles the band has arrived at this moment ready to dance, happy, inspired, rested, healed, coddled, and generally all shined up for public display. Charlie Hernandez and his army get the gear into position; Billy Francis and his staff get the band to the gear.

"Phil, Brad, walking in five."

Down the hall in two further casbahs are my bandmates, each

of them completing their preshow rituals. In my case these are mostly concerned with the physical component of my work. I have to hit the stage running. So I'm prowling in circles swinging my arms like Tarzan until Brad gives me the nod. Then I lurch out of my lair and into the white concrete hallways. We're walking. Each band member has a posse of staff and crew. We converge in the cavernous loading bay, just out of view of the stadium field. It's kind of industrial back here, but just beyond those curtains are the tens of thousands of the multitude. The stage is set and waiting.

With the three of us convened, Charlie starts the show. "Roll Bob," he commands.

The towering sound system that has been tinkling nicely as the stadium filled up during the evening now roars to life with Bob Marley's "Get Up Stand Up."

Everybody in our crew is heartily sick of this classic track after hearing it at the start of every show, but we're all synchronized to it. It's our countdown.

As the Wailers wail, we're plugging into the closed audio environment of our earplug monitors. The crew are running audio through our headsets, checking that we can hear each other. The guitar and bass are being strapped to their masters and the signal from each instrument is being checked (again).

At a moment of Charlie's choosing, we are summoned to the stage. We start across the field, guided by a thicket of flashlights, which are visible from some areas of the stadium. It's very quiet in our earplugged world, but we can feel the voodoo rising. Eighty thousand souls are welling up around us.

We dart into the stage, and the black curtains close behind us. We're now in the belly of the beast. Our stage appears to be a flat oval dish, but behind the drums, it slopes up slightly. This rise is achieved with very shallow steps that create a kind of duck blind, through which the crew can watch the action. Right now we are down in there, peering out at the audience. It's huge and expectant.

Andy is about ten feet away, on the other side of the submerged percussion riser. He's at the foot of the short stairway up to his hatch. Sting is next to me preparing to go up my stairs through my hatch. His is over on stage right but he uses this one at the show open. We take turns exchanging ritual gestures and invocations with Jeff, whose station is close by. Pressed into a notch in the gear, trying to take up as little space as possible is a video cable grip, an Asian woman whom I never see except at this time of day, every working day. We exchange the same formal bow that precedes every show.

The Marley track starts to fade. Charlie, Dug, and Chris are assembled behind the percussion riser. They regard me with exaggerated indulgent invitation. I eagerly join them and we form a circle around a specific spot on the deck. Same spot every night. The three crew bosses are holding flashlights in the dark.

▲ Jeff in the duck blinds

"Kill house lights!" barks Charlie. There has been a rising thrum from the multitude out there, but now there's an explosion as the giant klieg lights around the stadium go dark. The flashlights are focused on the spot.

"Go . . . chase!" orders Charlie, and the three forty-something heads-of-department simulate a flashing light show on the deck beneath us until, "Restore!" and the lights briskly converge again on the sacred spot. Dug stands aside with a beatific smile, Chris Sup and his mate pull aside the gong, while Charlie adopts the posture of the very suavest maître d':

"Mr. Copeland, at your leisure."

CHAPTER 35

AFTERSHOW RITUAL

JULY 2007
TORONTO

Getting used to this touring life.

■ ■ ■ **N**ot a bad show. It's great not to be doing a runner. Walking off the stage and along the hallways of the arena back to the dressing room is always (almost) very cheerful. My shirt has turned

to ice within seconds away from the hot stage lights so I fumble with my wires, radio packs, and belts as we walk so that I can get the damned shirt off. Sting is ten feet in front of me, sauntering along with Billy in attendance. I have no idea what his or Andy's postshow ritual is, or what they're thinking right now after spending two hours on a stage together in front of a lot of very aroused people. We disappear into our suites and are gone.

Brad and I arrive in my casbah and he pours a shot of choice tequila as I pull off my soggy clothes and head for the shower. Within two minutes of leaving the stage I'm in a shower of bliss. Hot at first as I soak and glorify in the moment and then colder to stop the sweating. It's exhilarating to play shows, but there is an excitement lag. During the show the business at hand (music, songs, arrangements, and so forth) is distracting from the fundamental coolness of the thing. But under the hot stream of water the thrill sinks in. I rerun the show in my head and revel in the moments of brilliance, while helping myself to absolution for the fuckups.

Since I'm in a shower designed for hockey players I'm thankful

▲ River Plate Stadium, Rio de Janeiro, by day

that, unlike teams, bands win every game. Even if there were difficulties during the show there is always the reward from the audience. At least with this band, there is no such thing as a dead show. The songs are just so ingrained into people's lives that when they hear us playing them they light up. So in the shower it's all good.

Looking around the team-sized shower room it's hard not to feel thankful for my job. It's a breezeblock rectangle painted white with white neon light and serious plumbing. It's the only part of my digs that Jaime Laurita's crew couldn't smother with pipe-and-drape. The Police area of the sport facility is swathed in silks and sexy lighting so that the players can shrug off worry and groove with joy. Sports players have to go out there and fight, so they don't get the mood lighting. We do, I think, use this building for fundamentally the same purpose. They go out and stage a ritual battle to arouse communal passions and tribal thrills. We do that, too, but don't have any opposition. If they slacken or blink, they lose. We're here to cruise. Don't get me wrong, rock music is an extreme effort, way beyond anything that would be possible

▲ Later that night

without the exhortations of the masses. But there's no one trying to stop us. What if they had a Super Bowl with just one team? Well, everybody wins!

People often say that this job looks like amazing fun. It sure beats rat catching, but it's strangely uneuphoric to be up there at the center of all that ritual. The state of mind is many opposite things all happening at once. My body is almost on automatic pilot. I'm not listening to myself, I'm fixated on the other players, switching my focus back and forth between them. During Andy's solos I'm right in there with him every step of the way. I like to pick up his phrases and articulate the rhythms of his ostinato figures. Crowds love that kind of interplay, but sometimes I go too far, and he's suddenly wondering where I put the groove. It's like if a pilot in his cockpit looks over and sees the mechanic trying to fly the plane. But generally he's pretty tolerant of the racket that I set up behind him and we keep good eye and ear contact for most of the set.

Sting is another story. We have a lot of conflict onstage. We both understand each other's issues perfectly but struggle to accommodate them, although it's finally getting easier to put our good intentions into practice. Sting has a concept in his mind of the ideal form that the music should take. It is our job to re-create that ideal in the physical world, on that stage. I have very little in my mind, ideal or otherwise. I don't count bars or look at a map. The patterns and arrangements are learned at a very deep level, where my conscious mind rarely goes. So when Sting, as an able arranger and bandleader, imagines a rhythm and asks me to play it, he never quite gets what he asked for. Anything that isn't what he wants is chaos to him. Working with me (on drums) requires an unreasonable tolerance for chaos. Strange how that contrasts with my composer gig, which is autistically meticulous. When I get on my drums I'm not the urbane but brisk professional anymore. I'm a hairy-assed silverback swinging through the trees.

CHAPTER 36

TUBA IN TURIN

OCTOBER 2007

After a day of searching the antique stores of Vienna, I have found the perfect birthday gift for the man who has everything: a beautiful brass tuba. The bass member of the brass family for the bass member of my band family. Perfect! It's a thing of brass beauty. By the time I've figured out how to play "Happy Birthday to You" on it, I want to keep it for myself. It is only the great love in my heart that commands me to reserve this treasure for my friend.

It happens that the birthday lands on the day of our show in Turin, Italy. This is going to be the best day of the tour. My Taranta gang are opening for us! Italy is the best country in the world, where my life is enriched every summer with my own little cozy music scene. Turin ain't Melpignano but anywhere in Italy still feels like a homecoming, particularly since my Salento tribe will be there.

The Stadio delle Alpi is an old building and the dressing rooms are just off center field; perfect for football teams to enter the pitch at the center line. It's nice that I can peek out from the players'

tunnel and watch my tribal friends banging up the pizzica for
massed Police fans. They never miss; even without me in the band
they rock the joint.

They finish their show in triumph and I'm heading back to the
silks when I run into Stingo. "Not bad!" he allows. I completely
failed during the last week not to oversell the Tarantas to my colleagues. He must have liked them, though, because he watched
most of their show. "But," he says, "they didn't play me 'Happy
Birthday.'"

"Aha! Well, I can take care of that!" says I. "Follow me."

When we get to my rooms I slip behind the curtain, pull out the
horn, and stride back into the room puffing "Happy Birthday to
You" on his shiny new toy. His face lights up with joy and before I
can even finish the tune he's grabbing it from me.

In a twinkling he's figured out "Tequila."

> *da Tent*
> *Dada*
> *Ten ten Ten*
> *Tant*

He's like that, our Stingo. Put anything that makes a sound into his hands and something beautiful will happen. For the rest of the preshow I can hear the tuba emanating soulfully from Sting world.

The walk is a little different tonight. The dressing rooms are at midfield and our stage is down at the far end. Between our world and the stage are the loading ramps and traffic systems for the crumbly old stadium. So we get into a little bus and take a ride around the works to get to the stage. To make sure that we get there without mishap, we have a full Italian police escort with flashing lights and sirens.

We are enjoying the drama as we snuggle up in the little van. All is well in Police-dom until we notice that we're on a freeway. The huge stadium, that blocks out the sky, is receding behind us. Um. . . .

With flags flying, our convoy takes the next exit, snarls up Turin traffic as we cross over the bridge, and descends the on ramp back down to the freeway toward the stadium. Full lights and sirens.

Soon we are home again in the stadium grounds, but our adventure is not over. We appear to be exploring the parking lots in search of a route to the stage—just like any fans at a show, but for the full lights and sirens. Then when we come to a T junction and the convoy halts. After an interlude, the lights and sirens go dark. We can only imagine the Italian fulminations in the lead car. *Porko Dio!*

"Yeah . . . Billy? . . . are the band gonna play tonight?" squawks Charlie in the unit.

"Bit of confusion with the escort," replies Billy from the front seat. His voice is unnaturally low and even. We are enjoying this scene from *Spinal Tap* more than he is.

When we pull up to the stage, with neither bleep of light nor murmur of siren from our escort, we're twenty minutes late for the show.

Soon we're saddled up and we start up the drill. As the show opens my heart is bursting with adoration for the splendid Italians. It's a really big show, with many of my personal chums in the crowd. I'm feeling perfect.

With joy in my heart I look to my brethren, that we may ignite the evening together. Andy gets it, he's right in my groove. Over on the right, however . . . oh, great. Sting's got a problem. Not much mystery to it, it's the usual. Me.

Let the joy shine forth, I soothe, seeking to deflect the dart of anger that zings past my ear. But it's no use. The other ignition sequence has begun.

First he starts waving his bass at me—often a good thing, but not this time. He's facing away from me, out to the crowd, but he's clearly trying to get my attention. Instead of playing the damned thing, he's trying to conduct me with it. I've got nothing better to do than to figure out how I may cease to displease my beloved comrade, but you know what happens next.

In my mind I'm running through the lengthy list of known displeasures. There's always the tempo thing, but right now he's rushing, not me, damn it. Then there is each and every instance that I hit a drum or cymbal God Damn it. And he's probably blaming me that he lost the plot at that last turnaround. . . .

No, no, no. There is only love. We are sharing the blessing of music with all of these enraptured Italians who love us. In fact there is kind of a heightened urgency to the show. When the punter blinders come up, I can see right to the back of the stadium. One hundred sixty thousand arms raised. The voodoo is way high tonight.

Andy takes a solo. He can feel the excitation. As he ramps it up and up, I'm raging with him. OK, so the tempo gets a little overheated. When we get back to the song Sting has to snatch at the lyrics in the brighter tempo. Well, I know that's going to piss him off.

And it does; now he's got Tourette's syndrome. He doesn't want to miss a precious word of his blessed song, so he's singing like a bird, but after every line of soaring beauty, his head twitches round to spit venom. There's an urgency to it. It's *really* important that he get his message across to me. It's vital that I not miss any drop of his outrage. Since I'm strenuously avoiding any outward sign of acknowledgment, he must employ ever larger gestures. I'm just focused on Andy. The riff is clear: lock and groove.

But I fail to completely ignore it when he half turns, takes his left hand off the frets and starts to make whacking gestures to indicate when I should hit my backbeat. What?!

Now we have eye contact for the first time all night. He's mouthing curses at me, as if he thinks I'll be persuaded by this to mellow out.

Pumped up as I am by the show, this strikes me as the most heinous crime imaginable in stagecraft. Particularly since there are only three of us it's very important not to frag your own team. I'm stunned. My body is strenuously engaged in sacred ritual and someone is shooting at me. *What?!*

No time for any little silvery ringing, we're straight into the clanging gongs of Armageddon.

I'm surging. Love and adore *this* you fucking piece of shit! I actually have the perfect tools in my hands for this sentiment. Hard wood, strong drums, and 500,000 watts of amplified rage. The stadium full of screaming frenzy doesn't calm me down much, either.

You fucking—*Fucking—Fuckkkkinnng bastard!*

I'm in a whiteout of fury. My cymbals are flattened against their stands and the drums are clacking because I'm hitting them too hard. There are white and red flashes behind my eyeballs. Splinters are flying off my sticks, and I'm slaughtering whole civilizations.

STEWART COPELAND

Jeff is in my headset. "Feeling a little happy tonight?"

I'm screaming unintelligibly into my head mic as we come to the end of the set. I charge down my hatch, and Brad is there with cold Gatorade and towels. The stadium around us is quaking with tumult. As the multitude screams its approval, Brad is carefully managing my mood. Of course he agrees one *hundred* percent with every imprecation that I hurl over to the Sting zone under stage right, where Beelzebub and Billy are head-to-head, no doubt having a similar conversation. But he's sharing my rage in kind of an upbeat way, steering me more toward humor than violence. Better a sardonic sneer than a murderous lunge, because we still have one last song to play.

I normally burn up just about every available calorie of energy that I possess during a regular show. When we go back out for our final song, I've got just enough fuel left to carry it manfully before flopping down the hatch and limping back to the silk. Tonight there is a whole new source of energy. The desire to rend, rip, claw, or cudgel conjures up hidden reserves and the Devil himself is torching the stadium. This may be Turin, but these folks are the descendants of Romans. They can smell the blood. They get it, and the conflagration consumes everything.

We take our bows with glassy smiles and I storm back down my hatch. When I get to the little love van, ready with my sardonic sneer, there's no sign of the Adversary. Billy and Brad have rustled up separate conveyance. But Andy is here, and he's in a genial mood. I'm not. My comradely congratulations (through gritted teeth) on his towering performance quickly accelerate into a contrasting opinion of our singer. By the time we get to the dressing rooms I'm speaking in tongues and pounding the upholstery, taxing the suspension system of the little van. Andy appears fascinated by the stitching on the back of the driver's hat. He's regretting that he took out his earplugs and left them with Dennis back at the stage.

Within the hour, I'm hosed down, dried off, and wallowing in

endorphins. Vittorio is here! And Titti, and Mauro and Giovanni and Eugenio, Stephano, Sylvia, Silvio, Antonio, Ninfa, Emanuele, Alfredo, Enza, and the whole Salento tribe. Long into the night we carouse and laugh. We only have this one show in Italy so everybody I know is here.

NEXT MORNING, IT'S A beautiful sunny day as I cross the hotel lobby, but in the back of my mind there is some unfinished business. Billy is there.

"Fancy a coffee?" he asks, uncharacteristically.

"Sure."

We wander over to the lobby café and Sting is there with his posse. Fiona and Trudie are twinkling to each other and waving their eyebrows at their husbands while gazing heavenward. I settle in close to the Jovian jowl.

"Give me back my fucking tuba, asshole."

"Can't. I trashed it."

Aaaahhh . . . music is thicker than blood.

CHAPTER 37

FOUR BEERS AND THE PRESIDENT

OCTOBER 2007
MILLENNIUM STADIUM, CARDIFF

It's gradually getting less weird on this tour. Our lives are engineered to keep band contact to a minimum so we mainly see each other on the plane and in the bus on our way from the airport to the sound check. Conversation in the bus is easy because it's too bumpy to read and we are physically within earshot. The best part is that it's usually dumb shit, although it is also a good place for clear conversation about band matters. When we get to the gig we each head back into our corners. After a quick look at our dressing rooms we head out to the stage, and when we get up there it's all business.

We're still doing sound checks, longer into the tour than most other bands bother with. It's good to get the blood moving and to tinker with the toys. Sting always has some new noodle to gnaw at.

The second best part of the day is the post–sound check nap. It's strangely nonvoluntary. The body knows by now what's coming up in a couple hours so it just shuts down. Coma. At 6:30 the bear crawls out of hibernation. Protein is the first demand. In Band

Dining Jaime has a spread of calibrated nutrients for the three athletes. There's some fancy-looking stuff spread out for us but I'm tearing at the red meat, gradually waking up my own flesh.

Usually, after Band Dining, it's time to start suiting up. But tonight I have to do some promotion for the South American leg that we have been coddled into adding to the tour. We're going to swing through Mexico, Argentina, Chile, and Brazil. Amy intercepts my stroll back to the dressing room and guides me along the cavernous stadium hallways into a room with a crew. It's a camera team from Chile, who just need a few words from me to promote our concert down there. The charismatic presenter of a TV show back in Santiago is here with his microphone and vibe. We get some fun repartee going while the camera turns. The TV guy is playing for his viewers back home (so am I) and very soon everybody has what they need.

Amy moves me to the next room, which is the same deal, only it's a crew from Argentina. Easy enough, same gags, same shtick, only now my favorite country in the world is Argentina. Flattery is the easiest shill, so it always helps to have a little specific local color to refer to when flogging tickets in distant lands. It so happens that with Argentina, there is an easy one. They have just re-established their historic flair for female leaders by electing the quite babeliscious Cristina Fernández de Kirchner as president.

But the cameras are down now and the team is stowing its gear as I step back out into the hallway. Now is when I get to strap on my gear and tool up for the big ride. The Argentine TV guy is still at my side as we stroll past the stacked flight cases and off-duty crew back to Police world. Just ahead is the pipe and drape, which is the telephone booth for my transformation into drum god. We are leering about his new president when I suggest that after a beer or two she could qualify as hot—too bad about that Chilean president though, "now that would take at least four beers!" Well, of course, the Argentines love that, but the Santiago crew are still loitering in the hall and they catch the quip.

Days later, word comes in from head office that the Latin press is full of outrage that some damned rock drummer has been casting aspersions on the dignity of the estimable President Michelle

▲ Sound check, contemplating the set list.

Bachelet of Chile. Turns out that the lines on her face are hard-earned. Her father died under torture, and she herself was tortured by Pinochet's goons. She is altogether too saintly a figure to have to put up with being questioned about her rock babe rating by her own national press. I hate to annoy heads of state, so I write a groveling letter and hope that it blows over by the time we get down there in a few weeks.

When I was a kid my daddy used to conduct his nefarious manipulation of local potentates with cocktail parties at our modest Ottoman palace in the hills overlooking Beirut. With the city sparkling below, an Armenian jazz band grooving on the terrace, and a briefcase full of CIA dollars in his office, he would cultivate eager dictators-in-training. Leaders of conscience were pretty thin on the ground in those days and the practices of empire had not yet been discredited. It was all about the colonels.

In the 1950s my father and his cowboy chums seemed to be doing a pretty good job, maneuvering the resources of their patch of the cold war world. Very simply, the Muslim oil was flowing west to us rather than north to the Soviets. The CIA had a pretty good record of putting "*our* sons of bitches" (as my dad fondly called them) into power around the Middle East. Even the great lion of pan-Arab nationalism (Baathism to you), Gamal Abdul Nasser, was in the pay of our guys. It's hard to fathom now, but the Shah of Iran was looking like a good deal back then. My dad and his friend Kermit Roosevelt had heinously installed a Peacock Throne on top of ancient Persia (Iran) and the second-largest source of oil in the world was ours. It all went splendidly until Khomeini.

While President Bachelet is no Khomeini, she is directly the heir to the same kind of foul play that my father practiced. In fact, during our first swing through South America back in the day, both Argentina and Chile were still under the dictatorship of American Empire–era juntas. In Chile we could feel the cold hand of autocracy on our shoulders from the moment we arrived. I think the militaries only let us into the country because they liked the name of our band.

Back in 1982 we had enjoyed much success from throwing verbal bombs wherever we went in the "free" world. It was all pretty harmless fun casting aspersions on cultural icons and taboos. It was expected of us. In fact, we had to disguise our true nature as rapacious capitalists by leading the charge of cultural revolution.

So we may have been a tad callow when we got to our first press conference in Viña del Mar. On the table before us, along with all of the microphones, were the flags of England, the United States, and Chile. These were swept aside by the preening rock band—regrettably, including the Chilean one. I dimly recall that it was the mighty hand of our singer that did the sweeping. He's always been antinationalist. As we spouted our usual boisterous cant we noticed a distinct lack of echo in the room. Instead of the usual jocular banter we were getting flinty-eyed scrutiny.

Before we exposed ourselves as deviant insurrectionists the state media had whipped up a tide of enthusiasm for us and the big outdoor festival that we were set to play. There were happy mobs outside the hotel and when we got to the show the vibe was electric, but the atmosphere backstage with our local contacts was cold. Right in front of the stage was a seated section of privileged brass and behind them was the common herd of Chilean people. During our show Sting pointedly projected right over the heads of state to the folks behind the barrier—who went wild. The oligarchs found themselves between the snarly rock band and the raging proles.

It was really only rock-and-roll exuberance, but the folks in the money seats didn't look to me like they were enjoying the show. I could see from the drum riser that they were looking over their shoulders. The fancy women looked scared and the fancy men were making hard eye contact with the men in uniform who were everywhere. When we finished the shows the junta was still intact, so we were allowed to leave town next morning without hassle. But the papers tore us to shreds. There was a story about how Sting had insulted national honor by having his microphone disinfected. And then how he kept spitting on the Chilean stage (which was actually true—for some reason most singers who also play an instrument expectorate prolifically).

So here I am again in 2007, causing trouble and annoying a nation. When we arrive this time, after a raucous ride in Argentina, the atmosphere in Chile is brand-new. The only hassle we have on arrival is Nadine Barner's strange supply of macrobiotic grains and unguents. The customs guys have a party trying to figure out what drugs to arrest her for.

Since it's a day off, Brad and I venture out for a stroll around Santiago, taking in some sights and doing a little retail therapy. It's a very nice city and strangely reminds me of Santa Monica, California, of all places. It's something about how the hills loom over the suburban shopping street. We end up at a cozy little restaurant for dinner, sample some of the native cuisine, and share our genuine enthusiasm with the chef, who comes out to have his picture taken with us. When one camera comes out, they all do, so the next ten minutes are spent signing autographs and smiling into camera flashes. No big deal, after a damned fine day and a great meal, I can absorb this idolatry without breaking stride.

Next morning Brad brings over the newspaper. There's a picture of Sting looking his usual handsome self surrounded by security staff, and a goofy picture of me on the streets of Santiago in the arms of the people. My Spanish is not too *hablo* but with Brad's help we discern from the article:

"Copeland demostró su célebre humor. . . ."

Well, that's promising. At least they got the humor part. But later on we get to it.

"Michelle Bachelet . . . cuatro cervezas . . . affaire con ella. . . ."

Oh boy. Reading on we get to:

"Sting . . . Bachelet . . . privada o una audiencia. . . ."

Ha-ha! Sexy ole Stingo scores! I wonder how many beers it took *her*. At the gig, in Band Dining, he shows me the trophy. For heroic services to . . . we're not sure what, he gets a big green sash and a magnificent medal, which he attaches to his bass strap. It's about three inches across, bigger even than the Chevalier des Arts that we all got in France. Oh well, maybe if I hadn't been such a knavish fool I coulda had a sash and medal, too.

▲ He gets this all the time. Check the medal on the bass strap.

CHAPTER 38

RAGING KUMBAYA

JANUARY 2008
NEW ZEALAND

Strange things happen Down Under. We're on tour with Fergie, and Rage Against the Machine is touring with Björk. Our tours are on parallel paths across the subcontinent.

Brad and I are heading for the main stage flashing passes at every layer. This isn't our show, but we have a good hand, and are making our way in when Brad's buddy on the Björk crew catches up with us. With him is Rage's tour manager. The band would like to say hello to me before they go onstage . . . any minute now. Why, sure! The festival audience is screaming with rage in the background as we head into the Rage compound, which is a group of trailers pulled into a square, laager style.

As we slip into their world I imagine that we'll be interrupting some kind of wild anger-inducing ritual. I mean what do you say to guys who are this pissed off? Here, suddenly in my face, is one of the scariest bands on earth. And hey, we're all goofballs! It turns out that back in the day they were all of an age as to be Police fodder. Before they got mad, I guess. And they are not mad now, either. We are immediately engaged in an orgy of mutual salutations of respect, slobbering our praises of one another. But it's time for them to do their show and the crew are calling, "Ready On Deck!"

Well, now that we're with the band, Brad is able to parley this all the way up onto the big stage and right to the front of the wings. We're about six inches from the edge of the light. If I stick my foot out it'll be part of the show. Now, for my humble taste in rock music, Rage Against the Machine is How You Do it. Back in L.A. I took my sons along to see them play the Forum, as a fine example of shamanistic principles. See how hard they hammer it down, my sons; this is the Right Stuff.

But I didn't realize then, from out in the audience, just how pissed off this band is. There is just *so* much Injustice in the world to be angry about. From the moment Tom starts it up, it's heavy, hard, and angry, and forty thousand kids are going nuts. We get a nice response at our shows, very emotional in fact, but this crowd of wild youth is unleavened by nostalgia. Dang! If these guys come to one of our shows, they had better do, like, eight hours of yoga first.

ALTHOUGH THERE ARE GIANT distances involved down here, it's actually a pretty small world. A couple of days later in Brisbane, floating through the marble-and-silk byways of the Palazzo Versace Hotel, who should I meet, but those heroes of the downtrodden, Rage Against, well sometimes, the Machine. This is a cultural mismatch. Now I know that I own their reputation.

Days later, on the streets of Sydney, there's their singer and angry poet Zack again. Is he . . . shopping? Did Zapata shop? Ha-*ha!* I remember when I used to be professionally angry. To be fair, even though there is Hunger and Injustice in the world, a great meal at a fancy restaurant is still a great meal, no matter how socially outraged one might be. OK, so they're extremely angry for two hours every day or so on behalf of the Unfed. It's just not healthy sometimes to fully live the life of the avatar that you create. Can you imagine being a member of Slipknot twenty-four-seven? From my hoary vantage point I forgive these lads probably more than they do themselves. It's OK to be Happy Against the Versace. I promise not to tell.

Couple of days later, my new chums are at our show. After our thing I go out to band dining to look for them and I find Tim, who has fought his way through every movie star in Australia, talking bass with Sting. Bless his heart, he's prodding Stingo about his plectrum. You see, when we were rockers, Sting used a plectrum. But every bass player reaches a stage in his or her development when they eschew the pick and pluck their fat strings with their fingers. It's just more sophisticated that way. That's how Stanley Clarke does it. There is no bass player over thirty who would be caught dead using a pick.

Problem is, Sting wrote many of our classics in that earlier, more callow, stage of his evolution. The music around a song like our "Bring on the Night" is built on that particular effect of a pick chugging up and down on the string. It's just not the same with fingers. I, like every drummer, have been pleading with my bass player to drop the sophisto and pick up the pick again, at least for a couple of songs. I love to be here now, watching the heaviest bass player of his generation hassling my guy, the heaviest musician of my generation, about it.

Back in my room over a round of tequila shots with the visitors, I'm inquiring about their reunion experience. They have a similar history of conflict in their band. Not sure what happened, singer ran off, or the band reformed with someone else. Anyway, there was drama. As I prod, I realize that we're having a little band therapy right here and now in my dressing room. The humidity is rising and I have a sudden fear that I have raked over coals that should have been left. I must heal the world.

I rise up and draw my guests to their feet. "C'mon, guys, band hug!"

They're a little leery at first but are too polite to resist. When we are all huggy and loving, a song wells up in our throats.

"Kumbaya, my Lord, Kumbaya . . . !"

We're all singing. Even Zack—who professionally as a singer doesn't sing—is singing!

My life is complete. My career is made. I actually have Rage Against the Machine singing "Kumbaya" in my casbah. It doesn't get any cooler than this.

"So, Zack, have you forgiven these assholes yet?"

"Kumbaya, my Lord. . . ."

It's all so mellow now, and we're passing around the tequila again when Brad Wilk, who has been sitting quietly, decides to throw a bomb.

"So, Stewart, did I read somewhere that you hate jazz?"

It takes a moment or two for the sacrilege of this information to penetrate the warm fuzzy atmosphere. But one by one, the Ragers process this thunderbolt and fall silent. Soon conversation has stopped. They are regarding me with baleful dread. This is my favorite cue.

"Well, yeah . . . the only problem with jazz . . . is that it sucks."

Whaa??!!!

Suddenly Love Against the Machine is raging around my silks, rending their garments, pulling their beards, and beseeching me to withdraw this blasphemy. Aw, man! This jazz gag *never* gets old.

"Yeah, you see, if you really want to be a 'musician' but have no talent, just practice for twenty hours a day and play jazz. It's almost as good as real music. Ha-ha! Because of course, jazz is the last refuge of the un—"

That's as far as I get. I now have Zack and Tim leaning forward with urgent fervor.

"Surely, you get Parker—" pleads Tim.

"No, he needs to hear some Coltrane," interrupts Zack implacably.

And they're arguing over which is the critical jazz that can save this old sinner. Coltrane? Parker? I forget which was which. Young

Wilk has climbed back into his slot, smirking darkly. When they pause for breath, I hit them with another.

"Well, I guess some jazz doesn't suck. I was brought up on Stan Kenton and Dave Brubeck...."

"*Aaarrrrggh!* Stan K-k-k-k-enton?! *That's* not jazz!" They howl with desperate indignation.

Now they're Raging against me personally. Who knew that Rage has such exquisite taste in jazz? There's only one solution. I rise up, arms outstretched.

"Kumbaya, my Lord...."

They're out of their seats in a flash, and we join in another round of this great song. Whaa*hooo!* Kumbaya! One thing about these guys, mad or glad, they do have a sense of humor. They may have crap taste in music but hanging with these guys is a total rage.

Now that we can talk, we quiz each other on what other music is cool or not. I don't want to disappoint anyone out there, so their yeas and nays are classified, but I can happily report that my good buddy Les's Primus makes the cut. It was hard to discern from up in my ivory tower, but it seems that Les was seminal to a lot of wild music.

We get talking on all kinds of things, politics mostly, and Zack generously forgives my CIA past. I promise him that my dad had *nothing* to do with Allende, Bay of Pigs, Contras, or any of the other Latin political meddling. All my daddy's dirty deeds were done in the Middle East. And he was extremely rare in his advocacy of the downtrodden Palestinians at a time when it was close to career suicide.

But there's one last ideological hurdle to overcome. I do have some plutocratic artifacts in my own past that must be faced.

"We've been through a lot together, Copeland," says Zack, son of a Mexican revolutionary. There is a glint of mischief in his eye.

"I'm just going to have to let you slide on the polo."

CHAPTER 39

SLAV ON A SLAB

JUNE 2008

Swinging through Eastern Europe.

As the Danube rolls past the river barge, and the greasy violins slice the night, my old buddies Paul Mulligan and Collin Dhillon are banging the tables and singing wildly to the Gypsy music. Andy and I are dancing the cha-cha, or whatever you would call this strange motion while the ancient Eastern melodies swirl around us. With a couple of spoons I'm able to join in the rhythm. There are maybe twenty players around us, heaving, surging, and dancing among the tables of this riverboat cafe.

We're a few miles downriver from Belgrade, beyond the glittery restaurants and down even further from the wild, throbbing, floating disco zone. We're alone on the dark river with our Gypsy friends. In the lamplight everybody is laughing or singing or banging something. I'm doing all three, forgetting briefly that this frail flesh of mine has obligations. These old bones are currently leased out to Tourzilla.

Next day in my hotel room, the price is paid for those few stolen hours of frivolous frolic. I'm admiring the skyscraper view of

Belgrade on a sunny morning-after-the-night-before as I reach over to zip up a suitcase. There is a click in my lower back that must have been audible down in the lobby, and I'm stuck. Locked in a cage of pain. I'm not aware of it yet, but I'll be pretty much holding this posture for the next week.

Brad is able to get me and my stuff down to the car because the full rigor mortis hasn't yet set in. The ride out to the airport gets the pain cycle moving, though. We've got the full flashing squealing escort; unfortunately for me, it's a particularly urgent Serbian team, but when we reach the plane I'm able to stretch out on the couch and relax off some of the spasm.

At a tiny airstrip in darkest Poland we are met by a fleet of Porsche Cayennes. On the one hand, it's pretty sleek. This is even plusher than what the German promoters send. On a better day I might have appreciated the swank of it all; but today the creamy leather bucket seats are a misery.

What's the point of a Porsche if it isn't to fly like the wind over the potholes of Poland? For forty minutes, unrelieved by traffic or traffic signals (flaming escort!) we lurch across the postcommunist tundra. By the time we get to the gig I'm sure they're going to have to cut me out of the car with a blow torch. I am locked up good.

I'm usually a good subject for chiropractors, who are generally very careful to prepare affected areas with calibrated massage and manipulation before applying their skill to specific joints. I'm optimistic that my tangle can be fixed.

The Katowice chiropractor shows up. One look at him, all mustache and gut, and it's not too hard to imagine that he's probably also the village barber, butcher, and dog catcher. He looks like a combination of Lech Wałesa and Homer Simpson.

With an air of confident authority he climbs right up onto the rickety table huffing, and without preamble drops three hundred pounds of Slav onto my back.

"Hup-*lah!!*" he shouts like the acrobat that he isn't, and lands like a cow.

"Hhyyaaaghhhnnnk!!!" I reply

The sound that we don't hear is the crunch of relief that is the signature tune of the chiropractic art. As I groan and writhe, Lech Simpson is beaming. After briefing the local staff importantly on the details of his recovery program, he exits in triumph.

Well, never mind, all I have to do now is play a show. Brad is able to go online and confirm that the evil-looking pills that the Butcher of Katowice gave us are indeed the painkillers (for humans) that I need. And that's pretty much the only remedy. I'm still in the same posture I was in when I zipped my bag this morning in Belgrade.

The show is an interesting ordeal. I'm wedged into my seat, with its backrest, so mostly I can do my job; but every now and then a reach for a distant crash cymbal will cross the wires in my back and an electric jolt of pain will paralyze me for a beat or two. Right there in front of a paying audience I'm being stabbed in the back and twisting randomly, swishing my sticks through air instead of drums. Sting and Andy chug right on and I'm able to climb back aboard the ship after a beat or two. Obvious fuckups, though.

And here's the strange thing. The crowd doesn't seem to notice! Maybe our reputation is so deep that moments of clanging chaos are thought to be artistic redefinitions of the space-time continuum. And they didn't even have to pay extra! Amazing what you can get away with when the voodoo is lit. But I'm strangely grumpy that they don't even honor my obvious pain with diminished but sympathetic applause. They're rocking along at full throttle, oblivious! Later, as we fly off into the night, Sting comes over to console me and I share this insight with him. He gets this a lot.

The voice is the most fragile instrument in music. On a world tour it's impossible to avoid the occasional sore throat. During The Police show Sting has four or five high notes that need to be hit big. They are landmarks for him. He's got to pace himself and take aim at these big ones. With a little bit of a sore throat, they are a challenge, but when he's caught onstage with real throat problems

▲ Brad in shades. Billy beyond in black shirt.

they croak big, right there in the spotlight at the focal point of everything. What amazes Sting is that the folks still cheer wildly. We're both uncomfortable with what this tells us.

In the next city, Leipzig, two hard-faced doctors come up to my room with black bags and sharp needles. They prickle me with cortisone for two days, which begins to straighten me out, but they warn me of side effects—such as irritability and flashes of temper. Good thing I'm in an environment where this won't be a problem.

CHAPTER 40

BURNING THE GOLDEN GOOSE

1984

I found this journal from back in the day.

Everything is different; nothing has changed. . . .

Life in my wildest dreams is beginning to depress me. This band is beginning to get on my nerves. It is at the apex of high but is beginning to outpace the mortal flesh. The world as we know it belongs to us, but we belong to this machine called The Police. From Bombay to Buenos Aires to Cleveland, the world, by which I mean the entire globe, is dancing under our feet. Across the continents, in all the capital cities, we perform our strange ritual and generate wild joy, then fly off into the night. We fly the seven skies and glimpse the world's great monuments as they flash by. We use them as props in our videos. The world we never see is the real world down there on the streets.

One day on my way out to the airport, the limousine takes a shortcut through a suburban neighborhood. Looking out the window at the nice, simple houses with cheerful gardens and happy pets, the thought crosses my mind that if I wasn't such a cartoon, I could live on a street like this. Right now simple pleasures just seem more appealing than exquisite adventures.

Walking down the street must feel better than all of this flying. Goofing off on a street corner seems better than the rarefied bubble that I live in.

Locked inside this bubble, Sting is getting more stir-crazy by the hour, although we're actually getting along pretty well right now. The shows are good and we've got nothing to argue about. We have all adapted easily to the opulent hotel life and have bailed out of any social contact with one another. I'm not actually sure what either of them do offstage these days. Andy is off with his cameras and Sting is nowhere to be seen.

▲ So don't even start . . .

CHAPTER 41

SINGAPORE SHOWDOWN

FEBRUARY 2008

The golden cage thing again.

There is still something not right. Andy and I get along fine. We have a healthy musical respect for each other and I can sense that he feels my pulse onstage. No matter how complicated his parts, he's always in my groove. But the point of this band is not my relationship with Andy. We're here for Sting's relationship with us.

We've been playing together for a year now and, for all of our disagreements, the crowds have been showering us with approval. Closer in, the wings are thronged with our esteemed musician peers, who are paying very close attention. With the critics we seem to be bulletproof. Rarely have so many loved so few, so much. So we're doing the right thing? On the right path?

Well, yes and no. It is a blessing beyond all blessings to be able to play this show that lights up the multitudes. Who could ask for anything more? Well, us. We're greedy to partake of the fresh new fruit that our imaginations place before us. We're all still growing. Having a sacred ritual to perform is all very good, but what do we do with new stuff? Over in my corner, I have a head full of music that is irrelevant to The Police. Or, more to the point, The Police is irrelevant to the churning, burning torrent that's swilling around, building up pressure, and becoming a big distraction after a year away from my studio.

Believe it or not, music is pretty important to the mental health of musicians. We can do it so well only because we go crazy when we don't. Bands are supposed to be—and this band certainly used to be—the perfect place to spit out new ideas as they occur, catch flyers from other talents, and run with whatever works.

My dilemma is that this just isn't the place for anything that's going on in my head. The music in my hands is what I'm here for, but the nonthinking, elemental, spiritual throb of my drums is being constantly interrupted by a cold stream of analysis and arrangement from the prophet. He has a perfect vision of what we should each be doing and my thing isn't it.

Fact is, I would starve as a session player. Even for my own film work I hire professional drummers to hit specific grooves, as the mission dictates. The only point of ever getting behind the drums

myself is to charge up a living, breathing audience, to close my eyes and look for the out groove that rocks the joint. Which is almost what I'm doing every night with The Police. Very close, but there is that constant cold current that keeps me from reaching Nirvana.

The Nirvana of which I speak is no impossible ideal, in fact it's the norm for me outside of this band. Piece of cake with the Tarantas. It is a constant irritant that I can light up the front rows but I just can't light up my bass player. He's got his own fire and that's all he needs.

His music is a cathedral of beauty, but it's implacable, unyielding, and set beautifully in stone. Whatever music he wants to make, I will definitely buy the record, but I'm the wrong guy to be playing it. There is a pink elephant, a shoe waiting to drop, a golden apple waiting to be plucked, a destiny hovering. Where is this band going?

We came together with a clear understanding that the mission is finite. Even when we started adding extensions to the tour, every added leg had a cutoff date. For the three of us it's uncomplicated. But we're surrounded by a world that is sustained by our produce. There is a momentum to this thing. Everyone wants to know what's next. There is no available point of view that shows this whole Police thing to be not an eternal golden goose.

One day I get a hunch about this. Maybe Sting still has the energy to continue harassing me after a solid year of it because he thinks he's going to be stuck with me. Maybe he's so resistant to collaboration because he sees a trap closing around him. Well, I certainly can sympathize. I've felt this constriction for a year now, but I entered it willingly, knowing that it would end. I'm still secure in this knowledge because it isn't me to whom people are looking for continuance. Folks assume that I'll be along for the ride. It's Sting who is getting the pressure.

If you love somebody, set them free. That's what Sting said the minute he was free from The Police the first time around, years ago. I think it's pretty good advice for right now, too. We love each other, so let's be free.

In a quiet moment before the show, I go over to Sting world and join him in his meditations. I've tried to formulate a coherent but untedious declaration of independence, but it just comes blurting out, something like:

"That little silvery bell has been ringing in my head for some time now. My high esteem for you has kept my hands from your throat, my axe from your handsome brow. But now I'm casting loose. You can go ahead and be as mad as you like, and I won't take offense.

"But you're going to be hearing some strange rhythms coming up behind you. Listen out for them or not. Suit yourself. With 500,000 watts of amplification and Andy to connect with, I'll be charging right on. Come along for the ride or not, I'm going home—via Nirvana.

"So I don't know what your plans are for the future, but this probably isn't the band for them. We're not the team that produced 'Roxanne' or 'Every Breath' anymore. The relationship that we have now only works in live performances—fueled by mass human frenzy. Couple of days in the studio and one of us is going to have mallets sticking out of his neck."

I have no idea at all how any of this is working or if I'm saying it right. I've known him for thirty years, but Sting is a sphinx. Maybe he doesn't believe me. I do babble earnestly from time to time, and he mostly just amiably tunes me out. There's no reason he should take this manifesto any more seriously than all of my other rantings.

Next morning, however, he surprises me by calling me in my room. Without elaboration, he thanks me. It's a short conversation and, as usual, leaves me mystified. Did he hear the part about strange rhythms? Cool thing is, there's no Sting problem anymore. Our future is untethered.

And so over the next few shows, as we tour across The Orient this new vibe sinks in. There are some flare-ups—we're both still volatile—but soon I can see that the reward of freedom is beginning to ease the punishment of chaos. By the time we get to Hawaii we are really loosening up. The two shows in Honolulu are scrappy as hell but who cares? We're trying stuff, throwing stuff back and forth. Real sparks are flying and great music is happening.

This really *is* a great band! Now I'm confused . . . no, I'm not. It's alive because it's over, because we can shrug it off. This is the same nihilism that set us free back in the day. It was the unfettered grooving in the dark under Eberhard's laser show that inspired us to open up the throttle and let the Valkyries take us.

After these Hawaiian shows we break for a month. They were supposed to be the end, but we were plushed into agreeing to one last push through Europe and the United States. I'm looking forward to it. This is going to be *much* more fun.

CHAPTER 42

TOAST IN THE MACHINE

AUGUST 2008

The fun part.

We're doing a runner tonight. We have to get out of Dodge before the roads choke up. After our last song, we wave, we bow, wave some more, then dart down the hatch into the stage, on our way to the waiting cars. At the foot of my hatch Jeff and Brad are pulling off the earpieces, head mic, wires, and power-pack belt. Then the slippery, soaking shirt. The three of us are headed for the cars, with Karen catching soggy vestments that are flying off of the retreating witch doctors. With the plugs out, my ears are suddenly back in the real world and the night is roaring.

As the multitudes ring we're escorted to the getaway cars by a festival of flashlights and a column of security. Local crew are hooting and hollering as we pass through them to the waiting squadron of vans and motorcycles. It's a giant disco of red, white, and blue flashing lights.

"Right here," says Brad, and I duck into a long, low white limousine. It's white because Billy likes to fuck with me. My colleagues are happy to pile into vans for the airport dash but I need

more space. I'm soaking wet, breathing hard, and everything within three feet of me is more breakable, including fragile fellow artists.

As the sirens wail we pull out of the gig, through the trucks and onto the highway. I'm buck-naked in towel heaven. Aaaahhh. . . .

Up the other end of the long white prom car is one of my more scurrilous buddies. He's completely in the flashing-lights moment, grinning from ear to ear with his eyes bugging out. He surrenders to fantasy, reaches into his jacket, and pulls out a spliff of marijuana.

"I've just got to do this!" he wails and lights up his cheroot.

He does have a point. It would be hard to imagine a more fitting punctuation to a Police concert. Riding with The Police, protected by the police . . . it's just screaming for a little law breaking! As he draws deep on his smoking cone, his eyes close and I can see his heart filling with love for the sirens and lights of the lawmen who surround us, who are here . . . to protect him. I'm tempted to ask the driver to radio the sheriff and ask him to slow down the posse because Mr. Copeland's guests would like to finish their joint before we get to the airport.

When we pile up the gangway onto the plane, my brethren are already there. Andy is settling into the midcabin, contentedly fussing with his cameras, books, and accoutrements. Sting is in the back with his colorful crew. I'm up at the front, where my own cronies drape themselves on the plush seats, bitterly ruing the parental advice that sent them to law school rather than down the path of rock and roll.

It's hard to recognize this band as the same three assholes who grumped out at Calgary. When we started the tour, it was all business. The three anointed ones would sit together at the front of the plane and make difficult conversation, while Billy, Phil, and

▲ Down!   Up! ▲

Brad maintained an atmosphere of funereal decorum around us. No one was allowed on the jet. No one was allowed near the stage. Even the dressing rooms and communal backstage facilities (gym, wardrobe, Band Dining, and such) were kept closed with the haloed air of a sacred grove. The Police are famously volatile. Let nothing arouse their demons.

The first crack in the armor was Sting's chum the vigilante philanthropist Bobby Sager. When he's on the plane, it's all easy company. Bobby's day job somewhere in the world is zillionaire philanthropy, but out here on the Dark Planet tour he brings us the gift of rock and roll. He just doesn't get the sacred thing. Pretty soon bringing chums aboard doesn't require three signatures and a cavity probe. Even my unpredictable friends Henry and Pete can raid Band Dining without getting Billied. My old polo chum Collin is On Tour. We all love how our civilian friends live the rock tour fantasy more than the bandsters.

So tonight there are three tinkling parties lighting up our flying tour bus as the moon carries us across the sky, over the horizon, and into the night. Just like the moon gods of yore.

THIS IS A WHOLE 'nuther tour. In Europe we're still playing stadiums and festivals, but by the time we get to our last jaunt across the United States we're into the tertiary markets. These are the places that we haven't already played ten times. Out here, instead of stadiums and arenas they have sheds, a form of venue unique to America. Half indoor, half outdoor; half seated, half wild. Since these structures are built for shows rather than games, the stages are hard-built. The bad news is that we have to leave our cool hot rod stage behind; the good news is that these stages sound fantastic. Some of them are in incredible locations, like the Gorge, in Washington state, and Red Rocks, near Denver.

There is something about how a fixed stage resonates, that connects the bass to the kick. Everything sounds better. Throw in a whole new attitude about music and we're starting to surprise again. The shackles are off and we're flying. We have deeply arranged parts of the set that Stingo can noodle with in sound check, and we have sections that are wanton chaos. Everybody's happy.

The atmosphere around the stage has loosened up. At the start of the tour Charlie would have Tazered anyone who came near the band while we were strapping up. Now it's a party.

A year ago we would urgently hug, exchange vows of love and encouragement as we waited for Charlie's nod, and then halfway through the first song of the set we'd be reaching for the flame throwers. Now we just make sure we can land a barb or two before the earplugs go in.

"You going out there in that?"

"Yeah. Is that one of Trudie's shirts?"

Sort of thing. But the music is lit. We're still hurling scatology at one another at every opportunity, but it's all sport.

STING IS STILL CAPABLE of mischief, however. One day we have a show in Las Vegas, and I take a detour to attend my son Patrick's graduation from UC Berkeley (my old alma mater). As soon as my loyal friend discovers my absence at sound check, he is straight down my hatch and sidling up to Jeff to rewrite my percussion loops. He just can't stop himself. He's a slave to music and is driven by his muses to organize every scintilla of it. This is the same arena in which, a year ago, we had a "band meeting" that was so rancorous that we missed sound check altogether. I forget what the problem was, but after yelling instead of sound checking we played one of the best shows of the tour. What is up with this band?

And don't even get me started on the time he sneaked down to the other end of the stadium to sidle up to big Mike and ask him to turn my percussion rack off in the PA. . . .

■

WHEN WE GET TO Portland, Les Claypool catches up with us and jumps aboard the tour for a couple of days. Les was a big Police fan back when he was a kid, which is one of the reasons that he called me to produce that Primus track years ago when I first met him. But in the post-Police years he didn't quite get Sting's solo work—took violent exception to it, in fact. Many were the times on the Oysterhead tour that I had to patiently explain to Les and Trey that if they knew Sting personally, or if they ever played music with him they would love and respect him as I do.

Sting's only awareness of Les is that he's another of my bass buddies (of which I have more than any other kind of buddy) and that one of my favorite T-shirts is Claypool swag. Sometimes the tiniest thing will motivate the most inspired show. Put Eric Clapton or Jeff Beck in the audience and Andy will burn down the house. Stingo is similarly affected. He doesn't need to know the pedigree—it's one of Stewart's guys, so let's show 'em who's boss. And at the Portland show Sting *is* the bass god. He's not too shabby as a singer either, but tonight he's on *bass*.

Les is won over completely. After our show he's ready to completely overlook "Desert Rose" *and* the lute. Like I said, Sting might be handsome and highbrow, but he's a motherfucker on that bass. No denying it. Les doesn't get the chance to share any of this love with Sting himself because we're staying in Portland tonight and have different places to go.

Next day there is strange weather at the back of the jet, and when Les goes past the bass god to grab a sandwich from the kitchen, the handsome jaw is set and the eyes averted. This causes some mystification but never mind, it's just a short ride up to the Gorge, where we're going to play one of the most spectacular venues in America.

Today is a sound check party, which means that a dozen or so contest winners are invited to attend our afternoon ritual. Things have become so casual that Sting has taken to inviting the fans up onto the stage to sing the songs while we play. It's actually something that we all enjoy. Having the folks around us gaping at the technology and cool stage stuff reminds us of how cool our job is. Today our job is particularly cool because the stage is set on the lip of a spectacular gorge and we're surrounded by huge natural scenery. As Sting pulls up the foxiest and least foxy babes to sing next to him on the mic, the thought crosses my mind, wouldn't it be great to get Les up here on The Police stage for a jam? Hah! That would be a whole new kind of awkward!

There is one fan this afternoon who suddenly, out of nowhere, hits the mic with a strong beautiful voice that echoes around the empty amphitheater and across the gorge. Dang! It's a big Cinderella moment and Sting invites her to sing "Don't Stand So Close to Me" at tonight's show.

Tonight Les is even more impressed. So am I, it really is a great show. But on the plane there is another brush-off. It's just one of those strange awkward moments of wrong timing. Sting can be, oddly, a tricky man to compliment. Some of his most explosive outbursts have been in response to mistimed praise. I have had my head torched many times for simply expressing satisfaction with a show. Oh well. After an unsuccessful attempt to communicate his approval Les saunters back up to the front whistling one of his strange tunes. It occurs to me that good old cuddly Claypool can be quite intimidating himself if you don't know him. Is this a time to pull out "Kumbaya"? Nah . . . Les is fine, Sting is fine . . . never mind.

So it's fine. But when we land and are leaving the plane, there is that inevitable little bottleneck at the forward passageway. Pressed a little too close together are two giants of the bass guitar. Les is impassive, but as host, Sting maybe feels a little obligation to break the ice. It's a little late, but better late than never, so Sting warmly delivers a little yoga tummy tap to his unexpecting guest.

Now, Les, as he'll proudly tell you, comes from a long line of car mechanics. The tummy tap is not a part of his cultural vocabulary. Before he can even register surprise, Stingo is down the gangway and gone.

Well now, Les is not so fine. What was *that?* He has been around the block many times in his rich and varied life, but no man ever gave him a tummy tap. All the way into San Francisco, Brad and I are reassuring him that nothing was meant by it. Yoga type people do it all the time. I even tap Brad a couple of times just to show how harmless it is. Les is unconvinced. He just can't imagine that so much talent can reside in such an inscrutable figure.

A few days later we have another buddy, Matt Stone, along for the ride and the whole experience is different. The timing is good! Matt, Sting, and Andy get along fine! Brad and I get a little carried away with the contrasting adventures and pretty soon we're scheming. It was Les after all who first introduced me to Matt years ago. By the time Les hears the tale from Brad, Matt, and me, it has evolved a little.

According to this new version, Matt's life has been transformed. Sting and he bonded immediately. Matt ditched Brad and me and spent the whole trip in the back of the plane doing yoga and breathing exercises with the golden one. Sting is teaching him how to play the lute. *South Park* is ruined!

■

WE'VE BEEN OUT HERE for a year and a half, and my, how things have changed. It took a while but I do believe we have arrived at the promised land. This is how it was always supposed to be. I get to go onstage with two titans of music playing songs that (1) are beautiful songs that beguile and challenge us night after night and (2) are hymns of glory to the gathered masses. Music that is known has a particular potency. If it has cool musical rips and curls, that raises the temperature, but when you get to play challenging and popular music with challenging and inspiring players this is as good as it gets. I'm playing with the big Tonka toys.

The first campaigns of the tour were about an enormous nostalgic reunion for an enormous number of people. It was about the flashing lights and the three-ring circus. This part is about a much deeper ritual of music. These shed audiences are very close up and we can feel, in this intimate environment, that every nuance has power. These are still big shows and the big gestures are still big, but the little things work, too. Tiny little nuggets of music protein can gladden the heart. Moments of repose can enchant and entrance. It's OK to cruise. And since we're cruising, when we let rip, it has a more focused fury. We're starting to surprise ourselves again. "Roxanne" is still "Roxanne" but there are whole new subplots weaving and turning every night.

The walk from silks to stage is a migrating party. When we get to the wings, our friends and guests keep on choogling around us. Charlie is doing the cha-cha with Bobby. He sniffs the air for the perfect timing to start the show. When the vibe is right . . .

"Roll Bob."

And the preshow rolls like clockwork. Only now, with Bob Marley tipping off the ceremony, we're easy skanking. Everybody is dancing. My percussion riser with the big gong doesn't rise on this stage. This is a regular flat stage and our gear is all just sitting there. Two amps and a drum set. After my lightshow with Charlie, Dug, and Chris, I just walk out there, jump up onto the riser, and pound the gong. Minutes later we're grooving on a regular stage like a regular band. Take away the nostalgia and the blizzard of production and we're on a level playing field. Just a band. But guess what. This is a much better band. I would pay money to go see this band. Probably even stay for the whole show.

It's amazing to remember the tensions of that first year. What were we doing to ourselves that churned us up like that? My theory is that the juju was so strong that it almost ate the witch doctors. Kinetic ritual is a two-way street. Our music gives us power but also has power over us. This music, with its long history, is very powerful.

CHAPTER 43

ELVIS IS LEAVING THE BUILDING

AUGUST 2008

Elvis Costello is not happy. He clearly doesn't like to have to do this, but he's dragged himself into my dressing room to pitch me on The Police appearance on his new TV show. It's a tough sell because the proposed recording falls on the second-to-last day of the tour. It's the day after three shows in a row and the day before our last ever show. I just know that no one will be in a mood for work that day.

So Elvis, all scarf and spectacles, is working me over. He looks like he's chewing toads. The flattery is finely calibrated, and I know why; he and Sting were spotted in a huddle earlier today and Elvis was no doubt getting driving instructions from Stingo. Those singer/songwriter guys might be jealous as hell of each other, but they're still thick as thieves.

This is actually our first chance to chat after touring together for some months. Everyone else in the Costello band and crew are like familiar tribal cousins. I had never met any of them before but they are the guys, or at least just like the guys that I grew up with

▲ Billy (lurking), Karen, Elvis, Elvis, Danny Q, Charlie, Elvis

in London. Elvis and The Attractions played all the same pubs and clubs that we did, carried their gear up and down the same beer-soaked steps, got hailed or hazed by the same journalists, ripped off by the same promoters, and had double-egg-sausage-chips-beans-and-a-slice at the same motorway diners. We were rivals back in the day so we didn't mix much then, but we're cozy now.

All except for Elvis himself. He's kind of a mystery. My hearty attempts at greetings have been met with uncomfortable evasion. There is a category of people in my life that is defined by a cautious body language in my presence. Such people adopt a defensive crouch, or evasively lean away as if to avoid catching beer or spittle from me. My jerky body movement and callow social style threaten such people, and with good reason. They are a magnet for my moving elbow, and they know it. They just know I'm going to spill my drink on them—and I usually do. Sting and Elvis are both in this category.

But one thing I can be sure of is that Elvis is an extremely clever man and the concept for the show that he's describing is persuasive. If he's doing it, it'll probably be way cool. Anyway, the answer was already yes from the moment he walked in. For the man who wrote "I Don't Want to Go to Chelsea," the answer is yes, and he can adopt any posture that makes him comfortable.

One reason that the shows have gone well on this leg of the tour is the big effect of Costello's band (now called "The Imposters") before we even get to the stage. They tear the place up and when we come out, the joint is already rocking. Also, to be surrounded by these tribal cousins reminds us of where we came from. It deflates the sacred temple that has been built around us. We're still swaddled in silk, but laughter is allowed. Goofy inconsequential banter is allowed. *I'm* allowed.

Steve Nieve, the Imposter keyboardist, has an idea of how we can make a hybrid arrangement of "Walking on the Moon" and "Watching the Detectives," so our sound checks on this last leg have merged. Instead of two sound checks for two bands, we just roll all the gear onstage and jam away the afternoon with two drummers, bassists, and guitarists, plus keyboards. It started out with just the medley that we had to organize for the TV show. But then another agenda cropped up. We want to throw in some extras for our last show at Madison Square Garden and have arrived at "Purple Haze" and "Sunshine of Your Love" as a kind of tribute to the great three-piece bands that went before us. So after running through "Walking on the Detectives," it's time to work out the extras for MSG. But the vibe is so mellow that no one wants to tell The Imposters to leave the stage. So when Andy hits the Hendrix riff, all seven players get on the groove. We actually fit together very well; it's that tribal connection. We come from the same place. It's the London sound. Even the two bandleaders fit together, still thick as thieves even though they have to share the baton.

It's the final countdown, counting the hours of stage time between now and last show shower. Twelve hours, ten hours, eight hours . . . we're all getting giddy. We're loving every second of this even as we gloat over every second burned. It's like the end of the perfect holiday in paradise. No matter how splendid the sojourn, it's time to go home.

The last shows of the tour proper are out on Long Island, NY. Then there will be the TV taping and then the last Police show ever, at Madison Square Garden in New York City. As a parting shot we raid the Costello stage during their show, dressed as three Elvises. Ha-*ha!* We dance around them while they play and enjoy a little simulated River Dance all over Elvis's foot pedals. Sting looks cool even in black wig and Elvis goggles.

Next day it's just two more hours of stage time—except for the TV show that Elvis slicked us into. It turns out to be the perfect way to spend our last day together. The music part is a breeze, and we even tape some of our seven-piece Hendrix and Cream, just for the fun of it. We spend the afternoon in the green room, watching the monitors and taking turns at interviews with Elvis in front of the small theater audience. There's a lot of happiness to ponder as we cheerfully throw brickbats at whoever is upstairs on camera.

The band gag of the last week has been that we look for opportunities to fire one another. "You're fired!" is our favorite refrain. We actually used to be pretty snappy with our band repartee but this whole tour we have hardly ever done a three-shot interview. This time, with Elvis as referee, the three blond heads manage to speak with one coherent voice: "You're fired!"

NOW IT REALLY IS just two hours of showtime before this band is over. Backstage at the MSG, in The Police pipe-and-drape world, the rooms are all clacking with good cheer. The B-52's hit the stage and wake up the house.

▲ The love circle

We've played here quite a few times this tour and way in the past, too. There was one time that the band vibe was so grim that each member had to be nursed up to the stage by teams of physical and spiritual therapists, murmuring incantations and rattling bones.

This time I've got Collin, Bruce, Rob, Mulligan, and even my son Scott, who has flown up from Alabama. My beautiful daughters, Eve, Grace, and Celeste are bouncing around the silks. Fiona has been wrangling the guest list from hell. One of our guests is Deborah Lin and her fiancé, Jim. I had fun describing them to Brad as a beautiful, tall supermodel with her boyfriend who looks kind of like Tony Soprano. He doesn't have much trouble picking her out of the crowd, and her friend looks *just* like Tony Soprano because Jim turns out to be James Gandolfini. The high point of the whole tour for Brad was to get an Italian neck clasp and kiss on the cheek from James. Even better than a Sting tummy tap.

The show itself has a few extra bells and whistles, best of which is the NYPD Drum Line, which kicks off the set with a crashing cadence based on "Message in a Bottle." The front rows are a combination of all the friends and fans that have been touring the world with us. Everybody is happy. There's not a trace of happy-sad. When we get to the end of the set, it's with the same relief as usual that I pull out my earplugs, swagger to the front of the stage, and wave good-bye. Thank you! Good *night!*

Then it's down the hatch and good-bye cool techno stage, good-bye blue Police drums, see you back in L.A. Jeff, and hello last show shower!

AFTERWORD

THE GREEN FLAG

2009

Since I'm too lazy to study physics, I've invented my own cosmology.

What is this shaman thing that I keep talking about? What does it have to do with music and why has it thrown me into so many of these adventures? To explain it I need to talk for a minute about kinetic ritual.

When humans gather together and shout or sing or dance as one body, there is a communal shift in brain chemistry. A collective human energy is ignited. It's not an energy like light or sound or "divine spirit," it's the raw horsepower of a united pack of humans. When we stomp or hoot together we unite. We can feel it and we are evolved to like it when this happens. As a coordinated pack, we can devour an individual or a smaller or less coordinated pack.

I'm making this up by the way, but I'm sure that instinct and brain chemistry must have something to do with it. Kinetic ritual releases the I'm-with-my-pack brain wave—which we like. We can jump higher and run faster when we feel that collective energy around us.

The part that I'm not making up is that to be at the focal point of the attention of massed humans is to be infused with some kind of extra power. Just on a raw horsepower level there is some kind of upgrade going on. Maybe it's something about how the body burns calories; the car just goes faster. Mentally as well, feats of coordination are enhanced by the pulse of collective consciousness. The fingers wiggle with increased coordination when in tune with the kinetic ritual.

So kinetic ritual is what happens when a group of humans stomp and hoot, or sing or march or dance together. Everybody likes the feeling of communal empowerment. This must be why we musicians, sports stars, actors, and politicians can make our livings. We draw humans together and charge them up.

My Pygmy friend, the Congo shaman, with his hoots and stomps, arouses the combined power of his little pack of humans and Barack Obama uses ritual imagery in soaring cadence to combine the power of millions of humans. Music is both a by-product of and catalyst for this phenomenon.

There is a green flag that is following us around the world. I recognize the insignia; it's my Rhythmatist rampant on green logo. Two images were sliced together in a recreative Photoshop moment to produce a handy logo for the fan-site, and now it has become a woven image. Not as grievous as a graven image perhaps, but near enough to ponder a behavior that is so feared by God as to be specifically banished in the Ten Commandments. There is a whiff of kinetic ritual in this behavior.

Something motivates a community of people that stretches around the world to send this green artifact on a tour parallel but distinct from The Police tour. It's not hard to imagine the lighthearted fun of this ritual behavior but why *is* it fun? Why is it fun to play with this flag as if it is sacred, to revere it, to sign it, and behold it as it travels across the land?

The flag is a manifestation of the human desire to be connected to a community. Part of that connection is the traffic in shared icons or . . . graven images.

My theory is that this recreation idolatry is a semivestigial trait derived from our nature as pack animals. We herd. We tend toward cooperation. This cooperation is greased by physical cues, which at one extreme are verbal discourse, but at the other extreme are dance and music. Ritual bypasses logic and motivates instinctive communal activity.

Maybe a by-product (ritual) of this by-product (music) is that which God so fears—worship. It's not the real worship of a real religion, but it playfully mimics the behavior. In the cult of the Rock Demigod, I'm an atheist, but it sure feels natural to behave like an acolyte. It doesn't matter how many dickhead guitarists I have known, when Jeff Beck walks in the room, I'm ready to start worshipping, and all I know about him is guitar mojo.

I hope God isn't too mad at us for all of this. The folks at the concerts aren't bowing down so much as rising up in exultation, but I'm just saying that I have an idea of what it feels like to be a golden calf.

Whatever is the meaning of this mojo, when the voodoo rises, people go into that ritual mode that bypasses logic, and strange things happen.

▲ Children of the flag. The original is on a stand behind the drums.

▲ This is who I really am.

APPENDIX

ISKANDAR—My childhood friend from the age of four to fourteen, when we lived in Beirut from 1955 to 1965. He was the son of a Palestinian refugee who worked for our family as maid, nanny, and cook.

MILES COPELAND, JR.—My father, an agent for the Central Intelligence Agency and founding member of its predecessor, the OSS. He worked in London and throughout the Middle East and played a critical role in U.S. activities in Syria, Egypt, Iraq, Iran, and Ghana. After retirement he wrote books. He died in 1991. I credit him for much of my musical appreciation and aptitude. He was a gifted musician himself, playing trumpet in his younger years under Glenn Miller, Charlie Barnet, and Ray Noble.

MILLFIELD SCHOOL—A cutting-edge Hogwarts and the coeducational boarding school in England where I spent most of my high school years, from 1967 to 1969.

MILES COPELAND III—My oldest brother, a manager, film executive producer, and a music impresario who founded the BTM record label and later, I.R.S. Records. As a promoter, he helped get The Police signed to a major contract and later managed Sting for many years.

IAN COPELAND—My other brother, a leading promoter and booking agent who helped ignite the New Wave movement in the United States. As a talent agent, he represented some of the most famous bands in rock history, including The B-52s, The Cure, Simple Minds, The Go-Gos, Nine Inch Nails, and R.E.M. He died in 2006, at age fifty-six, from melanoma.

LORRAINE (LENNIE) COPELAND—My sister, a filmmaker, author and now co-owner of the Ono Store and Café in Ono, California, population: single digits. Her 1988 book, Going International: How to Make Friends and Deal Effectively in the Global Marketplace, was a bestseller.

LORRAINE ADIE COPELAND—My mother, an archaeologist who specialized in the Paleolithic period and wrote extensively. Her books have always stopped me at the second word. They start with "The," followed by an unpronounceable fourteen-syllable word. She is Scottish and a naturalized American citizen who worked for British intelligence during World War II. She now lives in France.

KIM PHILBY—The British double agent who spied for the Soviet Union after World War II and became a friend of my dad in Beirut. I was friends with his son, Harry, before the entire Philby family disappeared in 1963, only to resurface years later in Moscow.

SAN DIEGO SCHOOL OF CREATIVE AND PERFORMING ARTS—A public arts magnet school where kids take specialized classes in theater, music, dance, the visual arts, video production, and stagecraft. It's where I first studied music composition under Dr. Mary K. Phillips, my teacher.

FRANCIS FORD COPPOLA—The famed director of The Godfather series and producer or director of dozens of other films. He called me out of the blue in 1985 when he was looking for someone to write music for Rumble Fish, which he was directing. I learned later that one of his kids had told him, "Hey, get that drummer guy from The Police." Francis always listens to his kids.

JEFF SEITZ—Despite his training as a classical musician (at Juilliard), Jeff joined me as a drum tech and became a recording engineer and coproducer thirty years ago and never left. He still sets up my drums wherever I need them, although we both barely remember how.

SONJA KRISTINA—Actress, singer, my former wife (1982 to 1991), mother of my first three children, she was the vocalist for Curved Air and continues to collaborate as half of a duo known as Mask, with another Brit, Marvin Ayres.

DARRYL WAY—British rocker, composer, and founding member of Curved Air, best known as a violinist, making the group one of the first rock bands to use one. The other original members were Francis Monkman (keybords, guitar), Sonja Kristina (vocals), Florian Pilkington-Miksa (drums), and Rob Martin (bass). Later members included Mick Jacques, Phil Kohn, and Tony Reeves. I played on two of their albums.

PAUL MULLIGAN—My brother Ian's best friend from our days in Beirut, he's a private businessman who put up £400 for "Fall Out," the first single released by The Police. He now operates 247 Jet, a corporate jet charter firm in Surrey, England.

NIGEL GREY—Grammy Award winner, recording engineer (extraordinaire) and producer for The Police's first two albums. He also produced albums for Siouxsie and the Banshees, Wishbone Ash, and lots of other groups.

KIM TURNER—He was the first tour manager for The Police, whose prime mission was (and he generally succeeded) keeping three blond heads from murdering one another. He was more like The Police referee.

BUDDY RICH—My first drummer idol and a master of technique, whichever one he used. He played with the biggest swing bands and stars of the 1940s and 1950s and continued performing through the 1980s. Once, at the Grammy Awards, he asked me for my autograph, for his daughter, Cathy. Imagine that.

JEAN-PIERRE DUTILLEUX—A filmmaker of the Fourth World who brought Sting and his wife, Trudie Styler, to the Brazilian rainforest in 1988 and was the founder of what is now known as the Rainforest

Foundation Fund. He was cowriter with me on the 1985 film, The Rhythmatist, on which my brother Miles was executive producer.

MOHAMED KHASHOGGI—An actor, producer, director, and son of the Turkish-Saudi arms dealer, Adnan Khashoggi, who was caught up in the Iran-Contra scandal. The family ranch in Kenya became the set of the Dutilleux film.

KULDIP DHILLON—"Sooty," to his chums although I variously know him as "Collin," "Kollin," "Kuldip," "The Hammer of Punjab" or "Damn it, where's the ball?!" One of my best friends, a polo-playing teammate and godfather to my daughter Eve. He's a real estate developer in England, whose son, Satnam, a partner in the family firm, plays polo at a professional level alongside the Prince of Wales and his sons.

MICHAEL SMUIN—Tony and Emmy Award–winning choreographer and codirector of the San Francisco Ballet for twelve years though 1985, a period that included Lear, a ballet I wrote and Victoria Morgan choreographed. Michael and I collaborated on Rumble Fish. He died in 2007.

DAVID BAMBERGER—A founder and general director of the Cleveland Opera, which became Opera Cleveland in 2006. It was home to the 1989 world premiere of my first opera, Holy Blood and Crescent Moon, just one of two hundred productions he has staged around the world. These days, he's head of the Cleveland Institute of Music's Opera Theater.

SUSAN SHIRWEN—Librettist for Holy Blood and Crescent Moon, which was loosely based on the theory that Jesus married Mary Magdalene, producing a short line of Frankish kings and a long line of mythology, not to mention The Da Vinci Code.

KATHY SCHENKER—Publicist for The Police and my first opera, Holy Blood and Crescent Moon, staged at the Cleveland Opera in 1989. She replaced my brother Miles as Sting's manager.

MY COPELANDS—Fiona and I have been married since 1991. We have three daughters together, Eve, Grace, and Celeste, and they are sisters to my three sons with my former wife, Sonja Kristina—Sven, Jordan, and Scott—as well as to Patrick, whose mother is Marina Guinness, a lass from Ireland. I'm also Grandpa to Sven's daughter, Kaya, and father-in-law to Jordan's wife, Ami.

JONATHAN MOORE—A renowned British stage actor, playwright, librettist, and opera director for film and television, he was Billy the Kid (and screenwriter) to my Jesse James (and music) in Horse Opera, a 1993 made-for-TV show commissioned by Channel 4 in London. The director was Bob Baldwin.

LES CLAYPOOL—Founder and leader of Primus, he's a master of the electric bass and developer of a distinctive slap technique. He teamed with me and Trey Anastasio of Phish to create Oysterhead, and later wrote and directed the jam band mockumentary, Electric Apricot: Quest for Festeroo, in which he played Lapland "Lapdog" Miclovich. Since then, he's written a book, appeared on-screen again, and composed songs for the Wii game Mushroom Men. The original Primus was Les, guitarist Todd Huth, and a drum machine. These days, it's Les, guitarist Larry LaLonde, and drummer Tim Alexander.

TREY ANASTASIO—Drummer, guitarist, and a founding member in 1983 of Phish, along with drummer Jon Fishman, guitarist Jeff Holdsworth, and bassist Mike Gordon. All but Holdsworth remain, his place now taken by vocalist and keyboard player Page McConnell. After a five-year hiatus, the band regrouped with an extended tour. Their fans are ecstatic.

GENE PROVENCIO—Former artists' relations officer for Tama drums, expanding their appeal beyond hard rock and heavy metal, he's now president and CEO of his own company, ProCymbal Inc., which makes products to keep cymbals clean. They're used by guys like Lars Ulrich of Metallica and Brian Frasier-Moore, drummer for Christina Aguilera and Madonna. He continues to serve as an independent consultant in the drumming world.

VITTORIO COSMA—Composer, arranger, and artistic director of La Notte della Taranta. Our band there was called Gizmo, and it included some of Europe's best musicians: Armand Sabal-Lecco, Max Gazzè, Mauro Refosco, and Dodo, as well as Dave Fiuczynski, an American guitarist best known as the leader of The Screaming Headless Torsos.

BRAD SANDS—Tour manager for Oysterhead, who had started with Trey Anastasio, the Phish guitarist. He also worked on The Police reunion tour.

MAURO COLOMBO—Tour manager for Gizmo and an emerging director.

SERGIO BLASI—Mayor of Melpignano, Italy, who made me an honorary citizen. So, he's my mayor!

DEREK POWER—My manager and friend of almost thirty years. He has represented actors, directors, novelists, screenwriters, and film composers, and has produced eight films of his own, including my 2006 Sundance entry, Everyone Stares: The Police Inside Out.

DEAD LIKE ME—A comedy-drama television series about soul saving on Showtime that starred Mandy Patinkin. I wrote the music. It ran two seasons, 2003 and 2004.

ENSEMBLEBASH—A British percussion quartet, formed in 1992 and influenced by the music of West Africa to create performances of contemporary classical, jazz, and musical theater.

INCUBUS—An alternative band from Southern California, formed in 1991, with three original members still active: Brandon Boyd (vocals, guitar, percussion), Mike Einziger (vocals, piano), and Jose Pasillas II (drums, percussion). Other current members are Chris Kilmore (turntables, keyboards) and Ben Kenney (bass). Andy

Summers and I joined them in 2004 for a show in L.A., playing some of The Police hits.

ANJELICA HUSTON—The great film actress, she directed the 2005 TV movie I scored, Riding the Bus with My Sister, which starred Rosie O'Donnell and Andie MacDowell. Rosie executive produced along with Larry Sanitsky.

MICHAEL THOMPSON—A great session guitarist who has contributed to many of my scores. In 1988 he played in the band I formed with Stanley Clarke, Animal Logic.

JUDD MILLER—A master of the electronic valve instrument, he's played on or scored hundreds of films and television shows, including twenty with me.

JESCA HOOP—Once a nanny for Tom Waits's children, she is a gifted singer, songwriter, and composer with a strong following in Southern California. I played drums on her debut album, Kismet.

FOO FIGHTERS—A group started in 1995 by post-Nirvana Dave Grohl, a virtual one-man band, who sings and plays guitar, piano, bass, and drums, although not at once. The current nucleus of the band includes three regulars, bassist Nate Mendel, who joined him at the beginning, Taylor Hawkins (drums), and Chris Shiflett (rhythm guitar), who joined in the late 1990s.

ARMAND SABAL-LECCO—The deepest bass player of all my many bass-playing friends. He's from Cameroon; his work with Paul Simon drew the attention of President Bill Clinton, who invited him to play at his 1993 inauguration. Armand has collaborated with a mighty list of musicians, including Peter Gabriel, Mike Stipe, Carole King, Stanley Clarke, Herbie Hancock, and your humble correspondent.

RAIZ—An Italian singer, former member of Almamegretta, a world reggae band from Naples, Italy. Raiz, a.k.a. Rino, left the band in 2003 to pursue a solo career.

MAX ABRAMS—My first big-time drum teacher and the author of fifty jazz tutorial books. I studied under him in London in 1966.

SERGIO FANTON—My drum technician for La Notte della Taranta and Gizmo tours and owner of a musical equipment rental empire, Notak.

STANLEY CLARKE—One of America's greatest jazz bassists, he has recorded dozens of solo and collaborative albums and written music for scores of feature films and television shows. He has also produced albums for stars like Natalie Cole, Marilyn McCoo, and Maynard Ferguson. He and I formed the group Animal Logic after The Police broke up, and we recorded two albums together, in 1989 and 1991.

GIOVANNI POLLASTRI, EUGENIO BRAMBILLA, LADY P—Friends, fans, and designers/maintainers of my Web site. Giovanni has been collecting news and pictures since 1980, which he later used to create an online community of fans. He sometimes serves as assistant promoter in Italy. As the graphics specialist, Eugenio is the architect of the Web site, designing and maintaining everything that appears on it as well as stuff like T-shirts and DVD/CD covers. Lady P, whose real name is Paola Attolino, is a researcher in linguistics at the University of Salerno and mater familias of the lyrics page on http://stewartcopeland.net, where she offers critical analyses of my lyrics.

AMY GREY—Founder of the publicity firm Dish Communications, she handled my film, Everyone Stares: The Police Inside Out and The Police reunion tour.

DOREEN RINGER ROSS—Vice president for Film and Television Relations at BMI, which represents me as a composer.

EBERHARD SCHOENER—He's a German composer, conductor, arranger, keyboardist, and conceiver of the outlandish. His recording with me, Sting, and Andy Summers was critical to the musical evolution of The Police. He began his musical life as a violinist and was the first to tour a Balinese gamelan orchestra in the West.

OLAF KÜBLER—A blues and jazz saxophonist in Schoener's band.

BILLY FRANCIS—Tour manager for The Police through our breakup in 1984. A Londoner, he stayed with Sting and returned as band manager for our reunion tour. He was more our consigliere, but his official title was tour manager.

PHIL DOUGHERTY—Guitar technician for Bono of U2, he was responsible for the one guitar Bono used. He later became Andy Summers's tour manager for The Police reunion.

ARGENTINA PRESIDENT CRISTINA FERNÁNDEZ DE KIRCHNER—The wife of the former president, Néstor Kirchner, she became the country's first elected female president in 2007 and second since Eva Perón served in the 1970s. She's serving a four-year term through 2011, which means I'll have plenty of time to say something else that requires an apology.

PRESIDENT MICHELLE BACHELET OF CHILE—The daughter of a brigadier general who died under torture after Augusto Pinochet came to power in a 1973 coup, she and her mother were later detained and tortured before their release in 1975. A pediatrician and epidemiologist by training, she served as Minister of Health and Defense Minister under President Ricardo Lagos and in 2006 was elected as the first female president of her country. It's doubtful she'll ever have a beer with me.

RAGE AGAINST THE MACHINE—Politically active band from Los Angeles, whose cast remains unchanged since its formation in 1991: vocalist Zack de la Rocha, guitarist Tom Morello, bassist Tim Commerford, and drummer Brad Wilk. One of the most influential

American bands for its political activism, RATM has always railed against U.S. foreign and domestic policies, using their music for social activism.

BILL ZYSBLAT—Accountant to the greats, including The Eagles, Simon & Garfunkel, and The Rolling Stones. Sting, too. He was the producer of The Police Reunion Tour (promoted by Live Nation).

STEWART COPELAND'S RAP SHEET

1973 Frolkhaven—At the Apex of High (Private Press LP)

Curved Air
1975 Midnight Wire
1976 Airborne

Klark Kent
1980 Klark Kent (10" Green Vinyl)
1995 Kollekted Works

The Police
1978 Outlandos d'Amour
1979 Reggatta de Blanc
1980 Zenyatta Mondatta
1981 The Police in the East/ The Police Around the World (DVD)
1981 Ghost in the Machine
1983 Synchronicity
1983 The Synchronicity Concert (DVD)
1986 Every Breath You Take—The Singles
1990 Their Greatest Hits
1993 Message in a Box (4 Disc Box Set)
1995 Live! (2 Disc Box Set)
1995 Every Breath You Take—The Classics
1996 Greatest Hits
1997 The Very Best of Sting and The Police
2007 The Police (Best Of) (2 Disc Set)
2008 Certifiable—Live in Buenos Aires 2007 (2 DVD + 2 CD Set)

Stewart Copeland
1985 The Rhythmatist
1988 The Equalizer and Other Cliff Hangers
1997 From *Rumble Fish* to *Gridlock'd* (Promotional Compilation)
2003 Orchestralli with Orchestra Ueca, Milano (DVD/CD)

2004 La Notte della Taranta (DVD/CD)
2007 Stewart Copeland: Anthology

Animal Logic
1989 Animal Logic
1991 Animal Logic II

Oysterhead
2001 The Grand Pecking Order

Soundtracks
Rumble Fish (1983)
9½ Weeks (1986)
Out of Bounds (1986)
Wall Street (1988)
Talk Radio (1988)
Earth Girls Are Easy (1989)
Noah's Ark (1990)
Men at Work (1990)
Rapa Nui (1994)
Silent Fall (1994)
Highlander II (1995)
Boys (1996)
The Leopard Son (1996)
The Pallbearer (1996)
Four Days in September (1998)
Very Bad Things (1998)
Little Boy Blue (1998)
Pecker (1998)
Simpatico (1999)
Boys and Girls (2000)

Composer Credits
1986 "King Lear," San Francisco Ballet, Michael Smuin
1988 "Emilio," Trento Ballet, Italy
1989 "Holy Blood and the Crescent Moon," Cleveland Opera (1992 Fort
    Worth Opera)
1992 "Horse Opera," Opera for Channel 4, United Kingdom
1993 "Noah's Ark/Solcheeka," Seattle Symphony Orchestra
1994 "Casque of Amontillado," Holders Easter Season, Barbados
1994 (and 1999) "Prey," Ballet Oklahoma
1999 "Kaya, Eve, and Grace," Catania Music Festival
2003 "La Notte della Taranta," Melpignano, Puglia (CD/DVD)
2008 "Celeste," Savannah Music Festival, featuring Daniel Hope (violin)

2009 "Retail Therapy," La Jolla Music Society's Summerfest
2009 "Ben Hur Live," European arena tour, score by Copeland

Film

1984 *Rumblefish*. Starring Matt Dillon. Directed by Francis Ford Coppola. Written by S. E. Hinton and Francis Ford Coppola. Executive producer, Francis Ford Coppola. MCA/Universal. [Best Score, Golden Globe nominee, 1984]

1985 *The Rhythmatist*. Starring Stewart Copeland. Written and directed by Jean-Pierre Dutilleux.

1986 *Out of Bounds*. Starring Anthony Michael Hall. Directed by Richard Tuggle. Written by Tony Kayden.

1987 *She's Having a Baby*. Starring Kevin Bacon and Elizabeth McGovern. Written and directed by John Hughes. Executive producer, Ronald Colby. Paramount.

1987 *Wall Street*. Starring Michael Douglas, Charlie Sheen, and Daryl Hannah. Directed by Oliver Stone. Written by Stanley Weiser and Oliver Stone. Producer, Edward R. Pressman. 20th Century Fox.

1988 *The Jogger* (short). Starring Terry O'Quinn. Written and directed by Robert Resnikoff.

1988 *Earth Girls Are Easy*. Starring Gina Davis, Jeff Goldblum, and Jim Carrey. Directed by Julien Temple.

1988 *Talk Radio*. Starring Eric Bogosian. Directed by Oliver Stone. Written by Eric Boogosian and Oliver Stone. Executive producers, Greg Strangis and Sam Strangis. Universal.

1989 *See No Evil, Hear No Evil*. Starring Richard Pryor and Gene Wilder. Directed by Arthur Hiller. Written by Earl Barret, Arne Sultan, and Marvin Worth. Executive producers, Earl Barret, Burtt Harris, and Arne Sultan. TriStar.

1990 *Hidden Agenda*. Starring Frances McDormand, Brian Cox, Brad Dourif, and Mai Zetterling. Directed by Ken Loach. Written by Jim Allen. Executive producers, John Daly and Derek Gibson. MGM.

1990 *Men at Work*. Starring Charlie Sheen and Emilio Estevez. Written and directed by Emilio Estevez. Executive producers, Moshe Diamant and Irwin Yablans.

1990 *Taking Care of Business*. Starring James Belushi and Charles Grodin. Directed by Arthur Hiller. Written by Jill Mazursky and Jeffrey Abrams. Executive producer, Paul Mazursky. Touchstone.

1990 *The First Power*. Starring Lou Diamond Phillips. Written and directed by Robert Resnikoff. Executive producer, Robert W. Cort. MGM.

1991 *Highlander II*. Starring Sean Connery and Virginia Madsen. Directed by Russell Mulcahy. Written by Gregory Widen, Brian Clemens, William

Panzer, and Peter Bellwood. Executive producers, Guy Collins and Mario Sotela. Miramax/Columbia TriStar.

1991 *Riff-Raff*. Starring Robert Carlyle and Emer McCourt. Directed by Ken Loach. Written by Bill Jesse. Producer, Sally Hibbin.

1993 *Seconds Out*. Written by Lynda LaPlante. Directed by Bruce McDonald.

1993 *Raining Stones*. Starring Bruce Jones and Julie Brown. Directed by Ken Loach. Written by Jim Allen. Producer, Sally Hibbin.

1993 *The Wide Sargasso Sea*. Starring Karina Lombard. Directed by John Duigan. Written by Carole Angier, John Duigan, Jean Rhys, and Jan Sharp. Executive producer, Sara Risher. New Line.

1993 *Airborne*. Starring Seth Green and Jack Black. Directed by Rob Bowman. Written by Bill Apablasa.

1993 *Bank Robber*. Starring Patrick Dempsey, Forrest Whittaker, and Mariska Hargitay. Written and directed by Nick Mead. IRS Films.

1994 *Airborne*. Starring Shane McDermott. Directed by Rob Bowman. Written by Bill Apablasa and Stephen McEveety. Producers, Bruce Davey and Stephen McEveety. Warner Bros.

1994 *Fresh*. Starring Sean Nelson and Samuel L. Jackson. Written and directed by Boaz Yakin. Executive producer, Lila Cazes. Miramax.

1994 *Decadence*. Starring Steven Berkoff. Written and directed by Joan Collins and Steven Berkoff.

1994 *Rapa Nui*. Starring Jason Scott Lee, Esai Morales, and Sandrine Holt. Directed by Kevin Reynolds. Written by Kevin Reynolds and Tim Rose Price. Executive producers, Guy East and Barrie M. Osborne. Warner Bros.

1994 *Silent Fall*. Starring Richard Dreyfuss, Linda Hamilton, and John Lithgow. Directed by Bruce Beresford. Written by Akiva Goldsman. Executive producer, Gary Barber. Warner Bros.

1994 *Surviving the Game*. Starring Ice-T and Rutger Hauer. Directed by Ernest R. Dickerson. Written by Eric Bernt. Executive producer, Kevin J. Messick. New Line.

1995 *Judgement*. Starring Matthew McConaughey. Directed by David Winkler.

1996 *Boys*. Starring Winona Ryder. Directed by Stacy Cochran. Written by Stacy Cochran and James Salter. Executive producers, Ted Field, Robert W. Cort, and Scott Kroopf. Interscope.

1996 *The Leopard Son* (documentary). Directed by Hugo Van Lawick. Executive producer, Tim Cowling. Discovery Films.

1996 *The Pallbearer*. Starring David Schwimmer and Gwyneth Paltrow. Directed by Matt Reeves. Written by Jason Katims and Matt Reeves. Executive producers, Meryl Poster, Bob Weinstein, and Harvey Weinstein. Miramax.

1997 *Good Burger*. Starring Kel Mitchell and Kenan Thompson. Directed by Brian Robbins. Written by Dan Schneider, Kevin Kopelow, and Heath Seifert. Executive producer, Julia Pistor. Paramount/Nickelodeon.

1997 *Gridlock'd*. Starring Tupac Shakur and Tim Roth. Written and directed by Vondie Curtis Hall. Executive producers, Ted Field, Scott Kroopf, and Russell Simmons. Columbia Tristar/Polygram.

1997 *Little Boy Blue*. Starring Ryan Phillippe, Nastassja Kinski, and John Savage. Directed by Antonio Tebaldi. Written by Michael Boston. Executive producer, Virginia Giritlian. Warner Bros.

1998 *West Beyrouth*. Written and directed by Ziad Doueri. Producers, Rashid Bouchareb and Jean Brehat.

1998 *Four Days in September*. Starring Alan Arkin. Directed by Bruno Baretto. Written by Ferrnando Gabeira and Leopoldo Serran. Producers, Lucy Barreto and Luiz Carlos Barreto. Miramax.

1998 *Pecker*. Starring Edward Furlong and Christina Ricci. Written and directed by John Waters. Executive producers, Joseph M. Caracciolo Jr., Mark Ordesky, Joe Revitte, and Jonathan Weisgal. New Line.

1998 *Very Bad Things*. Starring Christian Slater and Cameron Diaz. Written and directed by Peter Berg. Executive producers, Ted Field, Michael A. Helfant, Scott Kroopf, and Christian Slater. Polygram.

1999 *Made Men*. Starring James Belushi, Michael Beach, and Timothy Dalton. Directed by Louis Morneau. Written by Robert Franke, Alfred Gough, and Miles Millar. Executive producers, Dan Cracchiolo and Steve Richards. Silver Pictures.

1999 *More Dogs Than Bones*. Starring Joe Mantegna and Peter Coyote. Written and directed by Michael Browning. Producers, Ehud Bleiberg, Yitzhak Ginsberg, Miriam Leffert, and Brittany Taylor. Dream Entertainment.

1999 *She's All That*. Starring Freddie Prinze Jr. and Rachael Leigh Cook. Directed by Rob Iscove. Written by R. Lee Fleming Jr. Executive producers, Bob Weinstein and Harvey Weinstein. Miramax.

1999 *South Park, Bigger, Longer and Uncut*. Produced, written, and directed by Trey Parker and Matt Stone. Paramount.

1999 *Simpatico*. Starring Nick Nolte, Jeff Bridges, and Sharon Stone. Directed by Matthew Warchus. Written by Sam Shepard, Matthew Warchus, and David Nicholls. Executive producers, Sue Baden-Powell, Joel Lubin, and Greg Shapiro. Fine Line.

2000 *Boiler Room*. Written and directed by Ben Younger. Producers, Suzanne and Jennifer Todd. New Line.

2000 *Boys and Girls*. Starring Freddie Prinze Jr., Claire Forlani, and Jason Biggs. Directed by Robert Iscove. Written by The Drews. Executive producers, Jeremy Kramer, Jill Sobel Messick, Bob Weinstein, and Harvey Weinstein. Miramax/Dimension.

2000 *Skipped Parts*. Starring Drew Barrymore and Jennifer Jason Leigh. Directed by Tamra Davis. Written by Tim Sandlin. Executive producers, Mark Amin, Tamra Davis, and Mike Elliott. Trimark.

2000 *Sunset Strip*. Starring Simon Baker, Anna Friel, and Nick Stahl. Directed by Adam Collis. Written by Randall Jahnson and Russell DeGrazier. Producer, Art Linson. Executive producer, James Dodson. 20th Century Fox.

2001 *On the Line*. Starring Lance Bass and Joey Fatone. Directed by Eric Bross. Written by Eric Aronson and Paul Stanton. Executive producers, Robbie Brenner, Jeremy Kramer, Bob Osher, Andrew Panay, and Johnny Wright. Miramax/Zomba.

2002 *Deuces Wild*. Starring Stephen Dorff and Brad Renfro. Directed by Scott Kalvert. Written by Paul Kimatian and Christophen Gambale. Executive producers, Eberhard Kayser, Mario Ohoven, and Marc Sferrazza. MGM.

2004 *I Am David*. Starring Jim Caviezel and Ben Tibber. Directed by Paul Feig. Written by Paul Feig and Anne Holm. Producers, Davina Belling, Lauren Levine, and Clive Parsons. Walden Media/Lions Gate.

2004 *Amazon Forever*. Written and directed by Jean-Pierre Dutilleux. Gentleman Films.

2005 *Lovewrecked*. Starring Amanda Bynes. Directed by Randall Kleiser. Written by Stephen Langford. Executive producers, James Lance Bass, Derek F. C. Elliot, Kelli Konop, and Matthew F. Leonetti Jr. Media 8 Entertainment.

2006 *Everyone Stares: The Police Inside Out*. Produced, written, narrated, and edited by Stewart Copeland. Executive producers, Miles Copeland and Derek Power. A&M Universal.

Television

1985 *The Ewoks and the Droids*. Created by George Lucas. ABC/Lucasfilm.

1986 *The Equalizer* (pilot and three seasons). Starring Edward Woodward and Robert Lansing. Created by Michael Sloan. Executive producers, Stuart Cohen, James Duff McAdams, and Michael Sloan. Studios USA/CBS.

1989 *After Midnight* (pilot). Starring Marg Helgenberger, Marc McClure, and Ed Monaghan. Directed by Tony Richardson. Written by Ken Wheat and Jim Wheat. Executive producers, Allan Dennis and Barry J. Hirsch. MGM/ABC.

1990 *TV101* (pilot). Starring Sam Roberts and Brynn Thayer. Created, directed, and executive produced by Karl Schaefer. GTG.

1992 *Fugitive Among Us*. Starring Peter Strauss and Eric Roberts. Directed by Michael Toshiyuki Uno. Written by Mike Cochran and Gordon Greisman. Executive producer, Andrew Adelson. ABC.

1993 *Afterburn*. Starring Laura Dern. Directed by Robert Markowitz. Written by Elizabeth Chandler. Executive producer, Steve Tisch. HBO. [Best Score, Cable Ace Award, 1993]

1993 *Babylon 5* (two-hour pilot). Directed by Richard Compton. Created by J. Michael Straczynski. Producer, Doug Netter. TNT/Warner Bros.

1995 *Tyson*. Starring Michael Jai White and Paul Winfield. Directed by Uli Edel. Written by Jose Torres and Robert Johnson. Executive producers, Ross Greenburg and Edgar J. Scherick. HBO.

1995 *White Dwarf*. Starring Paul Winfield and Neal McDonough. Directed by Peter Markel. Written by Bruce Wagner. Executive producers, Francis Ford Coppola, Robert Halmi Sr., and Bruce Wagner. Cabin Fever Entertainment.

1998 *Futuresport*. Starring Dean Cain and Vanessa Williams. Directed by Ernest Dickerson. Written by Steve De Jarnatt and Robert Hewitt Wolfe. Executive producers, Deborah Raffin, Michael Viner, and Ron Ziskin. ABC/Amen Ra/Dove.

1998 *Legalese*. Starring James Garner. Directed by Glenn Jordan. Written by Billy Ray. Executive producer, J. Paul Higgins. New Line/TNT.

1998 *The Taking of Pelham 1-2-3*. Starring Edward James Olmos, Vincent D'Onofrio, and Donnie Wahlberg. Directed by Felix Alcala. Written by John Godey, Peter Stone, and April Smith. Executive producers, Pen Densham, Richard Barton Lewis, and John Watson. ABC Trilogy/MGM.

1998–2003 *Spyro the Dragon I, II, III, IV*. Universal Interactive/Sony Computer Entertainment America.

1999 *The Amanda Show*. Starring Amanda Bynes. Created by Dan Schneider. Nickelodeon.

2000 *Brutally Normal*. Written by Stephen Chbosky, Michael Goldberg, Will McRobb, Tommy Swerdlow, and Chris Viscardi. Executive producers, Greer Shepard and Mike Robin. Touchstone/The WB Network.

2002 *Breaking News*. Starring Tim Matheson. Created by Gardner Stern and Rhonda L. Moore. New Line Television, Pilot/Episodes TNT.

2003 *Dead Like Me* (pilot). Created by Bryan Fuller. Directed by Scott Winant. MGM/Showtime. [Best Score, Emmy nomination, 2004]

2003/4 *Dead Like Me* (multiples). Created by Bryan Fuller. MGM TV/ Showtime.

2005 *Desperate Housewives*. Starring Teri Hatcher, Felicity Huffman, Marcia Cross, Eva Longoria, and Nicollette Sheridan. Created and executive produced by Marc Cherry. ABC/Touchstone.

2005 *Riding the Bus with My Sister*. Starring Rosie O'Donnell and Andie MacDowell. Directed by Anjelica Huston. Written by Rachel Simon and Joyce Eliason. Executive producers, Rosie O'Donnell and Larry Sanitsky. Hallmark Hall of Fame.

2005 *Fisheye* (short). Directed by Jordan Copeland. Producer, Phil Otto.

2005 *The Life and Times of Juniper Lee*. Created by Judd Winick. The Cartoon Network.

ACKNOWLEDGMENTS

It was the fans on my Italian Web site who provided the primary impetus for this book. The occasional journals that I posted caused them to howl for more. But when the process started up in earnest, there were a few specific individuals who got me to the finish line. It was my manager (of twenty-seven years!) Derek Power who introduced me to publicist Amy Grey, who introduced me to agent Ed Victor, who introduced me to publisher Bob Miller, who figured out how to fashion these stories into a book. Many thanks to these great people.

Then came the actual writing part. I am indebted to my wife, Fiona, Jeff Seitz, and Brad Sands for jogging my memory, and to my chums Pete Griffith, Henry Gradstein, Johnny Moore, Donna Gradstein, and Marcia Dent for reading it and chuckling or yawning in instructive places.

My sister, Lennie, was the most exhaustive critic. She devoured every page and tore up my callow prose. She made me amend or defend every line but also gave me the most specific praise and encouragement. She *really* read my book.

My assistant Melisa Berger was the last level of filtration before letting the book leave the building and I'm grateful for her diligence. Many thanks also to Katie Salisbury for helping Melisa chase down the rights to the photographs.

Which brings me to the photographers, who were all very generous about letting me reprint their shots. The largest numbers were from Jean-Pierre Dutilleux and Danny Clinch, to whom I am particularly grateful, as well as to Charlie Hernandez and Kevin Williams from The Police crew. Their generosity allowed me to make this a picture book.

But really, the biggest hug must be for good old Derek Power, who put me into so many of these adventures in the first place.